AMERICAN MADNESS

Feral House
1240 W Sims Way #124
Port Townsend WA 98368

Designed by Jacob Covey

ISBN 978-1627310963
Printed in the United States of America
10 9 8 7 6 5 4 3 2 1

TEA KRULOS

AMERICAN MADNESS

The Story of the Phantom Patriot
and How Conspiracy Theories
Hijacked American Consciousness

"Ever since I got here, everyone has been trying to prove that I'm crazy. But no one has proven me wrong!"

—RICHARD McCASLIN,
court testimony

THE RABBIT HOLE

I n October of 2010, I was about a year into working on my first book, *Heroes in the Night*. That nonfiction book explores a unique subculture of people who call themselves "Real Life Super Heroes" (or RLSH). These are people who adopt their own superhero personas, including homemade costumes, and take on a wide range of missions, including charitable, humanitarian or activist efforts. Some of them also try to fight crime actively, often with mixed results. I had witnessed a scene of complete chaos when a costumed man named Phoenix Jones pepper-sprayed a group of people fighting outside of a bar in Seattle, which caused a confused brawl and the superhero ended up spending the night in jail. Others, like The Watchman in my hometown of Milwaukee, limited his crime-fighting to neighborhood block watch patrols in unusual attire. I had started a blog on the subject which had become popular and was hard at work trying to put a book together.

On October 2nd, I woke up and followed my morning ritual. I started brewing a pot of coffee and flipped open my laptop to see if any e-mails had drifted in overnight.

I did have a new message. It read:

Mr. Krulos,

My name is Richard McCaslin and I used to be known as the Phantom Patriot. I was the RLSH that set a fire in the Bohemian Grove on Jan. 20, 2002. You can read the "official version" of the story on Wikipedia. If you are interested in the whole story, please contact me. I can provide proof of my identity. I just found out about "Heroes in the Night" and would like to participate even though the "mainstream" RLSH community is keeping its distance from me.

Sincerely, Richard McCaslin

My first impulse was to roll my eyes and ignore it. Although I had found most of the RLSH I met to be surprisingly normal, I had already encountered a few cranks and pathological liars. One, Master Legend, claimed he was blessed with powers by a voodoo priestess. He had also posted a story about how he had defeated a couple of criminals after he had pulled a jalapeño pepper from his utility belt, chewed it up and spat it in their faces as a crude pepper spray, giving him the upper hand as he gave them "an all-night tour of Fist City."

Another RLSH, Neurocybe'X, claimed to have working knowledge of the ice planet Hoth (from the *Star Wars* universe). One person told me a long tale about his life that involved a secret government RLSH program that I suspected was ripped off from a Captain America comic book. I was sick of lying, attention-seeking trolls wasting my time with fabricated superhero antics.

But the thing that grabbed my attention with Richard's message was the bit about a Wikipedia page. I checked it out. The short entry said something about a Phantom Patriot engaging in a heavily armed, costumed raid of a place called the Bohemian Grove. I clicked on the entry for Bohemian Grove and scanned over the description. It said that the Grove was a private resort for men only, and only the world's richest and most powerful men. No media was allowed inside. They also practiced a mystery ritual in front of a statue of a giant owl. It mentioned an infiltration by a conspiracy theorist named Alex Jones. I had not heard of any of this.

I glanced at the time. I had other plans for the day, but my eyes were glued to my laptop, my curiosity in overdrive. I went out and wrapped up the errands I had to do as quickly as I could, and when I got back home, I opened my laptop again and got sucked into a "rabbit hole." That term is commonly associated with people lost in researching conspiracy topics, a reference to Alice chasing the White Rabbit and descending into Wonderland, where she explores a surreal dimension of madness, ruled by an insane tyrant. The term came into common use by conspiracy theorists after a famous scene in the 1999 movie *The Matrix*. Morpheus offers Neo a choice: he can take the blue pill and continue to live his humdrum life in a computer-generated simulation... or he can take the red pill and discover the awful truth about the Matrix-world they live in.

"You take the red pill, you stay in Wonderland and I show you how deep the rabbit hole goes," Morpheus tells Neo. "Remember, all I'm offering is the truth, nothing more."

I canceled everything else I had planned and spent the rest of that day (and many other random days after) reading and watching videos about the Bohemian Club and their exclusive redwood retreat, the Bohemian Grove, and the conspiracies associated with it. That led to more and more conspiracies, and the rabbit hole eventually extended for the rest of the weekend and pretty much the next nine years of my life as I journeyed through the alternate reality of Conspiracy World.

Prior to this, I had some knowledge of conspiracies, but not as much as I thought I had. As a teen, I was interested in UFO reports, so I had read several books on case files like Roswell and Area 51, which involved government conspiracy and cover-up. I had read a little bit about the JFK assassination and some articles on 9/11 Truthers and was always amused by supermarket tabloid reports about Elvis being alive and living amongst us incognito.

I was about to go to much darker places.

As I fell down the rabbit hole, I went on a trip to a place that was weird and frightening, sometimes funny, often sad, and occasionally dangerous.

The rabbit hole is a plunge that some people never escape from.

CHAPTER ONE

INTO THE GROVE

One night every July, a couple thousand men gather together in a dark, secluded area of a redwood forest in Northern California to witness a secret ceremony that has been participated in every year for over a hundred years. They are the most powerful men alive—former U.S. Presidents, congressmen, senators, CEOs, owners of sports teams, famous entertainers, media moguls, oil barons, top brass military: a who's who of the rulers of the world. This is the One Percent. These are the Masters of the Universe.

The Bohemian Club members (and their guests) assemble on one side of a pond to watch the ceremony. They sit in silence, with nothing but the sound of croaking frogs, until the pond is suddenly illuminated by the crackling torches carried by a solemn parade of men wearing monk robes. A funeral march played on bagpipes drifts in the air. The procession arrives at the 40-foot-tall statue of a foreboding owl perched next to the pond. The owl's stone body is covered with thick green moss and its giant eyes stare blankly across the pond. This is the Great Owl of Bohemia.

The leader of the procession, the High Priest, turns his back to the statue. He pauses for a moment observing his audience, then in a loud, stoic voice says:

"The owl is in his leafy temple. Let all within the Grove be reverent before him. Lift up your heads, oh ye trees, and be ye lifted up ye everlasting spires. For behold! Here is Bohemia's shrine and holy are the pillars of this house."

A metal gong is struck, making a loud clanging sound. A second priest delivers this single sentence: "Weaving spiders come not here." It's from Shakespeare's *A Midsummer's Night Dream*.

The High Priest continues to address the congregation, and for several long minutes he waxes eloquent about their environment, a large, private encampment called the Bohemian Grove. He delivers a poetic soliloquy about the congregation's forest surroundings and Mother Nature herself.

"The sky above is blue and sown with stars," his voice rings out, filled with nostalgia. "The forest floor is heaped with fragrant grit. The evening's cool kiss is yours."

The fire of the torches crackles. Now the tone of the ritual changes.

"Bohemians and priests!" the High Priest shouts. "The desperate call of heavy hearts is answered! By the power of your fellowship, Dull Care is slain!" This entity, "Dull Care," that the priest is referring to is an enemy symbolized in effigy, a mischievous imp that represents the worldly drags that these men despise—dull budget meetings and mounds of paperwork, insurance claim adjustments, parking, messy stock portfolios, and long talks with accounts receivable.

When the High Priest announces that this demon is dead, a loud cheer erupts from the crowd across the pond. Shadowy figures dressed in robes glide a boat toward the Great Owl of Bohemia. Inside the boat is what appears to be a human body wrapped in pieces of cloth like a mummy. Dramatic music soars through the air.

"Our funeral pyre awaits the corpse of Care!" the High Priest bellows as the boat approaches. The priests carry the cloth-wrapped effigy to the foot of the Great Owl. The High Priest addresses the effigy with disdain.

"Oh thou, thus ferried across the shadowy tide in all the ancient majesty of death, Dull Care, ardent enemy of beauty... not for *thee* forgiveness or the restful grave! Fire shall have its will of thee!" the priest shouts. "And all the winds make merry with your dust! Bring fire!"

The crowd cheers loudly again as priests come running to the High Priest with torches. But before they get a chance to torch the effigy, the air is filled with sinister laughter echoing through the redwoods. It is the supernatural voice of Dull Care himself.

"Fools! FOOLS! When will ye learn, that me ye cannot slay?" Dull Care's disembodied spirit voice mocks. "Year after year ye burn me in this grove, lifting your puny shouts of triumph to the stars. But when again ye turn your faces to the marketplace... do ye not find me waiting as of old? Fools! FOOLS! Fools to dream ye conquer care!"

"Say thou mocking spirit, it is not all a dream," the High Priest counters. "We know thou waiteth for us when this, our sylvan holiday, has ended. We shall meet thee and fight thee as of old, and some of us will prevail against thee and... some thou shall destroy," he adds sadly, thinking of fallen comrades driven insane by Dull Care.

"But this, too, we know—year after year, within this happy grove, our fellowship bans thee for a space. Thine malevolence which would pursue us here has lost its power under these friendly trees. So shall we burn thee once again this night and with the flames that eat thine effigy, we shall read the sign: Midsummer sets us free!"

The crowd applauds this thought loudly, but their celebrating is cut short again by Dull Care.

"Ye shall *burn* me once again?" Dull Care sneers. "Not with these flames which hither ye have brought from regions where I reign, ye fools and priests. I spit upon your fire!" A firework blasts and the priests' fire is extinguished.

The flustered High Priest now turns to the Great Owl of Bohemia to ask his advice on this escalating situation.

"Oh, Owl! Prince of all mortal wisdom. Owl of Bohemia, we beseech thee! Grant us thy council!"

Ground lights illuminate the enormous owl as he comes to life. The Great Owl of Bohemia's eyes light up, and he begins to sing to the congregation in a booming baritone. His song is a set of instructions informing the priests that only a fire that comes from the magic lamp attached to the statue can burn Dull Care.

"*One flame! One flame alone must light this fire,*" the giant owl croons, "*a pure eternal flame.*"

The priests light their torches.

"Oh Great Owl of Bohemia, we thank thee for thy adoration," the High Priest humbly says. He and the other priests move in on the effigy of Dull Care.

"Be gone, detested Care! Be gone! Once more we banish thee! Be gone Dull Care, fire shall have its will of thee!" The priests set Dull Care on fire.

The effigy roars into a fireball, and a loud screech from Dull Care is heard. The assembled men cheer loudly, rising to their feet. A long line of sparkling fireworks erupts along the length of the pond and the rousing strains of Grieg's "In the Hall of the Mountain King" plays loudly. For a grand finale, a set of fireworks explodes overhead to accompany the music.

With Dull Care defeated, the club members are free and the "greatest men's party on Earth" can begin.

AS I SAT AT my laptop drinking coffee that day I first heard from Richard, my first goal was to figure out just what this Bohemian Grove place that he had raided was all about.

The Bohemian Grove is a 2,700-acre encampment that stretches through the redwood forest on the Russian River outside Monte Rio, California (about 75 miles north of San Francisco). It is owned by the Bohemian Club, which operates out of a large red brick clubhouse that takes up most of a city block at 624 Taylor Street in downtown San Francisco.

The Club was founded in 1872 by a small group of San Francisco journalists, writers, and actors. San Francisco was a still a young city then and this group wanted to help promote the arts by starting a club that would stage play productions and readings. The term "bohemian" had the same implications then as it does today, a person who lives the lifestyle of a vagabond and artist.

The club founders quickly realized that for the club to flourish it would need to include men of money in addition to men of talent. The Bohemian Club, to the protest of some of its members, began to fill their ranks with bankers and wealthy patrons. It was the classic symbiotic relationship—the artists got patrons for their work, the businessmen got recognition for helping foster art and culture in a new city.

"I never saw so many well-dressed, well-fed, business-looking bohemians in my life," Oscar Wilde quipped after visiting the club in 1882.

In the club's sixth year, one of its founding members, actor Harry Edwards, announced he was relocating to New York. His Bohemian Club colleagues (now numbering about one hundred) decided to have a retreat in his honor on June 29, 1878, taking a day trip into the redwood forest.

"This festivity was hardly more than a nocturnal picnic arranged for the purpose of bidding farewell to Mr. Henry Edwards, better known as Harry Edwards, actor, entomologist, and sometimes president of the club," wrote Porter Garnett in his 1908 book on the Bohemian Grove, *The Bohemian Jinks: A Treatise*. Garnett was a typical Bohemian Club member of the time—playwright, critic, editor, and printer. As Garnett documents, the first Grove venture was little more than the Club members and a lot of booze:

"The camp was without many comforts, but the campers were well supplied with the traditional Bohemian spirit—the factors of which are intellect, taste, conviviality, self-indulgence, and the joys of life. They were also provided with blankets to keep them warm and a generous supply of liquor for the same purpose."

The club members had such a blast on the outing that they decided to make the trip a yearly excursion. They shuffled around for a few years before deciding to buy 160 acres of land called Meeker's Grove in the 1890s. It was a forest utopia, filled with old-growth redwoods and bordered by the Russian River. Here they began to develop Grove protocol and rituals which are still in place today. The Grove's longest-held rule is that women are not allowed as members.[1] And despite many club members in the media industry, reports and pictures of what goes on inside the Bohemian Grove are also banned.

The Bohemian Grove's reputation grew steadily. Writers Mark Twain, Jack London, Ambrose Bierce, and Bret Harte were all early honorary members. Teddy Roosevelt paid a visit to the Grove while visiting San Francisco in 1905. Membership expanded and so did the Grove.

The Bohemian Club continued to buy surrounding land until it reached its current size of 2,700 acres by 1944. Garnett recalls that in 1908 club members were still sleeping in tents, but that amenities included "a rustic building that contains the bar, and in the immediate vicinity are the writing-tent, the barber-shop, and the bath-house." These buildings were upgraded and improved, and the camp's comfort level rose steadily. Today, tents have been replaced by cozy cabins, which are divided among approximately 120 different camps. These plots have names like "Mandalay,"

---

1 "Women are strictly forbidden" is the sole sentence on the policy in Porter Garnett's Bohemian Grove book.

ABOVE: Bohemian Club members and writers Porter Garnett, George Sterling, and Jack London at the Grove sometime between 1904-1907.

"Cave Man," and "Hill Billies," with 10 to 30 members per camp. Many camps have their own traditions and special drinks and dishes. One camp does an annual "Bull's Balls Lunch," where they eat fried bull testicles.

The first documented U.S. president to be a Bohemian Club member was Herbert Hoover. In 1954 he was given an award dinner when he had reached "Old Guard" status—members who had been with the club 40 years or more. Hoover delivered a speech at the dinner, declaring that the Bohemian Grove was "the greatest men's party on earth."

Since Hoover, almost every Republican president has been a Bohemian Club member. Several prominent Democrats have been members, too, like Jimmy Carter and California Governor Pat Brown. Despite claims otherwise, there is no proof Bill Clinton or Barack Obama are part of the membership. In fact, when a heckler shouted something about the Bohemian Grove to President Clinton while he was stumping for Hillary, he responded:

"Bohemian Club! Did you say Bohemian Club? That's where all those rich Republicans go up and stand naked against redwood trees, right? I've never been to the Bohemian Club, but you oughta go. It'd be good for you; you'd get some fresh air."

One picture taken inside the Grove, and a smoking gun for conspiracy theorists, shows a lunch meeting of men at a table amid the redwoods outside of the Owl's Nest camp. A man, political campaign manager Harvey Hancock, is standing and giving a toast. Sitting to his left is future president Richard Nixon. On his right is future president Ronald Reagan. It would later be confirmed that Nixon and Reagan had a candid discussion at the Grove to talk about which one of them would make a presidential run first.

Nixon's appraisal of the Bohemian Grove seems to be mixed. He recalled that he gave one of the best speeches of his career at the Grove, which he credited for energizing his presidential campaign. After he became president, he had to decline attending the Grove to give a talk after the press got wind he would be there and hounded him for making a private speech as sitting president. Nixon sent a telegram to the Bohemian Club's president, apologizing that he couldn't make the summer encampment. He wrote that while anyone could aspire to be president of the United States, "few could become president of the Bohemian Club." The telegram was on display at the Bohemian Club's library for years.

But the Watergate Tapes revealed a more candid opinion, one that hints at the rumored secret sexual escapades that sometimes took place in the shade of the Grove's redwoods. Nixon was recorded commenting:

"The Bohemian Club, that I attend from time to time—the easterners and others come there—but it is the most faggy *goddamn* thing you can imagine, that

San Francisco crowd that goes there; it is just *terrible*! I mean, I won't shake hands with anyone from San Francisco."

BESIDES THE NIXON/REAGAN STORY, the most dramatic moment in Grove history (and another conspiracy stepping stone) is from 1942. Although the busiest time of the year at the Grove is the July Midsummer encampment, club members can arrange access to the resort year-round. As such, in September of 1942, a group of scientists named the S-1 Committee met privately in the Grove during the heat of World War II. Led by Nobel laureate and co-inventor of the cyclotron, Ernest O. Lawrence, the S-1 gathered to discuss the future of a program they were working on: the Manhattan Project.

Lawrence's group spent September 15 and 16, 1942, inside one of the Grove's clubhouses (which they carefully searched for spy surveillance devices) overlooking the Russian River. There they "reached the agreements destined to shape the entire future development of the project."

Atom bombs were deployed to Japan and destroyed Nagasaki and Hiroshima in 1945. Somewhere between 129,000 and 226,000 people died.

THE MIDSUMMER ENCAMPMENT STARTS the second or third weekend in July every year. Members fly in from all over the world, landing at a small private airport outside Monte Rio, and from there they shuttle down a forest lane named Bohemian Avenue, cross through a security checkpoint, and carry on into the resort. The members meet up and get settled at their camps—Ronald Reagan's camp was Owl's Nest (also popular for military and defense contractors), Hoover and Nixon were members of Cave Man (lots of oil company executives), both Bush presidents were part of camp Hill Billies (mostly Texas businessmen).

THE CREMATION OF CARE

AFTER AN OPENING NIGHT feast, the men file down to the lake to watch the Cremation of Care ceremony, the Midsummer encampment's longest running ritual and a bonding experience for the members and their guests. After all, the ritual is supposed to be for their eyes only.

"Here the burden of dead Care is placed on the funeral pyre, and the High Priest of Bohemia ascends a rustic rostrum whence he delivers the exequial oration," Garnett explains in his 1908 book. "He recalls all the injuries that have been inflicted upon the world and particularly on the Bohemian Club and its members by the foul and pestilential demon, carking Care, and gives thanks to the gods of Bohemia for deliverance from the malign influence."

The ceremony is changed with script modifications and different cast members over the years, but overall remains the same. For several years, the voice of the Great Owl of Bohemia was provided by "the most trusted man in America," *CBS Evening News* anchor and longtime Bohemian Club member Walter Cronkite.

Another year, 1996, Cronkite was part of a

joke. As club members filed down to the Cremation of Care ceremony, they encountered three Bohemians in the ceremonial monk robes doing a spoof on a popular Budweiser commercial, where three frogs croak out "BUD," "weis," "ER."

"CREEEE," croaked Walter Cronkite.

"MAY," added Clint Eastwood.

"-Tion," finished George H.W. Bush.

The owl is the official emblem of the Bohemian Club and is found decorating everything in the Grove, from signs to stationery. The Bohemian Club headquarters in downtown San Francisco features a cornerstone with an owl engraved on it and the club motto, "weaving spiders come not here."

Besides the owl, another symbol of the Bohemian Club is their patron saint, Saint John of Nepomuk, who was a confessor of the Queen of Bohemia. The story goes that he was executed by the King for not divulging the secrets of the Queen, making him a saint of Bohemia and secret-keeping. A statue of the saint, imported from Bohemia, is on display near one of the Grove's clubhouses.

ABOVE: Great Owl of Bohemia statue (left) and stage area. CREDIT: WIKIMEDIA COMMONS.

WORLD-CLASS ENTERTAINMENT

AFTER THE BURNING OF Dull Care, club members are encouraged to relax and enjoy the many days and nights of entertainment ahead of them inside the Grove. There are two major theatrical performances created specifically for Grove entertainment each year: the Grove Play, also known as the High Jinks, and the Low Jinks.

The High Jinks is a grand-scale play that features a cast of up to a hundred people in addition to an elaborate set and other production values. Between cast, set builders, the orchestra, and stagehands, upwards of three hundred people produce the play. The playscript is written by Grove members and usually includes adventure, fantasy, or historical themes. Porter Garnett wrote the 1911 Grove Play, *The Green Knight: A Vision. Rip Van Winkle* was staged in 1960. *Casanova* was the 2011 Grove Play.

This is just one of the things that the Grove members' wealth can buy—an elaborate, enormous production performed for one night only inside the Grove, with a production price tag that can easily run up to $150,000 or more.

To balance such a refined performance, a second production is also put on each year called the Low Jinks, which is a bawdy, crude, vaudeville-style production. 1968's Low Jinks was a horny word pun: *The Sin of Ophelia Grabb.* Since women aren't allowed to participate in the Grove, the Low Jinks performances include men in drag, acting out roles like "Bubbles Boobenheim," a showgirl turned art patron who appeared in the 1989 production, *Sculpture Culture.* The Low Jinks' raunchy comedy is another good reason why photography in most Grove areas is forbidden. No powerful man wants pictures circulating of him secretly wearing fishnet stockings and a stuffed bra doing an awkward Rockettes-style can-can dance.

In addition to these two performances, there are two evenings of professional entertainment called "Little Friday Night" and "Big Saturday Night," which have traditionally closed out the encampment and feature performances from major music and comedy stars. Everyone from Bing Crosby to members of the Grateful Dead have entertained at the Grove.

There are lots of other activities offered: swimming, boating, skeet shooting, fly fishing, nature tours, bird watching, recitals, and an annual display of art by Bohemian Club members.

Finding prostitutes is another extracurricular activity, not endorsed by the Bohemian Club but available to its members if they know where to look. "Jumping river" is the term for going to nearby cities like Monte Rio and Guerneville to find the bars where the ladies of the evening hang out. There was a crackdown on prostitution in the 1970s by the local sheriff's department, but the large meeting of wealthy men still attracts many prostitutes from California and Nevada each year.

One Grove activity that has drawn a group of protesters who gather outside the gates every year is the club's private speeches known as "Lakeside Talks." These occur daily during the encampment, delivered in front of the pond, as the Great Owl of Bohemia looks on in the background. These candid, off-the-record speeches have been a Grove tradition since 1932, with speeches delivered from future and past presidents, prime ministers, chancellors, treasurers, military personnel, entertainers, astronauts, the rich, the famous, and the powerful.

In 2013, for example, the lineup of guest speakers included retired Army General Stanley McChrystal, former commander of American forces in Afghanistan. He gave a speech titled "About Leadership." Conan O'Brien gave a talk on the topic of "Success, Failure in Surviving the Media Revolution." Other speakers included Paul Otellini (former CEO of Intel), Stanford University President John Hennessey, Jorge Quiroga (President of Bolivia), political commentator David Gergen, talk show host Chris Matthews, and William Reilly, former Environmental Protection Agency administrator.

SNEAKING IN

BY NOW, YOU MIGHT be wondering where some of these more candid details about life in the Bohemian Grove come from. For almost one hundred years there was little media on the Grove, outside of occasional society column pieces and accounts written from inside the club circle. Starting in the early 1970s, curiosity about the secret club led to a steady group of bold journalists who infiltrated the Grove with varying degrees of success.

The first two people to publish accounts of this sort both released books on the subject in 1974, with different approaches, but a similar idea—to report on what life in the Bohemian Grove was like. G. William Domhoff, now a research professor at University of California, Santa Cruz, scrutinized available materials at libraries and historical societies and spoke to employees who worked at the Grove. He published a sociology book titled *Bohemian Grove and Other Retreats* that analyzed the Grove and its membership, as well as similar groups like the Ranchero Visitadores. He also exchanged information with another author who was working on a book about the Grove at the same time. *The Greatest Men's Party on Earth: Inside the Bohemian Grove* was written by John van der Zee, who got a job as a waiter during a summer encampment to secretly gather a sense of Grove life undercover.

These books drew the attention of activists and the times began to catch up with the Bohemian Grove. The group had largely been white men, but as civil rights began to gain a foothold, they began recruiting minority members. They refused to budge on their "no girls allowed" policy and feminism found them to be a ripe target.

The Bohemian Club was sued for discrimination in 1978 by the California Department of Fair Employment and Housing. A judge sided with the Grove in the case, noting that Grove members "urinate in the open" which would be too much for female members to handle. After a series of appeals, it was ruled that the Grove must hire women employees (but not members) in 1986. The Grove complied but has always relegated women to kitchen and valet jobs, away from the actual camps.

After reading the Domhoff and Zee accounts, anti-nuke activist Mary Moore saw a common banner under which she could unite various activist groups and started the Bohemian Grove Action Network (BGAN) in 1980. The group began to stage protests at the front entrance of the Grove during the Midsummer Encampment every year. They chanted and held signs protesting a range of issues—equal rights for women, no nukes, save the whales, world peace, etc.—trying to flash a message to the world's most elite men as they cruised into the Grove. On one occasion they performed a "Resurrection of Care" ceremony, hoping to help the entity get back on his feet.

BGAN also became the Grove's longest-running network of infiltrators. With the help of disgruntled Grove employees, they gathered membership and guest lists, programs of events, maps, pictures, and anything else they could get their hands on. This has all ended up plastering the walls of Moore's home office in nearby Occidental, California. Outside of the Bohemian Club itself, Moore probably has the best archive of materials related to the Grove.

"For obvious reasons, I can't go into much detail how we got it," Mary Moore told me in an interview, in 2012. She was 77 years old that year and still operating BGAN, although her activities had slowed down. "We have had sympathetic people who are workers up there. One man, who is dead now, so I can say his name, was Don Heimforth. He was a gay man who was pretty high up in the union, so he wasn't afraid to speak out. In the early days, he was the one who brought us membership lists, programs, schedules. Really great guy, we worked with him for our first decade. He later became ill and died of AIDS."

The Network was key in helping curious journalists sneak into the Grove, using BGAN connections to get them in through service entrances. The first of these was journalist Rick Clogher, who snuck in and out of the Grove over a four-day period in 1980 and wrote an article, "Bohemian Grove: Inside the Secret Retreat of the Power Elite," which appeared in a 1981 issue of *Mother Jones.*

One of the most successful infiltrations, again with help from BGAN, occurred in 1989. Journalist Philip Weiss slipped in and out of the Grove for seven days during the Midsummer encampment. He wrote about the experience for a November 1989 issue of *Spy* magazine, which focused on satire and investigative reporting. I reached Weiss, who now co-edits a website called *Mondoweiss,* and asked about his Grove infiltration. He admitted he was wary of being caught.

"I guess I was ready to suffer the consequences," he told me. "I had a deal with *Spy* magazine that they'd defend me in a trespassing case."

To help avoid that, Weiss made sure he blended in by always carrying a drink in his hand and a copy of the *Wall Street Journal* tucked under his arm.

"There are a few rules, the most famous one being 'Weaving Spiders Come Not Here'—in other words, don't do business in the Grove," Weiss observed in his article. "The rule is widely ignored. Another unwritten rule is that everyone drink—and that everyone drink all the time. That rule is strictly adhered to."

While inside, he witnessed the typical Bohemian Club antics of partying and passing out in the ferns on the forest floor. He also attended Lakeside Talks and eavesdropped on Henry Kissinger while he made a phone call at the Grove's bank of payphones. He even got to meet Ronald Reagan, who had just finished his second presidential term earlier that year.

"I told my editors that Ronald Reagan was going to be there, and they said, 'You got to talk to him.' And I said 'Well, what do I say to him?'" Weiss recalled. "And my editor said, 'Tell him you named your son after him, lie to him.' That was my editor's brilliant idea and he made the piece with that."

Weiss got Reagan to confirm the rumor that the Grove was the spot where he and Richard Nixon had a chat about which one of them would make a run for the presidency first.

Despite Clogher's and Weiss' articles, not all infiltrations have been a success.

In 1982, BGAN helped reporters from *Time* magazine sneak into the Grove, but their article was killed, and a recording they made of a Lakeside Talk by Henry Kissinger was also rejected by NPR.

BGAN also helped Dirk Mathison, a writer for *People* magazine, get into the Grove in 1991. He witnessed a Lakeside Talk by Dick Cheney titled "Major Defense Problems of the 21st Century" and another by former Attorney General Eliot Richardson, but on his third day in the Grove he ran into an executive he knew from Time-Warner, who escorted him to the gate. The article was set to run in an August 1991 issue, but the story was killed.

Landon Jones, *People*'s managing editor, said the reason was that Mathison "hadn't been in the Grove long enough to get a complete story and because the story had been gotten by questionable means—trespassing."

The most infamous of Grove infiltrations happened in 2000. Journalist and author Jon Ronson (who went on to write books such as *The Men Who Stare at Goats* and *The Psychopath Test*) snuck into the Bohemian Grove with the help of an accomplice and wrote about the experience for a book titled *Them: Adventures with Extremists*. Ronson was also profiling a conspiracy theorist named Alex Jones, who was just beginning to launch his career at the time. Jones and his producer Mike Hanson snuck into the Bohemian Grove separately on the same night with a camera hidden in Hanson's duffel bag. We'll be talking more about Mr. Jones and that infamous night soon, but for now it's worth noting that after the videotape footage was edited by Jones' conspiracy brain and turned into a documentary, we can speculate that security at the Bohemian Grove was tightened and infiltration attempts were quickly shut down.

In 2009, for example, *Vanity Fair* contributing editor Alex Shoumatoff (wearing "haute rustic" clothing to blend in) decided to sneak into the Grove to see the Cremation of Care ceremony and then check out reports that the Grove was lumbering its own old-growth redwoods. After making a critical faux pas—sitting in the section reserved for the Old Guard (the men who have been members for 40 or more years)—Shoumatoff was quickly rounded up, photographed and arrested for trespassing.

In 2011, the crew of *Brad Meltzer's Decoded*, a reality show that explores secret history and conspiracy theories with a team of investigators, did an episode on the Grove. They paddled down the Russian River in canoes and climbed up a cliff into the Grove, where they were immediately arrested for trespassing.

In addition to the Alex Jones infiltration—which probably caused embarrassment and annoyance—there were a couple of other reasons security had tightened up. After September 11, 2001, there was a general sense of heightening security. And the third and most compelling reason certainly had to be the heavily armed raid of a man wearing a skull mask, Richard McCaslin, on January 20, 2002.

ABOVE: A studio portrait of
Richard from his press pack.

CHAPTER TWO

SUPERHERO-IN-TRAINING

A fter I read up on the Bohemian Grove, I e-mailed Richard back. I told him I was curious to hear about his life and his raid on the Bohemian Grove. He told me he would send me a "press package." Later in the week, I received a thick manila envelope, which I eagerly opened.

Inside was an autobiographical comic book story Richard had drawn during the six years he spent in prison. There was a sheet of color photocopies of photos of himself dressed in his "Phantom Patriot" costume before his raid. He was wearing a grinning rubber skull mask, blue jumpsuit, combat boots, and was holding a huge rifle. Also included were some court documents and a 12-page handwritten letter, the first of many I would receive from Richard.

He also included a studio photo portrait of himself in normal attire. Dressed in a blue and white striped button-up shirt, his arms folded, and an awkward grin, he looked like a typical clean-cut, middle-aged Caucasian male. He looked more likely to be a teacher or a salesman than a conspiracy commando.

Paging through the letter, I found a detailed account, written in a determined cursive hand. Picking up a page, I could feel the deep indentation of his handwriting on the other side of the sheet. Richard underlines certain words for emphasis (I've changed underlines to italics here) and throws quote marks around anything he finds dubious.

"I choose not to keep a computer in my apartment," Richard wrote to me. "It's too distracting and addictive. Besides, the Secret Service, FBI and NSA already have files on me. I'm not going to help them spy on me by broadcasting every aspect of my life on the Internet."

Eventually, after he was off parole and traveling, Richard did reluctantly switch from pen and ink to e-mails, of which I received a steady stream, some long and detailed, others brief messages. I was to meet Richard in person three different times in three different cities in 2011, 2012 and once again in 2015. I also filed a Freedom of Information Act request with the United States Secret Service, and after years of waiting, they sent me a 172-page file on Richard. Several parts were redacted, and 14 entire pages were withheld, but the available files showed that the USSS had thoroughly examined every bit of info they could obtain.

Through all this I began to piece together the story of Richard's life.

CHURCH AND TV

RICHARD MCCASLIN WAS BORN in the small town of Zanesville, Ohio on June 20, 1964 at Good Samaritan Hospital.

Zanesville, according to best-place-to-retire.com, is a "community comprised of a thriving central city, well-groomed residential areas, rural rolling hills, and picturesque villages. It is a charming, historic community filled with many treasures."

Richard's appraisal is a little more flat.

"Zanesville is a typical Midwestern town," Richard says. "It's a good place to raise a family, but it never recovered from the '80s recession, let alone this one. The culture leans toward 'redneck' but there's a surprising amount of doctors and lawyers there, too."

Named after pioneering road builder and land speculator Colonel Ebenezer Zane, a Revolutionary War veteran, the town is now home to approximately 25,500 people. It served as the capital of Ohio from 1810 to 1812 and is about 55 miles east of Columbus, close to the east border of the state. It was once known as the "pottery capital of the world," and Richard mentions two unique landmarks. The Y-bridge, on the National Register of Historic Places, was once name-dropped by famed aviator Amelia Earhart, who noted that it made Zanesville "the easiest recognizable city from the air" before disappearing into the ether.

The other noteworthy location, Richard says, is the Muskingum County Animal Farm. In October 2011, the owner of the private zoo terrorized Zanesville by setting his collection of 56 lions, tigers, wolves, leopards, bears, and primates loose before shooting himself. But other than that frightening day, life in Zanesville is peaceful, Richard says. The "quiet little town" has left Richard with some happy moments but these are outweighed by unpleasant memories.

Richard was born to Ned Richard and Elsie Lucille McCaslin, who lived on farmland on the outskirts of Zanesville. They had been married for 14 years and were childless.

"I came along unexpectedly. Mom, 41, had a cyst on her ovary. Dad wasn't pleased and always thought of me as a burden," Richard wrote to me. He describes his father as a hot-tempered disciplinarian who would tell Richard he "wished he had never been born" when he was angry with him. This had been passed down—Richard's father was "still pretty frightened of his own father," even when Richard's grandfather was 90 years old.

"He remarked how he had learned early in life not to anger his father, because of his father's temper," a psychologist (with their name redacted) noted in a report for the Secret Service. "He reported, moreover, how this led to his father hitting him a couple times, but without his having suffered any bruises or fractures when his father did so. He also noted along these lines how his father would likewise hit his mother."

Richard describes his mom, on the other hand, as the "good parent."

"Mom worked at JC Penney's until I was born. Her sister finally got Dad a job at General Electric," Richard wrote. His dad worked as a forklift driver in a GE warehouse. "My childhood was rough, but not for the usual reasons. My parents appeared to be 'saints' (Evangelical Christians), but they fought constantly, mostly over money. Dad was a High School dropout who lived with his parents until he married mom in 1950. He was 30, she was 28 and on the rebound. Ned actually got 'cold feet' *after* the wedding and tried to abandon Elsie on their wedding night! His parents sent him back."

Richard says the two main family activities were "church and TV." He was baptized at the First Christian Church in Zanesville.

"We watched *tons* of shows. It's easier to tell you what we *didn't* watch. We watched *Laugh-In*, which was risqué for its time, but I couldn't watch *Charlie's Angels*. Strangely enough, *Wonder Woman* was okay because she was a comic book character. Mom didn't watch soaps, but she got hooked on TV evangelists."

At a young age, Richard found his greatest passion: reading superhero comic books. He still remembers the first one he bought.

"It was a classic Neal Adams/Denny O'Neil *Batman*, 'The Return of Two-Face,'" he says. But Richard had a problem—his parents were less than thrilled by the new hobby. [2]

"Dad thought that comics were a waste of money," Richard says. "Mom thought the superhero ones were too violent. In the mid-'70s, she actually got me several of the Christian comics published by Archie Comics in a futile attempt to wean me off the superhero stuff! I wasn't allowed to buy 'new' comics, but I got them sporadically at Christmas, birthdays, flea markets, and school carnivals. I'd also 'sneak read' them at the drugstore and grocery."

When Richard was 14 he received a treasure chest of comic books when his neighbor's trailer burned down.

"The kid who lived there had a sea trunk of comics. Rodney's dad caught the trailer on fire (cigarettes) and the only thing the fire department salvaged was that sweet trunk of comics. It was scorched and wet, but Rodney said me and my friend Mike could have it."

The two kids, thrilled out of their minds, pushed the trunk on their bikes over to a nearby friend's house. This friend had an old chicken coop in his backyard, which had been renovated into a clubhouse. The boys climbed up onto the clubhouse roof and spread out the wet comics to dry in the sunlight. The first couple layers of books were so badly water-damaged that they were nothing but pulp, but as they dug further, the bounty of salvageable comics spread across the entire roof.

"Mike took most of the Marvels—*X-Men, Marvel Team-Ups* and *Two-in-Ones*, I took the DC ones like *Teen Titans*, and *Warlord*. Also, *John Carter, Warlord of Mars*. We took the *Superman* and *Action Comics* to the Ohio State Fair and traded them for other stuff."

The collection helped propel his comic-mania.

"I have read thousands of comics since the late 1960s," Richard wrote to me. "My childhood favorites were *Batman, Captain America* and *The Phantom*. Being an only child perhaps I subconsciously related to characters like Clark Kent, Bruce Wayne and Peter Parker."

Reading the comics captivated Richard's imagination, and he soon began to draw his own crusaders.

---

2 *Batman* #234, August 1971. The cover says: "The Return of Two-Face—Twice as Evil—Twice as Dangerous." Cover price is 25 cents.

"When I was little, Dad would get little notepads from work and give them to me in church, to keep me quiet," Richard says. "At first, I drew cowboys and Indians, soldiers and monsters. Once I started getting into comics, then that's what I drew. I started creating my own characters around age seven. Super Robot, Explosion Man, Nitro Man, Bobcat, Marvelite, Fury, Cat Boy, Patriot, etc. I started doing actual sequential comics in color pencil in high school. My main hero was Bobcat. I also had a 'showcase'-type book called Star Comics."

Another hobby that Richard would get into when he was older was creating costumes, something he inherited from his mother. He recalls that she made him a bee outfit when he was a toddler, and when he was around age six, she began making him costumes—an elephant, a cowboy, an astronaut—for the annual Homecoming parade in nearby Adamsville.

"Finally, I convinced her to make a Batman outfit." Richard wore the costume in the Homecoming parade and found a friend who admired his costume, Tommy Mozena, who would be Richard's friend for years. "The following year I was Shazam with my cousin Treva as Isis."

"HIGH SCHOOL PRETTY MUCH sucked for me," Richard tells me in blunt terms about his alma mater, Philo High School, located seven miles south of Zanesville in Duncan Falls. "I had to wear glasses for astigmatism, so I looked like Peter Parker, or young Clark Kent: basically, bully bait. Fortunately [Richard adds a question mark in parentheses here] I inherited Dad's temper and natural ability to fight. By sophomore year, most of the bullies left me alone although new ones would crop up time to time and I'd have to deal with them."

Despite this, Richard had successes in school—he made first chair playing trombone in the junior year school band, played football his senior year and got mostly As and Bs in class, making the National Honor Society with a 3.8 GPA. His favorite subject was history.

"So why did it suck, you ask? Because I never had a date," he explained to me.

This was to be a reoccurring theme in his life—a depressed, lovesick desperation for a relationship that would eventually lead to a disturbing obsession.

A psychiatrist's report on Richard for the Secret Service report notes:

"Mr. McCaslin describes in our 3/18/02 interview how his parents were extremely repressed with respect to issues of sex and did not say a word about anything sexual to him. He notes how then, when he was 15 years old, his mother put a 1912 Health & Hygiene Manual on his bed without otherwise having said a word to him. His notes how this attitude toward sex carried over into a certain level of inhibition and shyness on his part in his relationships with girls as he was growing up and even later on."

"I had a huge crush on one of the girls that sat next to me in several classes (majorette, homecoming queen, the usual)," Richard said, adding that this classmate "jump-started his puberty."

"She would flirt with me, but she had a boyfriend. We had an odd relationship for years. I was in boot camp when she wrote to me to tell me she was getting married," Richard wrote. He would later tell a Secret Service psychiatrist that receiving the wedding invitation left him "heartbroken and having him for the first time in his life consider suicide."

Later, Richard sent me a 16-page timeline of his life, and the year 1981 has a single entry:

1981: Feb: Ask girl out on a date for the first time. [Name redacted] cancels at the last minute on Valentine's Day. One season of football.

Richard's lack of a love life perhaps fueled his comic book passion and he began fantasizing about his own costumed persona. He sketched out an alter ego that he called The Stranger in 1981. What further encouraged this idea was seeing an ad for a book titled *How to Be a Superhero* in the back of a Marvel comic book.

"The little ad might have been on the same page as the x-ray specs and whoopee cushions," Richard wrote me.

I read a copy of *How to Be a Superhero* while researching my book *Heroes in the Night*. Here's what is known about the book—it was published in 1980 by a mystery man calling himself "Night Rider." Copies are rare. The book has a distinctly homemade feel, and offers short lessons in designing costumes, preparing for patrols and choosing weapons. The publisher is listed as "GEM publishers" with a PO Box address in Morgantown, West Virginia.

"I was so impressed by the book that I actually drove to Morgantown hoping to find this Night Rider guy," Richard recalls. "It was only a couple hours' drive from Zanesville." Richard spent a long night slowly cruising around back streets and alleys of Morgantown before heading back home.

"Of course I never found him," Richard says. But the concept of a "Real-Life Superhero" had left him star-struck.

AFTER GRADUATING FROM HIGH school in 1982, Richard took his cue from Captain America and joined the military, enlisting with the Marines for a three-year stint. He had several reasons for joining.

"I wanted the training to maybe become a Real Life Superhero. I didn't want to go to college. The recession was in full swing and there were no jobs." And perhaps most damning of all, "My dad said I had to get out of the house when I turned 18 that summer." Then he adds, "OK, part of it was to impress the majorette, who wasn't married yet, but she didn't want me to go. This was shortly after the Iran hostage crisis and many Americans thought that we would start a war to get some 'payback.'"

Richard signed up and reported for boot camp training at Parris Island, South Carolina and then infantry training at Camp Lejeune, North Carolina.

"A lot of my time in the Marines *sucked*," Richard says. "Boot Camp and Infantry Training School was mostly humiliation, indoctrination, and physical pain... the whole 'tear you down, then build you up' bullshit. Classic brainwashing, but I expected that. As long as I was learning a useful skill, it was worth it."

"My test scores in Infantry Training School were high enough that I could apply for Force Recon (Special Forces); however, at that time it would have meant a one-way ticket to Beirut. Even back then, this 'peacekeeping' mission made no sense. Reagan was doing a favor for the Pope... *really*? I chose barracks duty instead and got sent to Cecil Field Naval Air Station, a naval airbase and nuclear depot in Jacksonville, Florida. I guarded nukes for the next two and a half years... *boring!*"

After arriving at Cecil Field, Richard was assigned to share barracks with three other Marines. I tracked one of them down, who agreed to talk to me about Richard as long as I didn't use his real name. I'm calling him "John Smith" here.

"He was a bit odd, as was evident to us all," Smith recalls. "He had a thing for comic books. He had a huge collection, and had his folks send down a lot of it, along with his mom's famous cookies, which we all appreciated. Other than this, however, he fit in and got along with everyone." Smith adds that he would describe his personality as "nice, didn't give anyone shit, however, he was very headstrong."

Richard spent his spare time with his first and only girlfriend, a Filipino woman named Sara he met when he started attending a local Baptist church. "Her parents considered me a catch, but we just weren't compatible, so I broke it off," Richard wrote. A Secret Service report reveals more details:

"Mr. McCaslin describes how he and [Sara] dated off and on over a period of about six months, but with the relationship never having gone anywhere. He denies that they ever had sex. He reports how his parents visited with [Sara's] parents when they came to visit him in Jacksonville at Christmastime of 1983, with [Sara's] parents having invited his parents to dinner and getting the notion that his parents were wealthy. Mr. McCaslin reports how his own parents were generally awkward around other racial types than Caucasians and just did not like [Sara]. He reports how his relationship with [Sara] was not that good anyway and indicates how [Sara] did not love him."

Richard broke up with Sara, he says, about a month later.

Richard also continued to pursue comic books, making a weekly trek to a shop in Jacksonville named Xeno's.

"Before I got a car, it was kind of a bitch to get there. The base was 15 miles outside of town. The buses didn't go all the way out and taxis were a fortune. I bought a bicycle and made an all-day trek of it!"

As his duties in the Marines dragged on, Richard made a decision.

"Halfway through my enlistment, it became clear to me that I wasn't going to re-enlist. I was tired of taking orders from brainwashed idiots. 250 Marines had died in Beirut for *nothing*! Military personnel were just cannon fodder for politicians and corporations. When my enlistment was up, I got out before a real war started."

Richard was released in 1985 and honorably discharged in 1988.

THE ADVENTURES OF THE LYNX AND IRON CLAW

AFTER RETURNING HOME TO Zanesville from Jacksonville, Richard decided it was time to make the plunge into actual "real-life super heroics." In 1985 he created a costumed persona, The Lynx (based on his childhood creation, Bobcat), and even recruited a teenage sidekick, Denny, or as he was soon to be known, Iron Claw. Denny was ten years younger than Richard, the brother of Richard's friend Tommy, whom he had met dressed as Batman in the Homecoming Parade when he was a kid. Tommy, one of Richard's few friends, had died tragically in a motorcycle accident, and afterwards Richard had become a surrogate older brother of sorts to Denny. Richard made the costumes and Denny, already trained in the family trade of blacksmithing, made some steel claws.

"One thing that cemented our friendship was that after my brother died, Richard went into the Marine Corps," Denny explained to me in a phone call, "and my mom was friends with his mom and they thought it would be nice if I would be his pen pal, because the Corps can be rough and lonely. So I wrote him for three years."

After Richard returned from the Marines, the duo did a few costumed patrols in Zanesville.

"And at least once in Columbus as I remember," Denny recalled. "Costumes were kind of rudimentary, and we couldn't find any bad guys to beat up. I've worked steel since I was seven years old in my grandpa's shop, so I built claws like the Wolverine that I wore around. It was... an adventure," Denny laughs. "I was just 13 or 14 at the time. It was fun, it was exciting, but back then..." he pauses, recalling the patrols. "Well, I was too dumb to be scared, how does that sound? We were rebels without a clue back then."

The duo made an appearance at the November 1985 Mid-Ohio Con, where the guest of honor was famous comic book illustrator John Byrne. They wanted to be in costume when they arrived, so they changed into their superhero costumes (while it was snowing out) behind a barn near the convention venue, the Richland County Fairgrounds, a Midwest variation on the classic phone-booth costume change.

Denny soon gave up on the superhero lifestyle and fell out of contact with Richard in the early 1990s for a couple of decades. I asked him what Richard was like back when the duo was together.

"Well..." he hesitates. "It was like life got in the way of his comic books. He didn't focus on a career, but he didn't get married or have kids, so he didn't need one, I guess. It's like he was stuck in an old *Batman* episode or something. Back then, we'd drive around, then park and walk around and look for a drug dealer or people getting mugged, there was none of this conspiracy theory stuff back then." He told me he had heard "a little bit" about Richard's Bohemian Grove raid.

"He's still got relatives around here, so you hear bits and pieces." He hesitates again. "Look, I really like Richard, don't get me wrong. But some of his ideas now kind of scare me a little bit. I guess being married and having three kids does that sometimes."

Denny now works as a maintenance welder at a power plant and still does blacksmith work and welding on the side. He has five acres of land just outside Zanesville city limits. His family raises chickens, pigs, and a few calves. It was late on a Saturday afternoon when he called me from the blacksmith workshop in his barn. He told me that he and his children had just finished the day's chores.

"I got a 1947 Ford tractor here I got torn apart I'm going to work on for a while and then go in. Tonight we got a cowboy movie, a Louis L'Amour movie I'm going to watch with my family. To me, that's contentment. But that's me, and I know it takes different people to make the world go 'round.'"

STUNT SCHOOL

RICHARD MOVED TO COLUMBUS, Ohio in 1986 to pursue a job as a guard with Brinks Armored Cars but found out the company was planning on downsizing. He also thought there might be something more superheroic in his future, and after spotting an ad in the back of a magazine, he decided to follow a dream and attended the Kahana Stunt School in Chatsworth, California in the summer of 1987.

The school was run by Kim Kahana, a successful stuntman with a life story that rivals any of the hundreds of movies and TV shows he performed in. Kahana, born in 1930, got his start as a knife and fire dancer in a stage show called Samoan Warriors (he is actually of Japanese and Hawaiian descent). He had fought in the Korean War and was awarded a Silver Star, Bronze Star, and two Purple Hearts. In one instance he had been shot by a firing squad and thrown into a mass grave. He crawled out and escaped. Later, a grenade attack left him blind in one eye.

To add to Kahana's amazing lore, he survived a plane crash that killed 32 people in Texas in 1955. He says he walked away from the crash "without a scratch." Kahana studied a variety of martial arts, and when he saw two men assaulting a woman in a parking lot, he killed both of them with his bare hands, ending one of their lives with one well-placed karate kick, according to a newspaper report. After the war, he found work as a stuntman, and acted as the stunt double for Charles Bronson for many years. He worked on films like *Death Wish, Planet of the Apes, The Omega Man, Smokey and the Bandit*, and *Jeepers Creepers,* and a wide variety of TV shows, including *Kung Fu, Charlie's Angels, Fantasy Island,* and the *Six Million Dollar Man.*

Kahana also played the character of Chongo, a Tarzan-like character who swung around on vines and communicated through birdcalls and other noises, on the children's adventure series "Danger Island," a segment of *The Banana Splits Adventure Hour* (1968–70). Chongo teamed up with afro-sporting Elihu Morgan (played by Rockne Tarkington) who would often call out to him, "Uh-oh! Chongo!" This became a show catchphrase and one that followed him for years. Random people would shout it out to Kahana as he walked down the street until the show fell out of popularity.

Kahana taught his first stunt class in 1972 and had opened a stunt school open to the general public in 1977. A 1982 *New York Times* article reported on the type of students Kahana was looking for:

"'If your friends tell you you're a little crazy,' he says to those who sign up for his course, 'then you're for me.' Privately, he adds, 'because I'm a little crazy, too.'"

Richard excitedly signed up. He moved to California, bunking with an aunt and cousin who lived in the area on the weekend, and stayed "on campus" during the week. His class consisted of about nine other people, including a man from Vermont named Lon Gowan, who would become his best and, at times, only friend over the next decades.

"There was also a kid from Japan and a couple local guys," Richard recalls. "A brother and sister came from Florida, as well as a (woman) teacher from somewhere out of town."

My first conversation with Lon Gowan was in a phone call in 2013. Richard had just paid him a visit at his home in Los Angeles while traveling a few months before.

"I'm not sure how I found out about it, I had a friend who was a stunt person while I was living in Vermont," Lon says. "It was a decent experience, it was fun, a good time, but I don't really even put it on my résumé that I went there. I don't see it as a stepping stone to where I am as a professional performer and stuntman."

Lon hit it off with Richard, who he describes as "an introvert, it takes a lot to get him talking." Their friendship was forged in surviving Kahana's grueling and dangerous curriculum.

Kahana's Chatsworth stunt school had two locations—a martial arts dojo in town and a training course in Kahana's backyard.

"Kahana had hands-on classes in stage combat and martial arts, tumbling and trampoline, high falls, car hits, horse stunts and firearms," Richard says. "The car hits were brutal! Kahana had an old Dodge Dart that he used for this, we practiced getting hit and rolling over the hood and laying on the roof, as Kahana slammed on the brakes and we rolled off. Even with pads on, there were minor injuries. I pinched a nerve in my shoulder and Lon and I bumped heads hard when we tried a double roof slide. Due to my USMC training, Kahana had me lead the morning exercises and supervise the firearms training, up in the mountains."

Richard also remembers another interesting stunt he saw at Kahana's home training center.

"Kahana had two dogs. One dog was a Chihuahua (that went skydiving with him) and it was always trying to screw the female Saint Bernard every time she lay down!"

I talked to Kahana, now in his 80s, by phone in 2013. He moved from California to operate his Kahana's Stunt & Film School in Groveland, Florida, with his wife, sons, and daughter. Kahana told me he couldn't recall Richard, which wouldn't be surprising as he's seen over 15,000 stunt students at his various institutes over the years.

AFTER THE HIGH OF completing stunt school, Richard soon found himself with a skill but no practical place to apply it.

"Stunt school was one of the better times in my life, though it soon became apparent that I wouldn't be able to pay the Stunt Union dues, which would severely restrict my chance of getting work in Hollywood. After we graduated, Lon and I kicked around Hollywood looking for work," Richard says. He found a part-time job at the Anderson Furniture store. Nothing else panned out.

"Living with my aunt and cousin was awkward, and I wasn't making much money at the furniture store, so I packed it in and went home."

Lon also returned home to Vermont but stuck with the show biz dream. He found some gigs in Vermont working on films and got his union card as a member of the Screen Actors Guild. In 1990 he moved to the Los Angeles area and began to find steady acting jobs and stunt work in films, TV shows, and commercials. He continued to train in acting and studied improv comedy at the legendary Second City in Los Angeles.

All of this led to a variety of gigs: he worked as the stunt double for Ray Romano and had stunt roles on shows as varied as *The Young and the Restless* and *The Late Show with Jay Leno*. He found bit roles acting in commercials and on shows like *CSI: Crime Scene Investigation, Agent Carter, Supah Ninjas,* and *General Hospital.* He also made appearances in movies like Bobcat Goldthwaite's 2011 comedy *God Bless America* (as "guy who runs in the audience and gets shot") and Jordan Peele's 2019 horror thriller *Us.* He also appeared in comedy sketches on shows like *Conan* and shot over 35 national commercials. He runs a walkie-talkie rental service with his wife, Julie Dolan, who is also a successful actress and musician. (She's appeared in several movies and has had roles on *Dexter, Gilmore Girls,* and has voiced Princess Leia on the *Star Wars Rebels* cartoon and in video games. She was also on the reality show *Rock N Roll Fantasy Camp.*)

"I was already part of the Screen Actors Guild when I moved out here, so it was a little easier for me," Lon says on why he made it in Hollywood and Richard didn't. "When Richard was auditioning for stunt shows, he didn't have an actor's background, and it's all performance. If you don't have knowledge of what that craft is, it's hard to get those shows. There's no book that tells you how to be successful. You can't say if you want to be a professional stuntman, do A, B, and C. It doesn't work that way. I'm not sure Richard works that way. He's very literal-thinking, in my experience, and that's the way he's able to get certain things done, like his creative projects, because he's very regimented. Another part of our profession is you have to be very, very social, constantly going out and meeting people. I think Richard came about his ability to be social later on, maybe when he was in prison. He really wasn't very social before then."

AFTER STUNT SCHOOL RICHARD drifted, struggling to find work and meaning. He traveled to Kissimmee, Florida and found a job playing a squire at Medieval Times, the restaurant where diners are treated to actors engaged in medieval fighting and dramatics. Richard was fired shortly after he started when he lost his temper with the show's villain, the Black Knight. The actor was manhandling Richard too roughly, so Richard punched him in the middle of the arena in front of the entire cast and audience.

Richard spent the next five years or so in Zanesville, working delivery jobs, including a local pizza chain called Four Star Pizza. After hearing that the business was looking to develop a TV commercial, Richard created a pizza-delivering superhero, the Four Star Phantom, in 1988. He created a costume (kind of a cross between Batman and Evel Knievel) and spent his spare time shooting footage of himself delivering a pizza on a four-wheeler to a pleasantly surprised customer (played by his mother). He even worked out a stunt where he did a flip off the porch and edited the scene to make it look like he landed on his four-wheeler (he actually landed on an off-camera mattress below) and cruised off. It never aired—his manager decided to hire an animator instead.

In 1992, Richard had saved up some money and decided to give Hollywood another shot, staying with a cousin in San Bernardino. He got his only visible extra role in the wacky Marx Brothers homage *Brain Donors* that year. You can see him at the 1:03:25 mark of the movie delivering a bouquet of flowers to an opera singer. He didn't get paid for the gig and his car got stolen.

"Once again I packed it in, with no intention of ever returning to Hollywood again," Richard wrote me. Back in Zanesville, he started a bounce house rental business but sold it off a couple of years later "for lack of profit."

DURING THE LATE 1980S and throughout the '90s, Richard developed another of his hobbies: cosplay, the art of recreating costumes of fictional characters. It helped pass the time while living in Zanesville. Today, thousands of people spend serious time and money to develop costumes of their favorite comic book, movie, and TV creations and flock to comic conventions around the country. Attending a costume contest at these events or watching reality shows like *Heroes of Cosplay* or *Cosplay Melee* will show you that cosplay is a way of life.

Today cosplay is sexy and hip, but when Richard started doing it, it was a rare hobby, and a signal that you were a huge dork.

Richard fondly recalls 1989, the year Tim Burton's *Batman* film debuted, and a great early cosplay achievement for him. Richard meticulously recreated the Batman costume, then painted and decorated his '84 Camaro as the Batmobile. Then he drove it over to the Zanesville McDonald's drive-thru, imitating a popular 1989 McDonald's commercial. The public appearance of Batman turned a lot of heads everywhere he went. After the first TV series of *The Flash* aired in 1990–91, Richard created a Flash costume, strapped on a pair of rollerblades, and zoomed along in the Zanesville Fourth of July parade.

One day I received a manila envelope from Richard packed with photocopies of appearances he had made in various fan-letter pages of comics and magazines, all from 1995.

"I spent the day at Wonder Con, digging through dozens of back issue boxes. I was able to find all the regular comics that had some of my costume photos in them," he wrote.

Among the collection was a photo of Richard dressed as the Dark Horse Comics hero X, in the fan-letter page of *X* #14. "Richard, all I can say is 'WOW!' I admire your creativity and attention to detail." The editors responded, nominating Richard's letter and picture "Most X-cellent Letter of the Month." Richard also dug up photos of himself dressed as another Dark Horse hero, Madman, in the *Madman Comics* #7 letter section, and as Malibu Comics character Night Man from *Night Man* #17.

Richard told me he also had photos that appeared in *Wizard* magazine, a publication that focused on news of the superhero comic industry from 1991 to 2011, which was considered mandatory reading by many comic book fans. I tracked down issue number 40 (December 1994), and among interviews with comic book luminaries like Neil Gaiman and Frank Miller, I found the costume contest spread where there was not one, but four pictures of Richard in costume, scrolling down the edge of page 51. He was standing on a pile of rubble stoically as Captain America, ready to spring from a tree branch as Wolverine, moving

—The Most X-cellent Letter of the Month—

Dear X-Press Mail,

You knew it was only a matter of time. After receiving fan artwork and homemade action figure photos, you probably wondered if someone would actually attempt to make the costume. Well, here it is!

After wearing the X costume, I made several observations. First of all, it takes forever to lace up everything. Secondly, one-eyed masks are lousy for your peripheral vision. Finally, don't lose the padlock key.

Your Biggest Fan(atic),
Richard McCaslin
Zanesville, Ohio

Richard, all I can say is "WOW"! I admire your creativity and attention to detail. I just hope you didn't poke out your left eye. For future reference to all readers, I really appreciate the cards, art, and, of course, the above photos. However, I do request you inform us on the work that went into your endeavors and the materials you used. My question to you, Richard, is how did you make the mask? I also wonder if you did the sewing or a friend? Anyway, congratulations on having the Most X-cellent Letter (and costume) of the Month!

ABOVE: Richard's letter page appearances as X, Madman, and Night Man

stealthily next to a wall as Spider-Man, and emerging from the brush, pistol drawn, as The Phantom. *Wizard*'s caption reads:

Way-Too-Much-Free-Time Award
Richard McCaslin, Zanesville, OH

Hey, let's hear it for the *Wizard* fans who have way too much free time and know how to sew. (Sew? Sew? C'mon, ditch that sissy sewing gig and do something manly, like get into a bar fight or something.) For going the extra mile, Rich here walks off with a copy of *X-Men* #30 signed by Andy Kubert, *Marvels* #2 and 4 signed by Alex Ross, a *Gen 13* #1 signed by Brandon Choi, a *Gen 13* #1/2, a Gold *Maxx* #1/2, and a set of the ten oversize Fleer Flair prints!

Richard later sent me a checklist of every costume he created, from his 1973 Batman costume from the Homecoming parade to costumes he made in 2015, a total of 54 handcrafted superhero costumes in total.

I AM BATMAN

IN 1995, RICHARD DECIDED to try his luck in Texas. On his timeline document he has an entry that reads, "Moved to Houston, TX, at the invitation of old Marine Corps buddy." That buddy, his former roommate at Cecil Field, "John Smith," remembers different.

"He called me (I have no idea how he got my number to this day) on a Saturday evening when my pregnant wife and I were traveling back into Houston and said 'I'm here!' from the payphone on the corner of Antoine and I-10 at a gas station. At that point I hadn't heard from him in several years. I had last saw him with my first wife, who also lived in Ohio, so we drove over to Zanesville and visited him one afternoon. He was living with his parents at the time."

Richard, seemingly randomly, decided he would crash at the Smiths' house for an undetermined period of time.

"He lived with us for several months, however, with an upcoming baby there were things to prepare for, and I soon asked him to find a place of his own. I helped him move into an apartment he found off Bissonnet Street," Smith says. Visiting him there one day, Smith discovered Richard had "been busy on things like martial arts, making his own custom costumes, but not working."

The two former Marines quickly drifted apart.

"He quickly became harder to get a hold of, and ultimately he never returned any calls. I drove by there one day and found an empty apartment and never heard from him again. I thought for the longest that he was pissed off at me for asking him to leave our house, but my wife and new baby took precedence. At the same time, I was a bit miffed after putting him up with a home, food, etc.... while he never got a job or offered to pay for anything. My wife and I would leave him in our home while we two went to work."

Richard's Houston experience began to change for the better in 1996, a high point in his life. His friend Lon, from stunt school, gave him a heads-up that Six Flags Astroworld in Houston was hiring stuntmen for a new Batman stage show. It was a dream job, and Richard got hired to portray one of his childhood idols—the Caped Crusader himself—for the show's 1996 and 1997 seasons. This version of the stunt show was built on the buzz for 1995's *Batman Forever*, starring Val Kilmer as Batman. In that film Batman, along with Robin (Chris O'Donnell), took on villains Two-Face (Tommy Lee Jones) and the Riddler (Jim Carrey).

The Batman stunt shows were franchised out to different Six Flags parks throughout the 1990s, hiring stunt actors to fill the main characters' roles. Richard's team would do four shows a day for three or four days in a row, then switch out with another team.

Richard performed one of the most dramatic parts of the show. As the Riddler caused chaos below, Richard would appear from behind a curtain in a box 60 feet above the audience. He would unfurl his cape and zip down a wire over the audience and behind the stunt show's set. Then a second stuntman, Dave, also dressed as Batman, would zoom around the set's lagoon in the Batboat.

"Meanwhile, I would change out of my Batsuit into a thug costume and get back onstage to fight Dave," Richard explained. Then Dave would shove Richard off the dock into the water—SPLASH!—and triumph over evil three more times throughout the day, before the park closed. Richard's pay rate was about a $100 a day.

Richard hit it off with his co-workers. He enlisted some of them to help him make a fan-fiction Batman film using the stunt show set after hours. The security guards reluctantly agreed to let the crew use the Batcave set of the park's Batman rollercoaster ("Batman: The Escape") as well as the stunt stage to shoot the video. Richard portrayed Batman, and his co-workers played other characters like Robin and their enemy, the Scarecrow. Unfortunately, footage of the fan film—*Batman: Legacy of Fear*—is lost.

One of his co-workers, Jef Johnson, who played one of the Riddler's thugs, also collaborated with Richard for a *Wizard* magazine costume contest. Johnson now works teaching and performing as a clown. He conducts workshops and has worked with Cirque de Soleil.

"It was for their annual Halloween issue [#63]," Johnson told me by e-mail. "They hold a costume contest and publish the cool and ridiculous. We were second-place winners; the grand prize went to Wonder Woman. Richard was Blue Falcon and I was Space Ghost."

Richard also talked two of his fellow cast members, Vicki and Leah, to dress up in KISS makeup and costumes for a fan-letter appearance in *KISS: Psycho Circus* #3, published in 1997 by Image Comics. "Vicki played Chase Meridian and Leah was a Riddler babe. We didn't date. They had boyfriends," Richard writes in pencil under the photocopy of the letter page.

Richard would work on these creative projects on his days off and to make a little extra money; he'd also pick up some delivery driver shifts for a company called Home Delivery Network. He befriended a fellow driver, Terrance, and the two began to dream up a low-budget, independent superhero film the two would star in titled *Crackdown and Jumping Jack*. Richard eagerly dived into the project and began drafting scripts and designing costumes.

Then, when his rotation would start again, he'd set the script aside and climb into his Batman suit to prepare for action.

"I really rubbed this in my parents' face because back in first grade my teacher assigned the class to draw a picture of what they wanted to be when they grew up," Richard recalls. "I drew Batman... really! My folks actually got mad at me for not drawing a fireman, police officer, farmer, etc."

A black cloud was about to drift over Richard's life, but for the moment he was happy. He was Batman! Every day, he would get to put on his costume, carefully grabbing the pointy bat ears on top of his head to adjust the mask. Then he would climb 60 feet in the air, stoically spread his cape like a pair of giant bat wings and swoop through the Texas sunshine. The crowd below stared up at him in awe, cheering the hero on.

He was there to save the day, a superhero soaring high above them.

CHAPTER THREE

WHO SHOT JFK?

O n November 22, 2019, I wandered around Dealey Plaza in Dallas, Texas, underneath a dull gray sky. It was the 56th anniversary of the assassination of President John F. Kennedy. I walked up to the corner of Elm and Houston, where you can look up and see the window where Lee Harvey Oswald fired shots from the sixth floor of the Texas Book Depository in 1963. The building is now home to the Sixth Floor Museum, a collection of artifacts related to the life of President Kennedy and his murder. Peering out the windows of the museum, you can see the vantage Kennedy's killer, Lee Harvey Oswald, had when he pulled off three shots from a Carcano M91/38 bolt-action rifle before ditching the weapon among the piles of boxes of books and making a meandering escape.

That is, of course, if you believe what conspiracy researchers refer to as the "official story."

While walking through the displays of the Sixth Floor Museum, an enlarged photo of the presidential motorcade that fateful day caught my eye. President Kennedy is grinning and leaning on the car door, smiling at the crowd of Texans who have shown up to catch a glimpse of him. First Lady Jacqueline, in her pink pillbox hat and matching coat, is smiling to the crowd on the other side of the car. Texas Governor John Connally and his wife Nellie are seated in front of them. A stern-looking motorcycle cop floats to the side of the vehicle. Nellie Connally is about to turn around and say, "Mr. President, you can't say Dallas doesn't love you." President Kennedy answers, "No, you certainly can't." Those would be his last words.

Shortly after this picture hanging on the museum wall was taken, the world would be forever changed and the course of history altered.

The belief in conspiracy in America goes back to the founding of the nation, and a paranoia of conspiracy, treason, and distrust of authority is deeply embedded in our country's DNA.

"Those who now dismiss conspiracy theories as groundless paranoia have apparently forgotten that *the United States was founded on a conspiracy theory*," Lance deHaven-Smith writes in his book *Conspiracy Theory in America* [emphasis his]. The founding fathers cited King George's plan for "an absolute tyranny" in the Declaration of Independence. In this case, deHaven-Smith writes, the founders' ability to use conspiracy thinking to read the writing on the wall and look ahead was an important political awakening. George Washington was also a Freemason, a fraternal organization that would evolve into conspiracy lore as the unseen hand that controls all aspects of government.

November 22, 1963, is not only the date that Kennedy is assassinated, but part of the American psyche is too. Kennedy dies, and modern American conspiracy theory is born.

After shooting the president, Oswald walked down a rear stairwell. He was confronted by a Dallas police officer who had rushed to the building and was in the second-floor lunchroom, but Oswald was let go as he was an employee of the Texas Book Depository. He walked out the front door, shortly before it was sealed, got on a bus which he rode for two blocks

ABOVE: The JFK motorcade in Dallas, November 22, 1963.

(getting off because of heavy traffic), then took a taxi to the rooming house he was staying at. He stopped in for a few minutes, then left.

At 1:15 p.m., 45 minutes after the shooting, Oswald was confronted on the street by Dallas patrolman J.D. Tippit. Oswald shot him four times with a pistol, killing him, then snuck into the nearby Texas Theatre, where a movie titled *Cry of Battle* was showing. Witnesses called police, and he was arrested at the theater. On the morning of November 24, less than 48 hours after Kennedy was shot, police were escorting Oswald to a truck that would transport him from city to county jail when a nightclub owner named Jack Ruby walked up to Oswald and shot him in the abdomen. He died of his injuries a couple of hours later.

The President's Commission on the Assassination of President Kennedy, commonly referred to as the Warren Commission (after its chairman, Chief Justice Earl Warren), investigated and determined that Oswald was the lone gunman.

Almost immediately, this finding was disputed as being fishy. Critics began compiling a list of things about the Warren Commission Report that didn't add up. Lee Harvey Oswald could not have pulled off all three shots in six seconds, they said, and the bullet trajectory didn't make sense.

Another conspiracy talking point is the handling of Kennedy's corpse and evidence immediately following the assassination. The Secret Service basically stole Kennedy's body from Parkland Hospital, where he was pronounced dead at 1 p.m. Before the hospital could perform an autopsy, which the law required, the Secret Service absconded with the body, brandishing their guns and shoving those that stood in their way. Evidence, like the suit President Kennedy was wearing, and the car he was shot in, was scrubbed clean. President Kennedy's body was shoved onto Air Force One, where Lyndon Johnson was sworn in as president in flight to Washington, D.C. At the Bethesda Naval Hospital in Maryland, a haphazard and confusing autopsy took place, with members of several intelligence agencies—the Secret Service, FBI, and CIA, all present and making demands.

The assassination had enough unanswered questions that possible conspiracies should have been thoroughly examined by the Warren Commission. Their conclusion was met with derision from the public (almost immediately, over half of Americans polled believed there was "some group or element" responsible for the assassination) and private researchers. Soon, books on the topic, speculating what really happened that day in Dallas, were hitting the shelves on a regular basis.

Mark Lane, a lawyer hired by Oswald's mother, wrote a *New York Times* bestseller, *Rush to Judgment: A Critique of the Warren Commission's Inquiry into the Murders of President Kennedy, Officer J.D. Tippit, and Lee Harvey Oswald*, published in 1966, that criticized the Warren Commission and suggested conspiracy. Edward Jay Epstein, an investigative journalist and political science professor, wrote a book critical of the Warren Commission the same year titled *Inquest: The Warren Commission and the Establishment of Truth*. Another book, *Six Seconds in Dallas*, by Josiah Thompson, followed in 1967. It was the first to explore technical faults with the assassination such as bullet trajectory, and suggested President Kennedy was shot from multiple angles. Since then, hundreds of articles and books have followed, and are still written on a regular basis.

The CIA stepped in and decided they needed to combat this war of words on the "official story." They decided they needed to derail these accusatory accounts of shady behavior by the government. They needed a term to discredit these people and chose "conspiracy theory." Although the term had been used before, the CIA are the ones who entered it into the popular lexicon.

Just mentioning those two words will usually get a knee-jerk reaction from someone, the classic stereotype of a tinfoil-hat-wearing, highly paranoid and delusional individual, a "moonbat," a "wingnut," a "nutjob," a "crackpot," a "bug-eyed weirdo." And that's exactly what the CIA wanted.

CIA dispatch 1035-960, dated January 1967, reads in part:

> There seems to be an increasing tendency to hint that President Johnson himself, as the one person who might be said to have benefited, was in some way responsible for the assassination.
>
> Innuendo of such seriousness affects not only the individual concerned, but also the whole reputation of the American government. Our organization itself is directly involved: among other facts, we contributed information to the investigation. Conspiracy theories have frequently thrown suspicion on our organization, for example by falsely alleging that Lee Harvey Oswald worked for us. The aim of this dispatch is to provide material countering and discrediting the claims of the conspiracy theorists, so as to inhibit the circulation of such claims in other countries.

The CIA recommended using media "assets" to help push against the conspiracy theory books on the JFK assassination by writing reviews and other articles that argued that the theorists were politically or financially motivated or "infatuated with their own theories."

"The CIA propaganda program was designed to interject a new group into the pantheon of political groups Americans employ to pigeonhole political candidates, issues, movements, and so on," deHaven-Smith writes in *Conspiracy*

Theory in America. "In this case, the group was called 'conspiracy theorists' and its beliefs were described abstractly as conspiracy theories about the assassination of President Kennedy. However, like other group labels in American politics, the conspiracy theory label was (and is) sufficiently vague and general to be applied to many other events, issues, and individuals in addition to the assassination of President Kennedy."

IT'S IMPORTANT TO NOTE that conspiracies or things that seem like conspiracy do happen. One example of a horrifying true American conspiracy is Project MKUltra. Along with predecessors like Project ARTICHOKE and related programs like MKSEARCH, the clandestine CIA program existed to find ways to control other people's minds, ideally to find a situation like a "Manchurian Candidate," a way to brainwash someone into killing a target without being able to be cognizant of the mission.

MKUltra ran for 11 years, with the CIA contracting work out to about 80 other institutions, including 44 colleges and universities, 15 research facilities, 12 hospitals, and three penal institutes, all to the tune of an estimated $10 million (close to $80 million in today's money).

The CIA administered drugs like LSD, hallucinogenic mushrooms, alcohol enhancers, marijuana oil, and many other drugs to subjects, some of whom were aware they were being dosed with a drug, and others who did not. The goal was to see how the drugs affected the subjects' ability to stand interrogation and torture, their ability to follow orders, and to see if any of the drugs would be useful as a "truth serum." Besides drugs, some of the other studies called for techniques like hypnosis, electroshock therapy, sensory deprivation, verbal and sexual abuse, and other forms of torture. In one particularly disturbing study, MKUltra kept patients high on LSD for 77 straight days. In another experiment, Dr. Frank Olson was unknowingly dosed with LSD by his colleagues, which led to him to descend quickly into madness over the next few days. The CIA sent him to see a specialist in New York City, but Olson ended up jumping out the window of his thirteenth-floor room in Manhattan's Hotel Statler.

Special CIA "safe houses" lured in marginal elements of society like drug addicts, prostitutes, criminals, and suspected spies or double agents. These people would unknowingly be dosed, and their behavior monitored by hidden cameras, audio recorders and people behind two-way mirrors.

A 1955 MKUltra document includes a wish list of 17 drugs effects they'd like to come up with, including "materials and physical methods which will produce amnesia for events preceding and during their use" and "substances which alter personality structure in such a way that the tendency of the recipient to become dependent on another person is enhanced."

This is not something made up by a science fiction writer or a conspiracy theory nutjob wearing a tinfoil hat. The story came to light in the late 1970s. In 1973, panicked by the Watergate proceedings, CIA Director Richard Helms ordered that all documents related to MKUltra be quickly destroyed. However, about 16,000 documents relating to the program had been incorrectly filed in the financial records and were discovered with a 1977 Freedom of Information Act request by author John Marks, who pored over the documents with research assistants for his book, *The Search for the "Manchurian Candidate": The CIA and Mind Control: The Secret History of the Behavioral Sciences*. Although Marks pieced a lot of the program together, the full scope of MKUltra will never be known, since the bulk of documents related to it were shredded.

THE ZAPRUDER MICROCOSM

AS PRESIDENT KENNEDY'S MOTORCADE cruised through Dealey Plaza, Abraham Zapruder, who owned a dress manufacturing company on the plaza, stood outside his building and filmed the motorcade with his 8mm home movie camera.

The Zapruder Film is probably the most scrutinized piece of film footage in human history. There is an entire cast of characters that live in this microcosm of 26 seconds of footage in the film (as well as other film and photos taken during those moments). These Zapruder Film residents include Umbrella Man, a man seen opening his umbrella shortly before the assassination. For years conspiracy theorists said he was signaling the assassin to fire or was potentially one of the assassins himself, shooting the president with a special trick umbrella with a gun in it. Why else would he be flaunting the umbrella on a sunny day? Umbrella Man was later identified as Louie Steven Witt, who had not been aware of his controversy. In 1978 he explained his umbrella had been an odd form of protest. Kennedy's father Joseph had been a supporter of Nazi-appeasing prime minister Neville Chamberlain, and Witt decided to heckle JFK about this legacy by flaunting Chamberlain's favorite accessory, an umbrella. As Witt admitted, he was in the wrong place doing the wrong thing at the wrong time.

Other Dealey Plaza characters include the Babushka Lady, an unknown woman wearing a headscarf and taking pictures; the Badge Man, a person possibly wearing a badge standing near the "grassy knoll," who conspiracists say is a second shooter in the assassination; and the Three Tramps, a trio of hobos arrested near the Texas Book Depository shortly after the assassination, to whom conspiracy theorists have assigned a wide range of identities and involvement in the shooting.

The list of possible suspects of who really killed Kennedy is a long one: the CIA, Secret Service, Vice President Johnson, the mafia, the Cubans, the Russians, or any combination thereof.

JFK ASSASSINATION CONVENTION

TO TRY TO UNDERSTAND the world of JFK assassination devotees better, I traveled to Dallas in November 2019. A couple of days after I visited the Sixth Floor Museum, I was just around the corner near the famous grassy knoll. There was a gathering of people having a memorial service on the date of the assassination. Although it attracted some random passersby, the majority of the people there were attendees of the seventh annual JFK Assassination Conference. This group, sometimes called "Assassinologists" or the "Assassination Community," doesn't believe the story outlined in the Sixth Floor Museum and history textbooks.

Most Assassinologists believe that Oswald was, as he claimed after he was arrested, "a patsy." Assassinologists believe the fatal shots came from a variety of locations, depending on their theories, but the most commonly accepted story is that there was a shooter in the Texas Book Depository and a second shooter hiding behind a picket fence in the grassy knoll area. Other theories suggest a shooter on the overpass bridge, or in an area known as the "south knoll," or from within the presidential motorcade itself.

At the memorial, there was an observed 56 seconds of silence at 12:30 p.m., the time when shots rang out in Dealey Plaza. A Marine captain played "Taps" on a bugle, and a woman named Beverly Oliver sang "Amazing Grace" and "God Bless America." Oliver says that 56 years ago, she was here in Dallas and is the person spotted on the Zapruder film known as the "Babushka Lady." Oliver claims she shot footage of the assassination on a Super 8 camera, but that the FBI confiscated it.

As Oliver sang, a woman next to me dabbed tears from her eyes. Judging by her age, she, like most people of her generation, probably remembers vividly where she was when she heard the news of Kennedy's death and the shock she felt. A woman named Judyth Vary Baker, organizer of the JFK Assassination Conference, distributed flowers to attendees. We lined up to lay them at a memorial marker on the side of Elm Street. Two Xs on the road marked the exact spots where the two shots hit Kennedy (a third shot missed). In between bursts of traffic, a few people ventured out to the road to lay flowers on one of the Xs, which were soon smashed and dragged by cars into a rainbow smear.

The memorial also featured short speeches. One of them was by Hubert Clark, who was a U.S. Navy Ceremonial Guard and one of Kennedy's pallbearers. He wrote a book titled *Betrayal: A JFK Honor Guard Speaks*, in which he claims that the casket the honor guard delivered to be buried was empty, known as the Kennedy Casket Conspiracy. Clark's speech prompted an angry older man to pace back and forth on the sidewalk near the memorial to chastise the audience, shouting that Clark's suggestion was "disgusting" and that the collective audience should "go find jobs" and "get a life" as he shook his cane in their direction until he tired himself out. A man in an Army uniform, carrying an American flag over his shoulder, recorded everything with a phone mounted on a selfie stick.

The short memorial speeches continued.

"People want to know the truth. They're not going to get it from the city. They're not going to get it up there," Robert Groden said, pointing toward the Sixth Floor Museum. Groden, along with his associate Marshal Evans, are familiar faces in Dealey Plaza. Groden has been an Assassinologist since 1963, one of the first, and sets up a display of articles and assassination photos in the plaza every weekend to talk with tourists and other visitors about the plot to kill Kennedy. Evans sometimes joins him, and they sell DVDs and books from their table. Groden has written books like *JFK: The Case for Conspiracy* (1976) and *High Treason* (1989), and was a consultant for Oliver Stone's *JFK* movie. Evans is the author of *JFK: The Reckoning*.

Groden met his future wife while tabling in Dealey Plaza, and then, after he popped the question, he married her there just a couple days before the 2019 conference began on November 18. The newlyweds spent their honeymoon at the conference, selling DVDs and books. His wedding is a happy Dealey Plaza moment for Groden, but being ticketed and arrested there 82 times by the Dallas Police Department probably is not.

With a Super Bowl happening in Dallas in 2010, Dealey Plaza had become overrun with people who would act as "tour guides" that would approach people and panhandle in exchange for pointing out spots like the grassy knoll and the places where Kennedy was shot. There was a crackdown on ticketing these people and Groden was included. The other people left, but Groden refused to budge and continued to be ticketed and harassed by the city for seven years. The DPD repeatedly cited Groden for "erecting an illegal sign," citing a banner Groden had made that reads "GRASSY KNOLL" with arrows pointing up the hill to the location. They've also cited him for selling in a park without a permit, but Dealey Plaza is not a park, and the city offers no such license. At one point, Groden was placed in jail and denied access to his medication, he says.

All 82 of the charges against Groden were dropped, and finally, a judge, tired of having the court's time wasted, told Groden he should file a civil rights suit against the city, and that's what he did. A judge ordered the city to stop harassing Groden while the lawsuit was pending, but instead of staying away from Dealey Plaza, the DPD began ticketing Marshal Evans instead of Groden, even though Groden told them it was his sign and materials.

In 2017, Groden settled for $25,000 from the city to drop his suit against them. He still has a lawsuit against the Sixth Floor Museum, in which he says he has e-mails that show museum executives conspired with Dallas police and park officials to find ways to get Groden and his conspiracy-peddling out of the plaza.

After Groden and a couple of other speakers, the memorial service began to wrap up. A musician named David Neal sang a conspiracy folk song titled "November '63," a Bob Dylan-like folk tune that outlines the assassination plot.

A HIGH HOCH RATIO

ASSASSINOLOGISTS HAVE PRODUCED hundreds, if not thousands, of books, articles, documentaries, and websites, and a subculture surrounding it. The annual JFK Assassination Conference takes place in Dallas every year, timed with the anniversary of the Kennedy assassination. A rival symposium, called the November in Dallas Conference, also takes place around the same time frame. When I attended in 2019, they had expanded to a four-day event in a ballroom at the DoubleTree hotel on Market Center Boulevard, a corridor of chain hotels and restaurants. The single-room setup had a stage at one end of the ballroom and tables of vendors with books and DVDs lining the perimeter.

Attendance was about a hundred people, mostly an older crowd (more than one speaker stressed the importance of trying to reach young people with "the truth") who were alive when Kennedy was killed. The talks and panels started around 8 a.m. and rolled on to 9 or 10 p.m. each day.

Every angle about the JFK shooting imaginable was discussed. The Assassination Community doesn't waste time with Kennedy Theories 101—everyone here knows that, so they head straight to the deep cuts. Speaker David Knight gave a talk titled "New Weapon, New Theory," in which he examined President Kennedy's mortal wounds and came to the conclusion that the gun probably used in the shooting was an ArmaLite AR-5 or AR-7 and not the rifle found in the book depository. A lot of theories revolve around the weapon used, the number of shots fired, and Oswald's ability as a marksman ("he couldn't hit the side of a barn with a bazooka," one speaker claimed). Single-bullet (or as Assassinologists dismissively refer to it, "magic-bullet") theory says that it's unlikely one of the three shots fired made it through Kennedy's neck and into Governor Connally's back.

Other speakers included Ryan M. Jones, the official historian of the National Civil Rights Museum, who spoke on similarities between the Kennedy and Martin Luther King Jr. murders, including theories of multiple shooters. Pat Hall is the granddaughter of the woman who owned the boarding house that Oswald lived at the time of the shooting and spoke to his character, saying he was a good person that was kind to her family.

The conference is organized by a woman named Judyth Vary Baker, who first got attention in the Assassination Community when she shared her story for the History Channel documentary series *The Men Who Killed Kennedy*. Her story was dramatic and sensational—she said she was Lee Harvey Oswald's secret lover and that they had worked together on a secret government bioweapons program to kill Fidel Castro in 1963. She was a witness to Oswald stepping into an unraveling plot to frame him as JFK's killer, which she chronicles in her autobiography, *Me & Lee: How I Came to Know, Love and Lose Lee Harvey Oswald*.

Me & Lee was published in 2010 by a small press from Oregon called TrineDay, which specializes in conspiracy books, and in particular, a focus on Kennedy assassination theories. Many of the conference speakers had a TrineDay book. TrineDay's publisher, Kris Millegan, had a gray mustache and ponytail and was sporting a tan suit with elbow pads and a bolo tie. He gave a talk titled "Life as the Publisher of Banned Books." Millegan pointed out that he doesn't believe his books have been banned so much as they've been "suppressed," and started his talk by proudly pointing out that his home, Portland, is a city that has rejected fluoridating their water supply. This classic conspiracy suggests that fluoride is used by the government to keep people brainwashed and docile.

In Baker's book, she details how she excelled in science in high school and hoped to follow a career researching cures for cancer. After a scientist who was also a CIA asset met her at a science fair, 19-year-old Baker was recruited to move to New Orleans in the summer of 1963 to work on a secret CIA project, which would develop a super cancer "cocktail" that could stealthily be administered to Castro.

It's well documented that there were hundreds of attempts by the CIA to kill Castro over the decades he was in power, as seen in the documentary *638 Ways to Kill Castro*. Under Operation Mongoose, the CIA hired hitmen and came up with ideas that were more outlandish than injecting him with a super cancer. Plans to covertly kill the Cuban leader bordered on being cartoonish, including operations to sneak him an exploding cigar; to rig a conch shell with explosives that Castro would encounter while scuba diving (one of his favorite pastimes); or to infect him with thallium salts, which would cause him to lose his famous beard and make the once-proud leader a laughingstock. One of the last attempts on Castro's life was in 2000 when explosives attached to a podium he was going to deliver a speech in Panama were discovered.

Baker says she randomly bumped into Oswald at a post office, and after some small talk, they found they were both working on the same secret project. Despite being recently married to Robert Baker, who was studying to be a geologist, Judyth says she began a passionate affair with Oswald (who was married to Marina Prusakova, a pharmacology student he met in Russia). The program they worked for provided Oswald and Baker with cover jobs at the Reily Coffee Company. Oswald worked in the coffee production plant while Baker did company paperwork. After punching out, they would shuttle between the apartments of scientists working on the super cancer program, conducting tests on lab mice. The entire plan goes sideways, and the group was told that they had a new target they were supposed to kill instead of Castro—President Kennedy. Baker says Oswald was an unwilling participant and was trying to save Kennedy's life, but ended up getting framed for the murder, while his real killers escaped.

Those who accepted have Baker's story and participate in her JFK Assassination Conference are, as her critic John C. McAdams, a Marquette University associate professor of political science and author of *JFK Assassination Logic: How to Think about Claims of Conspiracy*, calls them, "Team Judyth." McAdams and other critics point to multiple holes and contradictory information in Baker's story. She has little proof to back up her claims, saying evidence she has was either accidentally discarded or stolen over the years.

McAdams notes that a flaw in Baker's account is the dramatic ending. In an early draft of a book (before the project became *Me & Lee*) that was, she says, leaked, Baker writes about her last phone conversation with Oswald.

They talked about him being aware that he is somehow going to be set up, but he told her that he loved her and that if he somehow made it through, he wanted the two of them to meet in Cancún, where the lovebirds would "stay at a fine hotel."

The problem with this story is that in 1963 there was no Cancún. At that time, it was just a coconut plantation, with the future tourist trap's first hotels not being built until 1974. Rather than trying to pass this off as a typo or a mixed-up recollection (it's known that Oswald had a trip to Mexico City, and Acapulco was a popular tourist destination in the '50s and '60s) Baker decided to dig deeper, saying that she loved to study maps with Oswald, and they had seen the land marked Cancún and that Oswald's probable plan was to rendezvous there so they could go for a long hike through the Yucatán Peninsula.

Another of the things that makes Baker's story seemed far-fetched is what McAdams calls the "Hoch Ratio Test." That theory says the more characters known to Assassinologists involved in the tale, the less likely it is to be true. Researcher Paul Hoch stated in a talk:

"I suspect that the useful measure of the plausibility of an allegation could be derived from the percentage of well-known names. If a source claims to have met with David Ferrie, Allen Dulles, and Fidel Castro in Jack Ruby's nightclub, I'll go on to the next document."

David Ferrie, who also appears in Baker's story, is a pilot who was in the New Orleans Civil Air Patrol with Oswald and alleged by some Assassinologists to be the person who hypnotized Oswald to set him up as Kennedy's assassin. Ferrie was found dead by suicide in 1967. Allen Dulles was the head of the CIA and was forced to resign after the Bay of Pigs incident. He was later on the Warren Commission and is seen as one of the hands behind Kennedy's murder.

Baker's story tips the Hoch Ratio Test heavily. Her account says that she met figures of JFK assassination lore like David Ferrie, Jack Ruby, as well as CIA scientists Dr. Alton Oschner and Dr. Mary Sherman. All of these people, along with others mentioned in Baker's book, were long-established by Assassinologists to be part of the conspiracy by the time she wrote the manuscript. The connections between Dr. Mary Sherman, David Ferrie, and their science experiments (which led to the mysterious death of Dr. Sherman) were outlined in a book by Edward T. Haslam titled *Mary, Ferrie & the Monkey Virus* in 1997. (TrineDay published an updated version of the story, titled *Dr. Mary's Monkey*, in 2015.) Haslam went on to be TrineDay's editor for *Me & Lee*.

Baker is not the only one who is perhaps telling a tall tale. McAdams also dissects the story of Beverly Oliver, the self-proclaimed "Babushka Lady," who had sung at the conference's grassy knoll memorial. Like Baker, a lot of dates and details of her story don't add up, and she also sets off a Hoch Ratio Test warning light.

True or not, the dramatic nature of Baker's story caught the attention of musical producer Jason Trachtenburg, who developed *Me & Lee* into an off-Broadway musical of the same name. A live performance of a scene and one of the songs from the *Me & Lee* musical were performed as part of the Friday night conference dinner entertainment, followed by a full screening of a DVD of the production. Trachtenburg played Oswald, while others portrayed Baker, Dr. Mary Sherman, and others. It was a surreal experience to see a portrayal of Lee Harvey Oswald declaring his innocence in songs like "Believe You Me" to a room full of smiling people.

The next day Baker took the stage for her talk, "Lee's Secrets: His Last Days." The room was filled, as the audience listened with rapt attention. Throughout the weekend, I had spotted Baker giving hugs and having deep conversations with Assassinologists. She had developed a community, and here she was an essential and historical person. Baker's speech wandered, filling in odd details about Oswald's life. She spent several long minutes talking about Oswald's great love for milk, saying he'd order it in bars, just like his hero Hopalong Cassidy did. Oswald, Baker said, was a hero like Hopalong, and not the villain who had shot President Kennedy in the head that terrible day. He was a good guy, and we had all been deceived.

THE HOUR OF THE TIME

AS MISTRUST OF GOVERNMENT and conspiracy theories grew, some key terms came into use to describe the sinister cabal bent on world domination. These words, often nebulous about whom they refer to, include "globalist" (anyone helping orchestrate a one-world government), "New World Order" (made famous from a speech by George H.W. Bush, this term is seen as referring to a totalitarian government), and the "Deep State" (the people who secretly call the shots).

The idea of a Globalist New World Order, in which all nations and cultures assimilate into a one-world government, and which forces all citizens into a regimented lifestyle void of free will, is a driving force of many conspiracy theories. The United Nations and the European Union are seen by conspiracists as a starter kit for this concept, and you can find the fear of it resonating in "Make America Great Again" and Brexit.

Most conspiracy theorists do not label themselves as such and view the term as offensive or condescending. They prefer terms like "Patriots," "Truthers," "Truth Seekers," "Investigators," or "Citizen Journalists."

Since the JFK assassination, a growing number of players had been attributed to the "super-conspiracy," as multiple-tiered conspiracies are known. These groups, conspiracists say, are all connected to each other. Far-flung groups—the Catholic Church, the country music industry, Satanists, NASA—are all part of this conspiracy conglomerate.

The super-conspiracy also includes not only clandestine groups like the CIA, NSA, FBI, and ATF, but other agencies like FEMA and the CDC. More layers add groups said to be helping a globalist agenda like the Bilderberg Group (a group of political leaders and industry experts that has a private annual meeting, a tradition since the '50s) and the Trilateral Commission (founded by David Rockefeller in the '70s to improve cooperation between North America, Europe, and Japan).

Other historic groups said to be in on the conspiracy are the Illuminati, a secret society founded in 1776 that had dissipated by the end of the century, though conspiracy theorists say they still exist and are pulling strings today. Similarly, the Freemasons or Masons are fraternal organizations that still exist. They've long been thought to be part of conspiracies hatched in meetings at their lodges.

The Freemasons' infamy as a secret society can be traced to the story of disgruntled Mason Captain William Morgan, who said he was going to publish an exposé on the group's secrets, titled *Illustrations of Masonry*. In 1826 Morgan disappeared and was presumed to be murdered by the Masons, though mystery surrounds his last days as his body was never properly identified. Following the incident, a briefly lived Anti-Masonic Party formed, the country's first third party. Anti-Masonic Party presidential candidate William Wirt ran against Andrew Jackson and Henry Clay in the 1832 election. Most of the party's members merged to become the Whig Party.

CONSPIRACIES STRETCHED OUT OVER the years, and by the 1990s, mistrust in government exploded. Conspiracy theories proliferated, and militia groups grew, expanding into the 2000s (the number then decreased until Obama became president, when militia membership shot up again).

Several events added to the rising '90s disdain for government institutions. The Ruby Ridge siege, an 11-day standoff between the FBI and the Weaver family in 1992, started when Randy Weaver didn't respond to a bench warrant for illegally selling firearms. When he went to investigate intruders on his property, FBI agents shot his dog and his 14-year-old son, Sammy. An FBI sniper also shot and killed his wife, Vicki. Deputy U.S. Marshal William Francis Degan, Jr. also died in the shootout. Weaver eventually surrendered to save his daughters.

The following year, the Waco, Texas, incident started with the ATF trying to raid David Koresh and his Branch Davidians' compound to seize illegal weapons, leaving several agents and Branch Davidians dead. It turned into a terrifying 51-day standoff with the ATF and FBI that ended with the Branch Davidians' compound going up in flames. The government agencies say the Branch Davidians started the fires themselves, but conspiracy theorists say the FBI started the fire to burn the Branch Davidians alive.

During the '90s, two conspiracy theorists gained a level of popularity and made a major impact on conspiracy culture. They talked about similar themes but were stylistically different.

One was Jim Marrs (died 2017), who looked like an eccentric college professor. He had a neatly trimmed white beard, an Indiana Jones-style fedora, and was well-spoken, getting his start as a reporter in Fort Worth, Texas. His 1989 book *Crossfire: The Plot That Killed Kennedy* was adapted into Oliver Stone's 1991 film *JFK* and became a bestseller. He went on to write books on UFOs, like the popular 1997 book *Alien Agenda*, as well as alleged secret government programs.

The other prototype, Milton William Cooper (died 2001), a former Navy officer, got his start on UFO conspiracy, but moved to government conspiracy and became a voice of the militia or patriot (as they call themselves) movement. He authored the classic conspiracy bible *Behold a Pale Horse*, first published in 1991, which examined everything from the JFK assassination (he was killed by the driver, armed with a special gun that fired a shellfish toxin, Cooper wrote), as well as AIDS being a government made epidemic to kill minorities and gays, and the history of the secret societies. *Behold a Pale Horse* appealed to a wide range of people who disliked and distrusted the government, ranging from rural militias to the Nation of Islam, both of whom ordered copies of the book in bulk.

Cooper also developed a following (he claimed it was in the tens of millions, but probably smaller) for his shortwave radio show *The Hour of the Time*, which broadcast from 1993–2001. His personal style, talking about his family and their life in a reclusive home on top of a mountain in Eagar, Arizona, which he called Cooper Hill, endeared him to listeners and he fired them up with his diatribes about government corruption.

In the type of incident that would be repeated over and over, Cooper found out how influential he was and how seriously individuals might take his calls to action. In his Cooper biography *Pale Horse Rider*, author Mark Jacobson recalls how Cooper was working at an office on his patriot newspaper *Veritas* when two men who said they were fans dropped in for a visit. They chatted with him for a while, with one of them asking Cooper a strange question—did Cooper think he should shoot a cop if he was pulled over? A confused Cooper told him no. The men offered Cooper a copy of *The Turner Diaries*, which they had a large supply of, a 1978 novel by William Pierce (writing as Andrew Macdonald) that became an underground hit with white supremacists. In the dystopian book, a radical group overthrows a tyrannical government and starts a race war. The book had been part of the inspiration for a white supremacist group who named themselves The Order, taking their name from a fictional group in the book. After a string of armed robberies, the group murdered Jewish attorney and talk show host Alan Berg in Denver. One scene includes the bombing of an FBI headquarters.

Those two men visiting Cooper were Timothy McVeigh and Terry Nichols, who bombed the Alfred P. Murrah Federal Building April 19, 1995, killing 168 people and injuring almost seven hundred more.

McVeigh and Nichols said they were inspired for the attack by the Waco incident, reading *The Turner Diaries*, and by listening to Cooper on *The Hour of the Time*. After the Oklahoma City bombing, President Clinton called Cooper "the most dangerous man on radio," which Cooper took as a badge of honor.

In 1998 Cooper was issued an arrest warrant for tax evasion. He avoided multiple attempts to be served with paperwork, as law enforcement didn't want another situation like Ruby Ridge or Waco. But finally, after several complaints from neighbors (Cooper angrily chased one family off Cooper's Hill, stuck a gun in the father's face and accused him of being a spy), the Apache County Sheriff's Department attempted to arrest Cooper on November 5, 2001. When they entered his property, a plan to quietly arrest him fell apart. A shootout started just before midnight, and Cooper shot one of the deputies in the head. An officer fired back and killed him at his front door. Conspiracists say the shootout happened because the powers that be determined Cooper's voice needed to be silenced.

Cooper died at the same time a young radio and cable access host named Alex Jones was rising to become a conspiracy star in Austin, and Cooper's heir apparent. Cooper himself believed Jones had ripped off his act. Like Cooper, Jones was loud, angry, and paranoid. And like Cooper, he would be influential on people who would take dangerous, violent action, inspired by his words.

CHAPTER 4

ALEX *FUCKING* JONES

In 1998, Richard's life began a four-year downward spiral, beginning with the failing health of his parents. With two seasons under his belt, Richard returned to Astroworld for rehearsals for the 1998 Batman stunt show season in April. Richard got a troubling phone call in Houston—his mom had put his dad in a nursing home for Alzheimer's. He died shortly after.

Richard had a rough relationship with his father, but he noted that as he got older "their relationship got better." But his last memories of his father aren't good. His memory deteriorating with Alzheimer's, his father told Richard he didn't recognize him and that he "didn't have any children."

"That hurt," Richard said in an interview with the Secret Service. "It seemed deliberate he forgot me on purpose because he remembered the names of my second and third cousins.

"Mom's health was failing, too. A neighbor was coming over to the house to watch her while I was away," Richard explained. "I took a pay cut to come back to visit but was promised travel expenses. Once I got back, the show producer stiffed me on the travel expenses. I went 'on strike' and wouldn't come to rehearsals until I got reimbursed. They simply fired me and brought in one of their own people!"

Jobless in Houston, Richard decided to head to Hollywood and stayed with Lon for a short period in May and June. Lon helped him out again in this time of need, finding him a gig doing costume work at Universal Studios in Hollywood. Richard worked over the summer greeting tourists in costumes based on characters from the 1998 movie *Small Soldiers*. He returned in October to Universal to portray a zombie cowboy, joining a crew of Halloween characters wandering the park.

His mother's declining health led him back to Zanesville again. Back home, he got into a serious argument with his "scheming Aunt Eleanor," who he claims moved in with his mom and was "trying to take over the house." Richard says he had to kick the 83-year-old aunt out in the street, prompting her to call her son, who in turn called the Zanesville police.

"It almost backfired on her, when the cops figured out they got played. They almost locked her up," Richard says, still bitter at the memory.

His mom was moved into a nursing home and Richard, unemployed, traveled to Florida to try to find more stunt show work. He tried auditioning for Pirate Dinner Theater, Disney's Tarzan Show, and Universal's Marvel Island Show, but didn't get any callbacks. Richard claims he was "blacklisted" by the company that owned the Batman stunt show.

Richard returned to Ohio. Back home, he briefly attended a wrestling school in Cincinnati, the Heartland Wrestling Association, and even picked out a wrestling persona—Stealth Fighter—but this didn't go well either.

"I more than held my own against the punks who were in the class, but by the third week I had re-injured my shoulder," Richard says, referring to the nerve damage from Kahana's Stunt School. "I got some 'horse tranquilizers' for it but the doctor warned me repeated injury would cause permanent damage." Richard says he also discovered wrestlers were making as little as $50 a night.

"That wouldn't even be enough to pay for a hotel room. I decided to cut my losses and move to Austin," Richard says.

RICHARD MOVED TO AUSTIN in 2000. His main motivating factor was to reconnect with his delivery driver friend Terrance from Houston. Richard needed a creative project to balance the negative news he had been receiving. This film project, *Crackdown and Jumping Jack*, could have been just what he needed. Crackdown, to be played by Richard, would be a goggle-sporting, stop-sign-shield-wielding superhero. His trusty backup would be Terrance as Jumping Jack, a jack-o'-lantern-masked sidekick.

While he was shuttling around Ohio, Florida, California, and Texas, Richard was consistently working on the script, costumes, and other details. He got so into the Crackdown persona that he cruised on a few car patrols in Zanesville dressed as the character, "but nothing happened," he admits.

As time went on, Richard discovered his enthusiasm for the project wasn't shared by his partner.

"This Austin period was bad," Richard sums up. "Terrance had made several promises to help with movie production but once I got down there, he broke every one of them. Terrance told me that he had some friends with some video equipment that we could use. It never happened. He said he knew some people we could cast in the movie. They never showed up. I tried to teach him in stage combat and tumbling, but he had no talent for it. I couldn't afford to rent (let alone buy) the necessary video equipment and I didn't really know how to use it anyway. Terrance never offered to pay for anything. The project died and so did our friendship. Austin is a nice town to live in. It's just that most of my personal experiences at that time were bad."

Despite his previous vow to not return, Richard took another shot at Hollywood. He auditioned for a role as an FBI agent in the Sandra Bullock comedy *Miss Congeniality* (2000) but didn't get the part. He was also paid to spend a day on the set of *Spy Kids* (2001) to act as one of the monstrous henchmen known as Floop's Floogies. The scenes were later cut and recast.

"The extras were never actually used. The union stuntmen just filled the henchmen roles. We still got paid for the day." Richard says the extras mostly hung out with cult horror makeup and special effects artist (and actor) Tom Savini, who worked on the production, playing cards. Back in Austin, Richard found a job as a host and cashier at Owens Family Restaurant on I-35, the last payroll job he'd have for many years.

During this period of drifting, Richard's mother died. It was absolutely devastating to him. His parents' estate left him a sizable inheritance—about $675,000. But with both parents deceased, no siblings, and a recently soured friendship with his creative partner, Terrance, Richard had something that money couldn't remedy—loneliness.

In Austin, Richard found something to fill that void.

DARK SECRETS

ALEX JONES WAS RAISED in Rockwall, Texas, the son of a dentist and a homemaker. In a *Rolling Stone* interview, he says his first experience with authority being deceptive and hypocritical was in high school, where he'd witnessed off-duty Rockwall cops dealing drugs at parties. These were the same cops that did D.A.R.E. anti-drug presentations at school and drug-tested Jones and his football teammates. After his family moved to Austin, Jones took an interest in reading history. A major influence he found on his father's bookshelf was a 1971 book titled *None Dare Call It Conspiracy* by Gary Allen, a book that lays out the blueprint to the New World Order.

After high school, Jones attended community college in Austin and landed a job at radio station KJFK in 1996, where he hosted *The Final Edition*. He was fired in 1999, he says, for talking too much about "inside-terror-job stuff." But by then he had already realized and harnessed the power of the Internet to broadcast online and syndicate *The Alex Jones Show* to several other stations by himself. Jones called his new website platform InfoWars, and his strong online presence in the early days of the Internet is how he has consistently stayed ahead in younger demographics. His online reach gives him a wider audience than talk rivals like Rush Limbaugh and Glenn Beck and would eventually build InfoWars into a multimillion-dollar platform.

The Internet is also where he quickly developed a new nickname in forums, "Alex *Fucking* Jones"—"fucking" being such a versatile word that the nickname could describe awe, disdain, disbelief, or sometimes all of the above, depending on who was using it and in what context. "I'll pay good money if an actual living, breathing person who works at Twitter can seriously e-mail me and explain why my accounts were deemed more dangerous than Alex Fucking Jones," a writer at SomethingAwful.com posted after his account was banned as "hateful content" after joking about Nancy Pelosi eating children.

In the mid-'90s, Jones went to Austin Community College and began filling in for shows on cable access station Austin Community Television (AC-TV), which lived up to the city's unofficial motto "Keep Austin Weird."

The cable access station would be where he would first air his documentary projects. His first film, *America: Destroyed by Design*, was released in 1997 and focused on globalism and the Oklahoma City bombing, which Jones says was a false flag attack designed to look like the work of terrorists but perpetrated by our own government.

One of the first well-known Jones meltdowns was during his broadcasts leading up to New Year's Eve, 1999. Half-crazed with Y2K bug fever, Jones ranted about the impending apocalypse that was approaching the midnight hour. Jones reported that hundreds of thousands were dead in Chechnya, nuclear plants were melting down in Pennsylvania, world economies were collapsing, store shelves were empty and gas stations out of fuel, a police state was getting ready to mobilize, and other alarming catastrophes were happening around the world, all of it orchestrated by Vladimir Putin, Jones told his listeners.

"It is absolutely out of control, it is pandemic, ladies and gentlemen!" Jones said. It was exciting radio, but none of it was true.

In the year 2000 Jones created five documentaries, including *America: Wake Up or Waco* (which documented his efforts to help rebuild the Branch Davidian church as a memorial to those that died there in the standoff with the ATF and FBI), and *Police State 2000*, which "exposes the militarization of American law enforcement and the growing relationship between the military and the police." But his most sensational documentary that year was titled *Dark Secrets: Inside Bohemian Grove*. The brazen trespass into the Grove was an early boost to his cred as a conspiracy "Infowarrior," as Jones calls his loyal listeners.

In July 2000, Jones and cameraman Mike Hanson crawled through the woods and boarded a shuttle truck in the Grove's parking lot. Hanson was carrying a duffel bag with a camera hidden inside. Once they got in, they nervously wandered around, trying to act discreet, saying they were guests of the Texas-heavy Hill Billies camp when questioned by suspicious guards. They recorded the Cremation of Care ceremony in its entirety. The shaky, motion-sickness-inducing footage was cut together for *Dark Secrets*, which was broadcast on cable access and sold as a DVD and VHS.

The second party infiltrating that night was author Jon Ronson, who was documenting various conspiracy theorists and extremists, including Jones. After Jones flaked on him, Ronson sneaked in with a local informant

ABOVE: Alex Jones at a 2014 protest.
CREDIT: WIKIMEDIA COMMONS/SEAN P. ANDERSON.

by simply looking confident and walking in through the front gate. He recalled the experience in his book *Them: Adventures with Extremists*.

Ronson and all of the infiltrators I've spoken about up until now—Domhoff, van der Zee, Clogher, Weiss, and the Bohemian Grove Action Network—each has a slightly different take on the Grove, but ultimately more or less agree on one thing. They say the Grove is an exclusive, private club where the world's richest and most powerful men drink, party, enjoy world-class entertainment, and network in a relaxed atmosphere. And sometimes dress in drag and do the can-can.

"My lasting impression was of an all-pervading sense of immaturity," Ronson writes in *Them*. "The Elvis impersonators, the pseudo-pagan spooky rituals, the heavy drinking. These people might have reached the apex of their professions, but emotionally they seemed trapped in their college years."

Alex Jones' take on the Bohemian Grove is different from all of this. He says there is something more sinister going on there, like satanic rituals. He says the Great Owl of Bohemia represents the false deity Moloch, and that Dull Care represents a child being sacrificed as an offering to appease this ancient evil.

The *Dark Secrets* documentary opens with some dramatic, monster-stalking-you-in-the-woods music, mixed with images of the Cremation of Care ceremony. Alex Jones then appears and warns viewers about the shocking footage they will see.

"Could it be when you have all the power and all the women and all the land and all the art that you have to do something new—you have to go against the basic grain of humanity, you have to *get off* in a *sick way*?" Jones asks the viewer, using one of his favorite hooks—the speculative, rhetorical question. He then documents his trip to Monte Rio, California and his analysis of the footage shot from the duffel-bag-hidden camera inside the Grove. Jones describes the Cremation of Care ceremony as a "bizarre ancient Canaanite Luciferian Babylon mystery religion ceremony."

"Upon further research of the ritual you just witnessed, it becomes clear it is a mixture of the Babylon cult of Moloch fused with Druidic rites... mixed with Masonic rites from Scotland," Jones explains. He speculates that artwork on a Cremation of Care ceremony program, when blown up life-size, shows that a skull in the art is the "anatomical size of a baby or small child." He makes the claim again later, saying that the effigy could represent a child, "...or it could be real, ladies and gentlemen!"

Jones' own footage sinks this "child effigy" claim. The effigy, Dull Care, speaks to the Bohemians during the Cremation of Care ceremony, not with the voice of a child, but a sinister booming baritone of an adult. And is it realistic to expect that program cover art is going to have an anatomically correct skull on it?

Other conspiracy theorists have elaborated and added their own flourishes to the story. There is an underground chamber, they say, where sex slaves are kept shackled to the walls. There are claims that snuff films had been recorded in the Grove, and others have run with Jones' speculation that the Cremation of Care was just one of several ceremonies where actual people, even children, and not wooden effigies are being sacrificed at the altar of the bloodthirsty Moloch. Some have even said that an evil breed of aliens, the Reptilians, congregate there to plot their eventual world domination.

"I'M NOT CONCERNED THAT they're having a recreational two weeks," Mary Moore, of Bohemian Grove Action Network, says of the Grove members. "I could care less if they're dancing around in tutus or if they're having gay sex orgies. Who cares? I am concerned that a small group of men have so much influence and power and no matter what your issue is as an activist—environment, racism, nuclear weapons—you can find someone up at the Grove that is making a profit from it."

Moore strongly feels that the "conspiracy mumbo-jumbo" detracts heavily from her group's message. I could tell there was a reluctance for her to talk to me because she had been roped into one too many media pieces that mixed her message together with Alex Jones and other conspiracy theorists.

"We think their theories are pretty silly and there is no way they can prove them, it's all speculation... underground sex chambers where they keep women chained up and burning live babies at the Cremation of Care, I mean just really sensationalist, bizarre stuff!" Moore says. "And no, we don't want our image to be watered down with that kind of stuff, it makes us all look stupid."

Weiss, from *Spy* magazine, says he believes in conspiracies of power, but that the Grove isn't a necessary part of it.

"Maybe an incident happens there or an occasional important event, but I don't think that's why the place exists. I think those people can find each other anywhere. Like, let's say the Trilateral Commission is running the world. Why do they need the Bohemian Grove? There's too many idiots that would get in the way of them running the world there."

I asked Weiss if he felt the Cremation of Care ceremony, which he witnessed, was a sinister occult power ritual.

"No," he dismissed flatly. "It's just too fucking goofy."

"I HAD HEARD THE TERM 'conspiracy theory' but mostly in a Bigfoot, UFO, and aliens connotation," Richard told me. "I already knew the government lied about a lot of things (Vietnam, Watergate, etc.) but I didn't know there was a 'community' of like-minded people seeking the truth. Jones was compelling because he was 'in your face' about his stories and had actually traveled to several 'hotspots.'"

Richard, alone in Austin and watching AC-TV, caught a broadcast of *Dark Secrets: Inside Bohemian Grove* sometime in 2000, and he notes that it "changed his life forever."

"I had just about given up on the Real Life Superhero thing," Richard says. "Patrols rarely produce results. I needed a specific mission. What could be more appropriate than taking down a secret society of Satanists?"

As a conspiracy-minded Christian, who had been a young man in the '80s and '90s, Richard's thinking was shaped by a wave of paranoia known as the Satanic Panic. This episode of our culture was a time where the hand of Satan was seen in games like Dungeons & Dragons and other fantasy games, comic books, heavy metal music, and New Age practices. There was a widespread fear of Satanic cults who were said to be all over the country and engaged in rituals that included child sexual abuse, black magick, animal and even human sacrifice.

The Satanic Panic was largely launched by a now-discredited bestselling autobiography from 1980, *Michelle Remembers*, which details author Michelle Smith allegedly being forced to participate in these rituals. Smith, who wrote the book with the help of recovered memory from a therapist, recalls one 81-day-long ritual in 1955 that summoned the devil himself.

The Satanic Panic was spread further by hoaxes, circulating misinformation, and people looking for attention. The message of a secret Satanic Army was preached by televangelists and "God's cartoonist" Jack T. Chick, founder of Chick Publications. "Chick tracts" are small comic strip books distributed by an invisible network of people leaving them in public spaces. Chick began producing them in the 1960s and kept them rolling until he died in 2016 (Chick Publications continues to produce new tracts). Chick promoted the Satanic Panic as a conspiracy cabal of Satanists, the Catholic Church, witches, LGBT, secular teachers, atheists, Muslims, and others, often working together as a coalition of the damned. His targets shifted over the decades from *Bewitched* to Dungeons & Dragons to Harry Potter, but the Devil was always lurking somewhere.

Although the panic died down in the '90s, some of the effects lingered long after.

THE PHANTOM PATRIOT

RICHARD BEGAN DRAFTING NEW superhero ideas on paper in 2000. These were different from his younger creations, because his new heroes now reflected his new mission—to fight the "New World Order." He created a character called The Activist, who would be a protest character, but Richard dismissed him as "not intimidating enough." Another idea, the Austin Knight, a potential cable access show host as was scrapped as "too regional." He continued to sketch until he came up with a new character design he was happy with: the Phantom Patriot.

ABOVE: The cover of *Phantom Patriot #1*, illustrated by Richard McCaslin, August 2001.

"I got the skull mask in 1999 from a Halloween store in Cincinnati, Ohio. I used it for a Ghost Rider costume," says Richard of the most startling aspect of his costume—a grinning skeleton face mask. The rest of the costume consisted of a star-spangled bandanna he wrapped around the top of his head, and a navy-blue jumpsuit. The suit had the words "Phantom Patriot" sewn across the chest and symbols of a donkey and an elephant on his shoulders, each struck out with a red circle and slash. His belt featured the Phantom Patriot symbol as a buckle, a double mirrored letter *P*. Combat boots rounded out the look.

Richard's first idea with the persona was to make "symbolic appearances" in costume. He also produced a series of four comic-book-style zines filled with poems and illustrations that took a cue from Alex Jones, condemning the "globalist scum." His illustrated poems railed against the UN agenda, the mass media, the Federal Reserve, and the deceptive "Uncle Scam." He listed Infowars.com on each of the pamphlets' back covers. Over the course of a few months, Richard printed hundreds of these little zines, distributing them in a similar way to Chick tracts—leaving little piles where people might grab them, and handing them out in person.

Issue number one, a ten-page booklet with a cover date of August 2001, has this poem Richard penned about the Bohemian Grove in it:

BIRD IN THE BUSH
Bohemian Grove
What a happening place
Worship the devil
In front of God's face
Ritual sacrifice
Debauchery and sodomy
Everyone there
Should get a lobotomy
Owl of Babylon
Moloch by name
Stands as an idol
While two Georges bow in shame
As with the father
So with the son
Both believe earth
Should be ruled as one

Richard traveled to the East Coast, making appearances in costume at the Minuteman statue in Concord, Massachusetts, and the Boston Tea Party ship, as well as an appearance in Chappaqua, New York (where the Clintons have a home), leaving his pamphlets as a calling card. He considered visiting the Statue of Liberty, but "I had no idea how the security guards would react to a 'nutcase in a skull mask,' so I scrubbed that idea." He decided to head to Washington, D.C. and the White House instead.

"I parked my car several blocks from the Capitol Building. I put on my uniform and rode into the National Mall area on a BMX bike. I had a sign on the front that said, 'Stop the New World Order!' (subtle) I then proceeded to ride around the whole mall area—the Capitol Building, the Washington Monument, the Lincoln Memorial and the White House. There were plenty of people around. A few laughed and pointed, but most of them just stood and stared at me, slack-jawed. The one notable exception was a *little kid*. After being prompted by his father, he yells out the window of the car, 'You're a freak!' After circling the White House, I stopped and threw some pamphlets over the fence. There were Secret Service agents sitting in a car in the driveway. I'm not sure if they saw me, but I didn't hang around to find out."

After the East Coast, the Phantom Patriot appeared in Crawford, Texas, leaving copies of his zines on the property of President George W. Bush's ranch and again at a Masonic lodge in Waco, Texas. Part of the goal for these far-spread appearances was, according to Secret Service files, to make it appear as though there was a wide-ranging "Phantom Patriot Movement" distributing literature and cheering the hero on.

Richard felt that distributing literature and making "symbolic appearances" wasn't making a deep enough impact. He wanted to engage in a direct action that would transform himself into a bit of folklore, a hero like the Lone Ranger or Batman. He first thought of raiding the Bohemian Grove in 2001. He packed his Phantom Patriot gear into his truck to drive up to the Grove for a "recon mission" during the Midsummer encampment in July of that year, which he described in a letter:

The only maps I had were the regular tourist kind. I got most of my directions from the Alex Jones video. At the end of Jones' *Dark Secrets* documentary, he gives instructions on how to drive to the Bohemian Grove... I did a (costumed) recon of the front gate area and parking lot. There were people coming and going, but I didn't recognize anyone famous. I had my Glock .45 pistol, my Kabar knife and a camera. What I didn't have was a *plan*. I didn't want to risk sneaking in until it got dark (a couple hours later). Even if I did get in, then what?

I wasn't sure if the sacrifice "victim" for the Cremation of Care was a real baby or not. Even if it was, what should I do; rush in with "guns blazing" and rescue the baby? This was *real* life, not a comic book. Sure, I could have killed a few satanic pedophiles, but the odds of me getting out of there alive (with a baby in tow) were slim to none. No matter how it went down, it would be reported in the Illuminati-controlled media as a "terrorist attack against world leaders on vacation!" After mulling this over for a while, I reluctantly packed it in and drove back to Texas to regroup and rethink my mission.

Richard let his Bohemian Grove plans go for the moment.

"At that time, I wasn't quite ready to get arrested, let alone die for the cause," Richard wrote to me. "September 11 changed all that."

CHAPTER 5

TRUTHERS

"You think it was 19 guys that were living in a cave, armed with box cutters that knocked down them towers with airplanes... in nine seconds?" Matthew Naus asked me incredulously, his voice crackling. He smirked at me, indicating such a notion—known to 9/11 conspiracy theorists as "the official story"—is absurd. I glanced at the tables surrounding us in the café where we had agreed to meet. Everyone was ignoring us, or pretending to. Not that Naus seemed out of place; he looks like the most typical blue-collar Milwaukeean you can imagine. He was wearing both a Green Bay Packers baseball cap and a green and gold Packers sweatshirt—clear indicators that he was a proud Wisconsinite—and jeans. He had a neatly trimmed mustache and looked like he might work as a construction foreman or in a factory.

Naus had agreed to sit down and join me for coffee and tell me what he and a group of thousands of others—members of the "9/11 Truth Movement," who call themselves "9/11 Truthers" or simply "Truthers"—believe really happened on September 11, 2001.

On that date Naus was driving to his job as a middle school teacher in West Allis, a suburb of Milwaukee, when he heard news of the first plane strike over the radio. At the school, he and the principal wheeled out a television and watched in shock as the news unfolded.

At the time, Naus believed what he was seeing in these news reports: that members of al-Qaeda, under the direction of Osama Bin Laden, had hijacked four commercial airline flights and crashed them into the World Trade Center towers, the Pentagon, with a fourth headed to the White House crashing instead into a field in Pennsylvania.

But in 2005, Naus began to see things differently after he heard a segment on a popular radio show called *Coast to Coast AM*, which explores conspiracy theories and paranormal subjects. That episode discussed the collapse of World Trade Center Building 7, a 47-story structure that wasn't struck by a plane and suddenly collapsed at 5:21 p.m. on 9/11. Experts say that it was the pile-up of debris from the twin towers and eight hours of fires inside the building that led to the sudden implosion, but Truthers say it was clearly a controlled demolition. In the confusion and clouds of dust there are still unanswered questions about Building 7, which makes it a favorite talking point for Truthers.

After the show and his own research, Naus learned more about 9/11 conspiracy.

The most common conspiracies say that the twin towers, like Building 7, were brought down by controlled demolitions and not the airplanes that struck them. Conspiracy says that the Pentagon was hit with a missile and not an airplane, and that Flight 93, which crashed in Pennsylvania, was shot down deliberately or that the passengers were relocated, murdered, and their plane was replaced with a fabricated wreck site. More fringe theories suggest that the planes didn't exist at all and were holograms.

Opposing schools of Truther thought suggest that the government either stood down and let the terrorists hijack the planes (the "Let it Happen on Purpose" or LIHOP theory) or actively helped in planning the attack (the "Made it Happen on Purpose" or MIHOP theory). The reason 9/11 happened, Truthers say, was to have a catalyst to invade the Middle East for their oil, and so Bush could have revenge on Saddam Hussein. A secondary benefit would be destroying damning paperwork, a cover-up for evidence of $2.3 trillion in Pentagon money that was missing.

Naus was convinced by what he was reading and became a Truther and an active organizer within the movement. A Vietnam vet, Naus co-founded a group called Veterans for 9/11 Truth, following the lead of similar groups like Scholars for 9/11 Truth, and Architects and Engineers for 9/11 Truth. Later, he formed a Milwaukee-based group called Take a Stand for 9/11 Truth. The group held monthly protests in high-traffic areas of Milwaukee, organized meetings, and

distributed Truther literature and burned copies of DVDs. Naus also hosted a Truther-themed cable access program in West Allis titled *Meet the Truth*, with guests from within the movement.

To help illustrate his deep involvement with the Truthers, Naus had brought along a scrapbook for me to look at, which he thumped down on the café table. It was filled with photos of him at various protest marches, Truther conferences, and poses of him with prominent Truthers.

"Here, here's me with the guys who made *Loose Change*," he said, pointing to a couple of pictures. *Loose Change 9/11: An American Coup* is the Truthers' most popular piece of propaganda, viewed by millions of people online. Alex Jones was an executive producer.

Naus pointed to a picture of him and Jones together at a 9/11 protest in Manhattan near Ground Zero. Jones had quickly become a hero of the Truther movement when he predicted 9/11 happening months before it did.

As a *Rolling Stone* article reports, "On July 25, 2001 [Jones] looked into the camera and issued a warning that has become legendary among 9/11 Truthers. 'Please!' he implored. 'Call Congress. Tell 'em we know the government is planning terrorism.' Jones mentioned the World Trade Center by name and warned against the propaganda he expected to accompany the attacks. 'Bin Laden is the boogeyman they need in this Orwellian, phony system,' he said."

Jones opened his September 11, 2001 radio show with a tirade against the government,

ABOVE: 9/11 Truthers at a 2007 rally in Los Angeles. CREDIT: WIKIMEDIA COMMONS/DAMON D'AMATO.

saying that the buildings were brought down with controlled demolition.

"Look, here's Jones with Charlie Sheen," Naus says, turning a page with a crinkling sound, pointing at a photo of Jones and Sheen, arms around each other's shoulders, smiling at the camera.

Ignoring his coffee completely, Naus showed more photos—a picture of himself with Jim Marrs, the classic conspiracy theorist, at a conference.

"This is David Ray Griffin—he's written over ten books on 9/11. I did a 15-city tour for him in 2010, in fact, there's a part of one of his books where he thanks me for organizing his tour," Naus explained to me.

Truther groups have spread around the world, organizing meetings, protests, and conferences, and talking about the latest literature on the subject. 9/11 conspiracy books and DVDs are a cottage industry. There have even been candidates running for office on a "9/11 Truth Platform." New Jersey conspiracy theorist/politician Jeff Boss threw his hat into the 2012 presidential election ring and won 907 votes.

ON JULY 22, 2004, the 9/11 Commission published its final report on their findings of the circumstances of the terrorist attack. The Commission interviewed over 1,200 people in ten countries and reviewed over two million pages of documents from various intelligence organizations around the world. Their findings confirmed that miscommunication between intelligence groups left the country vulnerable, and after careful planning by Al-Qaeda, the terrorists were able to carry out their plan. The report was published and became a bestselling book.

When I asked Naus what he thought of the *9/11 Commission Report*, he made it clear he thought it was a poorly written fiction.

"Oh, I burn a copy every year," Naus told me, grinning widely. Take a Stand for 9/11 Truth, he explained, used to burn a copy on the date of the Boston Tea Party, December 16. The group cremated the book in a Weber grill in a city park, then dumped the ashes in Lake Michigan. December is not the best time of year to plan outdoor activities in Wisconsin, though, so they later switched the date to July 22, the day the commission published the report.

This new event, dubbed the "9/11 Myth Destruction Picnic," took place in a city park near the lake on a nice, sunny day. Perhaps energized by the good weather, Naus determined that simply burning a copy of the book was too lenient a sentence, so he bought several copies to destroy.

"We destroyed it six different ways," he explained. "We put it in a big jug of Kool-Aid, you know, like, 'you're drinking the Kool-Aid if you believe this.' Then we tarred and feathered it; we drilled holes in it because there are so many holes in the story. We shredded it and then I mixed the shredded pages into bullshit, cow manure," Naus laughed. "And actual bullshit! I went to the State Fair to find real bullshit!" He stopped to reflect on the day.

"Oh yeah, we peed on it! But we didn't really pee on it, because we didn't want to get arrested in the park, so we filled some balloons up with Mello Yello. Then we held the balloon necks in our hands," he told me, making a foreskin-pinching gesture, "to make it look like we were peeing on it. I have all this on film!" Naus told me, looking up his YouTube page on his iPhone.

AS TIME WENT ON, Naus suspected something bigger had happened and that the current popular 9/11 conspiracies were a "cover-up of a cover-up." In this way I found conspiracy theorists to be somewhat like hipsters—when a theory becomes too popular and mainstream, they head deeper underground into the rabbit hole to find the next idea. Naus began to question if planes had ever really hit the twin towers, especially after he began reading the theories of Dr. Judy Wood, who came to the conclusion that the towers weren't destroyed by plane impact or controlled demolition, but were secretly blasted by a controlled energy beam, technology that had been developed by Nikola Tesla.

Tesla is a conspiracy favorite, with various theories suggesting that his discovery of free energy from the atmosphere was suppressed by oil and energy companies; that he had established communication with extraterrestrials; and, relevant to Dr. Wood's theory, toward the end of his life he claimed he developed a death ray. Tesla's conspiracy lore deepened when the FBI seized all his papers after his death in 1943, hoping they might find something to give them the upper hand in World War II (they reported they didn't find anything useful and later declassified the documents). Dr. Wood's theory taps into the mythology of Tesla's death ray.

"Here, she explains it all in here," Naus told me, handing me a hefty, nearly five-hundred-page textbook titled *Where Did the Towers Go? Evidence of Directed Free-Energy Technology on 9/11*, self-published by Dr. Wood in 2010. "She lays out *empirical* evidence," Naus told me adamantly, tapping the table at the café with his pointer finger.

"The World Trade Center (WTC) towers did not 'collapse' on 9/11/01. They didn't have sufficient time to collapse because they were destroyed faster than is physically possible for a gravity-driven collapse," Dr. Wood writes.

The text is a strange collection of equations, charts, graphs, and photo analysis, strung together with random observations. One section shows a series of graphs that detail the rate a billiard ball should fall off the roof of World Trade Center Building 1, another chapter studies seismic impact. In another part, Dr. Wood examines the body language of people falling to their death from the twin towers, concluding that they were launched by an energy beam impact instead of jumping.

In her conclusion, Dr. Wood says that "the technology demonstrated on 9/11 can, indeed, split the world in half, or it can be used to let all people to live fruitful, constructive, and non-polluting lives through their use of free energy."

AFTER WATCHING SOME VIDEO FOOTAGE of Naus destroying copies of the *9/11 Commission Report,* I asked him if he thought we'll ever get a public disclosure of what he thinks really happened on 9/11. "Maybe not in my lifetime. I think what is going to happen is that the government is going to get dissolved. I think the one chance we have is we have good people in the military," Naus told me. "There's going to be a day of reckoning, but we're going to go through a lot more before then. There's going to be chaos in the cities and food shortages. They're going to block off areas—if people are killing each other in the cities, they won't give a shit, they'll just block off the roads to the suburbs."

If that turns out to be the situation, Naus plans to go out shooting if he has to.

"I'm not the type of person that is fear-driven. The only thing I fear is that I'm caught somewhere where I can't shoot it out with them when they come to take my guns and catch me. You know, 'Fuck you, you're taking my freedom away, go ahead and kill me, but I'm takin' out one of youse!' I'm afraid to get caught without protecting my freedom, but other than that I don't fear nothing at all. Most truth seekers are like that."

Somewhat dazed by his last statements, I parted ways with Naus at the café and start walking down the street.

"Hey Tea, wait up!" Naus shouted after me. I slowly turned around as he approached.

"Here, I forgot to give you this," he said, handing me a DVD in a paper sleeve. "This here is a documentary about the Apollo moon landing. It was all fake," he said, shaking his head.

I looked at the DVD, with a photocopied insert. It read *The Apollo Moon Hoax.*

"What they did is they got, uh, the guy who directed *2001: A Space Odyssey...*"

"Stanley Kubrick?" I asked.

"Yeah, Stanley Kubrick. They shot the whole moon landing in a Hollywood studio and Stanley Kubrick directed the whole thing."

OUR NATION SAW EVIL

ON SEPTEMBER 11, RICHARD says he was walking back home from the grocery store when he got the news.

"At a street corner near my apartment, a guy was selling rush editions of the *Austin American Statesman* with the story on the front. I got one, of course." The headline for the special report edition screamed "Our Nation Saw Evil," above a photo of panicked New Yorkers rushing down a street in a giant cloud of ash. The other two cover articles are headlined "Long, aggressive fight ahead for U.S., Bush" and "Airliners turned into weapons of terror."

"I wasn't all that surprised that something like this had happened, although I figured the 'terrorist' target in NYC would be the Statue of Liberty," Richard says. "Obviously, a bunch of third-world extremists couldn't have pulled this off. At least not by themselves."

Richard's conspiracy theory studies already had him amped up and made him an instant Truther.

"Correct me if I'm wrong, but *none* of the passengers' bodies on *any* of those planes were ever actually recovered or identified (probably killed elsewhere)," he wrote me. "The news just kept saying that everyone got burned up. *Bullshit!* Then to further insult the intelligence of their viewers, the teleprompter readers began reporting that copies of the Koran and the hijackers' passports had miraculously been found at Ground Zero! What really amazes me is that the majority of Americans still believe the 'official story' after all the hard evidence to disprove it!"

Richard continued to make symbolic appearances as the Phantom Patriot, on Congress Avenue and again on Sixth Street, a popular entertainment district, on Halloween.

He had some of his poems he had written for his pamphlets read on a cable access show, *Common Sense*, a conspiracy show hosted by George Humphrey and Rusty Fields, which aired on the same channel as Alex Jones, AC-TV. Jones himself gave Phantom Patriot an endorsement on air, Richard says, on a November 1, 2001 show.

But none of this was satisfying for him. He decided it was time to take direct action, like his comic book heroes. The world was different now. The ground had shook. Richard remembered his recon mission at the Bohemian Grove.

It was go time.

ABOVE: Richard in his
Phantom Patriot costume
with weapons shortly before
his Bohemian Grove raid.

CHAPTER 6

BURN THE OWL

"Moloch! Moloch! Nightmare of Moloch! Moloch the loveless! Mental Moloch! Moloch the heavy judger of men!"—Allen Ginsberg, *Howl and Other Poems*

E nergized by the events of September 11, Richard spent the next few months training for his plan to infiltrate the Bohemian Grove. He had three goals going in.

First, he wanted to disrupt any satanic rituals he might encounter and save victims who were awaiting a fiery death.

He also wanted to create a media whirlwind with the raid that would blow the lid off the Grove. Imagine the Phantom Patriot, surrounded by news cameras, relieved sacrifice victims in the background, law enforcement shoving the nation's most powerful men, now identified as baby-killers, into the backs of cop cars. At long last, Richard's day of triumph!

His third goal, in case nothing else panned out, was to fill the Bohemians with fear by burning their sacred Great Owl of Bohemia to the ground.

Richard chose a January date for his raid rather than the July encampment because he thought it would help him go unnoticed. He reasoned that only the more hardcore satanic Bohemians would be bunking at the Grove this time of year, instead of the more casual members who were there to drink and go fishing. Richard didn't have a particular reason for choosing the date, but later noted that some sources list January 20–27 as a period on the "Satanic Holidays" calendar marked for "abduction, ceremonial preparation, and holding of sacrificial victims," as a listing circulated on the Internet alleges. The listing isn't sourced and looks like it might be a leftover relic from the Satanic Panic.

Winter in the redwood forest was the perfect time for his mission, Richard reasoned. The Satanists would have their guard down.

Richard's first step to planning his raid was to brush up on his firearm skills. He took a pistol course at a Thunder Ranch in Texas, then attended a three-day SCARS (Special Combat Aggressive Reactionary System) seminar in Salt Lake City. After that, he decided he would pack up and move from Austin to Carson City, Nevada. He traded in his RV for a pickup truck.

"Carson City was more or less the closest Nevada city to the Grove," Richard explains about his destination. "I hadn't picked a particular date to do the mission, so I needed a place to stay until then. There was also a chance I wouldn't do it at all, and Carson City was a decent place to live."

BEFORE HE LEFT TOWN, Richard stopped by the AC-TV studios to talk to Alex Jones about the Bohemian Grove. Richard was looking for confirmation that he was on the right path.

"I met him at the public access studio where he did his show in Austin. I felt I should meet this guy before I went to the Grove," Richard wrote to me. "We discussed the Grove in general, but I didn't say anything about going there. If I got arrested, I didn't want him charged with conspiracy. At one point, he excused himself from the conversation, but he said he would be right back. At the time, I thought that AJ thought I might be an undercover fed. I decided to leave before he got back."

On his way to Carson City, Richard had a nerve-racking moment. While approaching the Hoover Dam, he noticed that traffic had crawled to a stop and that the Highway Patrol was doing a vehicle check. His mind wandered to the back of his truck, where he had a container with his recently purchased arsenal—guns, a sword, crossbows, and lots of ammunition. All of this was legally acquired, *but how to explain the Phantom Patriot costume?* And what was with this roadblock? Richard felt a panic. *Did they know? Was this set up for him*? But the Highway Patrol looked at his driver's license and waved him on. Richard passed the Hoover Dam and carried on to Carson City and found an apartment to rent.

During this period, Richard quit communicating with his friends. He kept all his plans for the Bohemian Grove to himself, fearing that if he talked to anyone about it, he would be incriminating them. With his family gone, and his few friends unaware of his location, he was alone in the world.

Lon had some contact with Richard while he was in Texas, "...but not a lot," he recalled. He had noticed that Richard had been getting more heavily "into religion and the conspiracy stuff had become more pervasive" over the last couple of years, but the conspiracy talk didn't alarm him.

"I've talked to people about conspiracy stuff before, and the thing is, everyone has them—some of the ideas are mainstream, and some aren't. I had a buddy of mine who told me the same corporation that makes Play-Doh makes carpet cleaner, and it turns out it's true!" Lon told me. "But is that a conspiracy or is it just a smart business move? When you get into the Illuminati and that stuff, you start to lose me, but it's hard for me to fault someone who believes that stuff, that's their truth, I just don't see it."

Later Lon would share his "Richard File" with me, hundreds of pages of legal documents and personal correspondence, including his last communication with him before the raid: a Christmas card sent to Lon and his wife Julie, post-marked January 9, 2002, just ten days before Richard headed to the Bohemian Grove, and after he had arrived in Carson City. It had included a check.

"I'm going through a weird time right now. Yes Lon... weirder than usual," Richard wrote to them, after thanking them for a card and explaining he had been traveling. "I inherited a large sum of money from Mom's estate. This year, I decided that I would share some of it with a few friends, while they are still young and poor enough to appreciate it. I'm sure that you two 'starving actors' have bills to pay."

After that, communication from Richard stopped.

"He didn't want anyone in on his actions, where he was and what was going on. Probably smartly so, because he probably knew there were a few people who would try to stop him or tip people off if he did that," Lon told me, pausing to reflect. "I'd have to call somebody if I knew he was going to do that, because I couldn't stand the idea that someone got injured in that process on purpose or by mistake."

On January 19, 2002, Richard decided it was time.

THE RAID

"I SPENT MY LAST 'free day' watching Mel Gibson's *The Patriot* on VHS," Richard says. Later, when questioned by detectives on who his role models were, Richard would tell them he had two: his mother and Mel Gibson, because of his roles in *The Patriot* and *Braveheart*. It's likely he also identified with Gibson's character in the 1997 thriller *Conspiracy Theory*, in which Gibson played a conspiracist who seemed like a paranoid crackpot until his theories began to unfold.

After watching the movie, Richard did an equipment check, loaded up his pickup truck and drove from Carson City up to the Bohemian Grove, about a four- to five-hour drive.

Richard entered the Grove around 9 p.m. that night wearing his Phantom Patriot costume with a Kevlar vest underneath. He was armed with a Crossfire MK-1 (a 5.56 rifle/12-gauge shotgun hybrid), a .45 caliber semi-automatic Glock pistol, a ninja sword, and a Kabar knife. In his backpack, he carried over one hundred rounds of ammunition, and a fireworks mortar tube and smoke bombs. In his truck, which he parked outside the Grove, were two crossbows and a billy club.

Later, while he was in prison, Richard documented his life-changing night and day inside the Grove by writing and illustrating a full-color, three-part

ABOVE: Art created by Richard McCaslin
shortly before his Bohemian Grove Raid.

autobiographical comic detailing his raid titled "Phantom Patriot: The Skeleton in America's Closet," part of a collection of comics he drew in a graphic novel called *Prison Penned Comics.*

Richard's artwork could undoubtedly be defined as "outsider art." However, his scrutiny of thousands of comic books has given him a strong working knowledge of how a comic book storyline works. His style is outsider art meets *How to Draw Comics the Marvel Way*, the classic instruction book young comic artists have turned to for guidance since the late 1970s. His page layout is well organized, but there is something weird about his artwork. His characters have eerie oval bug eyes with giant luminous irises and almost always are frozen in looks of anger, shock, or confusion, captured in a toothy half-circle frown. Things like hair strands and leaves on trees are oddly symmetrical.

In the original version of the comic, drawn while Richard was still a Christian, the panels are jam-packed with Bible verses—one page lists eight different verses as a footnote. Other scenes incorporate Bible verses drawn as part of the landscape as if created by an enthusiastic editorial cartoonist. One panel, for example, has 2 Thessalonians 1:6–9 (in a nutshell: God is just and will give trouble to those who trouble you) floating inside of a gray storm cloud.

The first panel of Part Two of the comic, "Confrontation," shows Richard clad as the Phantom Patriot sneaking through the redwood forest, holding his rifle and shining a flashlight on the path ahead of him. He has a thought bubble emanating from his head which contains a line from Henry David Thoreau's *Walden*: "I went into the woods because I wished to live deliberately!"

Richard explains his massive arsenal in the comic:

> Despite being heavily armed, it wasn't my intention to simply kill any Bohemians I might encounter. Many of them probably deserved to die for their various crimes, but that was God's decision, not mine. The weapons were for my protection, in case I was attacked by the Grove's security forces; which I assumed would shoot me on sight, or worse. There was also a slim chance that I might actually catch the Bohemians in their criminal activity. If I could make a citizen's arrest, without firing a shot, all the better.

Richard wandered around the giant redwoods until a path led him into the outskirts of the camp.

"For the next two hours I explored the empty grove, as my hopes of interrupting any occult rituals began to fade," a caption box in his comic explains. The illustration below the caption shows the Phantom Patriot looking in disgust at his weakening flashlight.

"Way to go 'Rambo,'" says the self-deprecating superhero. "You have plenty of ammo, but no extra batteries." Now completely in the dark, with the moon covered in clouds and the branches of the towering redwoods, Richard decided he was at risk of getting lost, so he sought cover to hide out until sunrise. He found a nearby cabin and kicked in the door. The comic gives a sound effect of CRASH! as Richard storms the cabin.

"I don't remember what camp it was. I tried to sleep, but it was fairly cold, so I mostly laid awake until first light."

AS THE SUN ROSE, Richard ventured back into the Grove, and after wandering down a path, he soon found himself face-to-face at last with his great enemy "Moloch," the Great Owl of Bohemia. It sat there ominously, staring blankly as the rising sun reflected off the lagoon in front of it.

"The Owl looked just like it did in Alex Jones' video, except a lot crappier. You'd think a bunch of billionaires would spring for something a little more elaborate," Richard says.

Up until this point, Richard had thought that the Great Owl of Bohemia was carved out of a giant redwood tree and had hoped to light it on fire and destroy it. But to his disappointment, he found it was made out of concrete. The statue is hollow on the inside. It's wired for electrical use, and a door in the back opens the hollow body, which serves as a storage shed, holding the Dull Care effigies and other props for the Cremation of Care ceremony.

ABOVE: The calling card left by Richard on the Great Owl of Bohemia statue.

"I wish I had brought a sledgehammer so I could have at least knocked down the altar," Richard told me. Discouraged, he decided instead to leave a message as a warning—a piece of paper featuring his Phantom Patriot logo, a circle and slash through a Bohemian owl logo and the Bible verse Leviticus 18:21—"You shall not give any of your offspring to offer them to Moloch, nor shall you profane the name of your God; I am the Lord."

Richard would have this piece of paper returned to him about a decade later, neatly sealed in an evidence bag.

With no satanic rituals upended and no burning owl statue before him, Richard's mission began to go off the charts.

"I hadn't traveled halfway across the country just to walk out of the Bohemian Grove without causing some real damage," he said. He broke into a nearby banquet hall, the one where Bohemians gather for dinner before the Cremation of Care. After making sure the building was empty, he found a bottle of degreaser. A panel in the comic shows him pouring a ridiculously large bottle of the chemical onto a table.

"I splashed some around the office and kitchen, then lit it," the caption reads, and as the Phantom Patriot looks back at the flames, a thought balloon drifts over his head. "That should be enough to put the fear of God in these perverts!"

But Richard's attempted arson was quickly doused as the building's fire alarm blared, and the sprinklers were triggered to extinguish the flames. This spot could have been where Richard's story ends. He wasn't sure if he should fight or flee.

"I briefly considered making my 'last stand' against Bohemian security and the eventual SWAT team right there," Richard says in the comic. "However, it dawned on me that if I were caught on the property, the corrupt local authorities might simply kill me and cover up the entire incident." Alerted by the fire alarm, a Bohemian Grove maintenance worker named Bob Hipkiss initially spotted Richard and followed him as Richard marched in a "strutting stride" toward the resort's gates and approached the security guard shacks. Hipkiss radioed security guard Fred Yeager, who was on duty. When Richard spotted Yeager, he pointed his rifle at him through the guard shack window.

Fred Yeager's court testimony recalls the moment.

"Well, you know, I— I was— I was— all I could just say I guess maybe this is it, good Lord forgive me and I didn't know what was going to happen. You know, I was pretty upset," Yeager testified.

Richard had spotted Yeager's phone and thought it might have been a gun. Yeager raised his hands. Richard stared at him with blank skull mask eyes, and then:

"Well, it was so strange," Yeager told the court. "He looked at me and then he dropped his left hand from the weapon and raised it and waved, and I just stood there kind of transfixed, and then he turned on a left face and proceeded in the same gait that he approached."

Richard had made it out of the Grove and into a parking lot area, where he encountered the local fire marshal in his pickup truck, who was stationed just a mile down the road and was responding to the fire alarms. When he saw Richard, he turned around and took off.

"He doesn't like my looks," the cartoon version of Richard ponders as the truck speeds away.

Several minutes later, Richard reached the main road and could see his truck, but he had a significant barrier—four police cruisers were surrounding it. The Sonoma County Sheriff's Department had responded to the Grove's 911 call and on the way, they motioned to two California Highway Patrol officers to follow them. Richard took cover behind a tree.

From a police report:

Man with a gun call, Bohemian Grove. I stopped my vehicle by a blue pickup truck parked on the side of the roadway. Since there were no residencies adjacent to the location of the truck, I considered that it might be involved in the incident. The subject's position was approximately ten yards to the rear of the truck, and in a loud voice, I repeatedly ordered the subject from his place of concealment to the roadway. Subject was out of my view except for a small portion of his shoulder and head that would occasionally come from behind the tree. I could also see the condensation of the subject's breath from behind the tree.

The four responding officers ducked behind their cruisers for cover. They continued to yell for Richard to drop his weapon and come out in the open. Richard didn't respond.

"Oh yeah. He was very quiet there," Officer Nenad Gorenec, of the California Highway Patrol, later told the court at Richard's trial. "I mean I could not hear anything else but the deputies yelling and us yelling. It was extremely quiet. I didn't hear a bird or anything. It was a very—very strange feeling in the whole area."

Richard was facing the most critical decision of his life—should he engage, or should he surrender? Two of the officers began to close in on his position, moving from behind their squad to a giant redwood tree stump for cover.

"I had to make a decision now!" Richard says in the comic. "If the SWAT team from Santa Rosa or Sonoma rushed up here on a Sunday morning, I was certain they wouldn't go home without my dead body." After "a few tense minutes," Richard decided to make his move.

"I decided to test the cop's integrity by stepping out into the road with my rifle pointed down, but still at the ready. If they shot at me, I could probably take a few hits to my Kevlar vest and still return fire."

From a police report:

Subject finally walked from his position, still carrying the rifle. When the subject came into view, I could see he was wearing a blue paramilitary uniform, a belt with what appeared to be a sidearm, I could see he was carrying an assault rifle with a high capacity banana-style magazine. Subject was wearing a full latex mask; the character of the mask was a skeleton skull. The subject slowly walked to the center of the road when he stopped, his rifle at a low ready, with the rifle held in both hands. He stood facing me, not responding or communicating, looking at the positions of the four officers on the team. He remained in this stance for approximately four minutes in defiance of my repeated commands to put the rifle on the ground.

"It looked like he was ready—ready to give us a hard time," Officer Eric Wayne Haufler of the California Highway Patrol told the court. "Ready to play ball."

Richard took a deep breath, his breath's condensation pouring out of the mask in the January air. He stood in the middle of the small country road. The morning breeze flowed. His breathing was shallow and filled his skull mask, which grinned quietly at the officers. He stood with his feet spread in a ready stance.

"A couple more minutes passed until finally, one of the officers asked me what I wanted. To my surprise, I detected a wave of fear in his voice. In fact, all four cops seemed visibly shaken by my appearance," Richard wrote.

It shouldn't have been a surprise. Sonoma County is a relatively peaceful place, and up until now, the biggest threat to the Grove had been a few nosy journalists. The Sunday edition of the Sonoma County-based *Press-Democrat* was being delivered in the quiet of the morning at the same time as Richard's standoff. The big front-page story, "Dejected Raiders left out in the cold," was about the Oakland Raiders losing a playoff game to the New England Patriots. Weather predicted a potentially gloomy day: high 56, low 30, chance of rain.

A gunman in a skeleton mask was out of place.

"We've had protestors and stuff at the Bohemian Grove, but I've been here 24 years, and I've never seen—and I don't think any of us will ever again see—a guy dressed like that come here in our careers," Sheriff's Lieutenant Bruce Rochester told the *San Francisco Chronicle* shortly after the raid. "Nobody's laughing. The deputies were scared, and we're all still scratching our heads."

While he stood there in the road, Richard's mind wandered back to his apartment in Carson City. He had left little behind—his comic books and a collection of photos of himself posing in various superhero costumes over the years. On the kitchen table, he had left a will. He named his friend Lon as executor of his estate. There was also artwork Richard had drawn of the Phantom Patriot raiding the Bohemian Grove, priests making a sacrifice to the Great Owl statue in the background. There was a poem he had written about his journey titled "The Battle of Bohemia." Next to this was an autographed picture of a beautiful young country music star, Chely Wright, whom Richard had met the year before. He was in love with her. Attached to the picture was a note with a Bible verse Richard had handwritten—Mark 8:36, "For what shall it profit a man if he shall gain the whole world, and loses his own soul?"

Now, the police car lights flashed silently in front of him. The giant, ancient redwood trees towered over the scene on both sides of the road.

"I wasn't really scared. I was prepared to die for the cause," Richard wrote to me. "This'll sound stupid, but at that moment I wondered, what would Chely think of me?"

BATMAN AND MINNIE PEARL

THE SECRET SERVICE FILE includes an analysis of the search of Richard's apartment in Carson City the day after his raid. The report notes that "the apartment was neat and clean, the refrigerator and kitchen cabinets were empty and there was no food." In the sparse apartment, they found comic books, weapons, and a Bowflex machine in the living room. They found a notebook labeled "Phantom Patriot Missions" on his coffee table which logged his symbolic appearances and had poems written in it. Next to the journal on the coffee table was the *Dark Secrets: Inside Bohemian Grove* documentary on VHS, as well as a Bible, and self-defense and martial arts training videos.

On his bookshelf, they found provocative reading material, and made a note of three titles: *101 Things to Do Til the Revolution: Ideas and Resources for Self-Liberation, Monkey Wrenching and Preparedness*, by Claire Wolfe; a guide to living off the grid titled *Bulletproof Privacy: How to Live Hidden, Happy and Free!* written by a survivalist with the pseudonym Boston T. Party; and *Knights of Darkness: Secrets of the World's Deadliest Night Fighters* by Dr. HaHa Lung, who specializes in ninjutsu and other fighting techniques.

Most attention-grabbing was a display on the coffee table.

From a police report:

> During the search of his apartment, I found a photograph displayed on one
> of the tables in the living room. The picture was autographed... Although I
> wasn't familiar with Chely Wright, it appeared she was a celebrity. What was
> disconcerting about the photograph is that it appeared to be set up as some
> sort of shrine. Below the photograph was 'Phantom Patriot' artwork inside a
> plastic bag.

LATER, I WOULD MEET Richard in person. By then, I had been corre-
sponding with him for over a year. While driving around the hilly streets of
San Francisco, he casually asked if I had heard of a singer named Chely Wright.
"No," I replied.

"Oh, she's a country music singer," he told me. I replied that I wasn't very
knowledgeable about country music, being more of a rock 'n' roll guy myself.
He said that he had had a "weird experience" with her. The thought got lost in
the day—a lot was going on. Later, he mentioned Wright and a "date" he had
with her again in an e-mail. This time I was curious enough to consult Google.
I paired "Richard McCaslin" and "Chely Wright" and searched. I got one hit. It
was an entry in a column called "Country Beat" for MTV.com, dated June 13,
2001. It read:

> Dinner with Chely Wright went for $14,500 at her celebrity auction and benefit
> June 12 at Nashville's Wildhorse Saloon. An avid Wright fan, Richard McCaslin,
> made the winning bid for dinner with the singer at the Nashville restaurant of
> his choice. The event raised money for Wright's Reading, Writing, and Rhythm
> Foundation, which provides musical instruments for schools.

Oh shit, I thought. *What now?*

DURING RICHARD'S DOWNWARD SPIRAL and while shuttling around
state to state looking for work and opportunity, he happened to catch a music
video on Country Music Television one day in 1999. It was a video for a hot
new single, "Single White Female," by Chely Wright. The smash hit was soon
number one on the country music charts. The video features a sophisticated

and sexy-looking Wright and her entourage singing the bouncy hit on a city bus while transit riders contemplate their relationship status.

"A single white female..." Wright sings, smiling, "is looking for a man like you!" Many men thought that perhaps Wright was addressing them personally and developed an infatuation with her. Richard was one of them. He thought she was a "beautiful woman" and he could "relate to some of her lyrics, specifically about being lonely," he told the Secret Service, adding that "he fell in love with her."

After talking briefly back and forth, Richard sat down and wrote a 23-page handwritten account he titled "My Memories of Chely Wright." He made a photocopy of the entire letter and mailed it to me in a manila envelope. It was instantly apparent flipping through the pages that this was not merely an account of a "weird experience" or a "date" but a celebrity stalking and that Richard was still unhealthily obsessed with the country star and his encounter with her.

After seeing Wright's video, Richard went to see her perform in concert a couple times, traveling to catch shows by her in Louisville, Kentucky and again in Belton, Texas.

He had just developed the Phantom Patriot persona, and in May 2001, he returned to Zanesville to collect his inheritance. It was an ugly homecoming. Richard writes:

2001: May: Put together Phantom Patriot costume and gear. Return to Zanesville to collect inheritance. Discover "discrepancies" in tax forms and other paperwork. Government took almost half of it! Cousin Beverly had (illegally) increased her "cut" as Power of Attorney. She was a notary public and worked for a judge (co-signer). She had probably been planning this since Dad died. I was staying (temporarily) at "old maid" cousin Kathy's house. She tried to borrow money from me, to pay off the house, even though she had plenty in the bank. I bought an RV and left town without telling anyone.

Richard found out about the Chely Wright Fan Club party she would be at in Nashville in June 2001 and made it his next destination. His parents deceased, his inheritance in his bank account, he was planning his first visit to the Bohemian Grove for July 2001. But the chance to meet Wright gave him pause. If he could meet her, he was sure they would "hit it off," he told the Secret Service.

"I was already planning my Bohemian Grove mission, but the summer encampment was still a month away," Richard wrote. "I knew that the odds of me getting shot or arrested in there were high. So in a way, meeting Chely in person was on my 'bucket list.'"

WRIGHT'S ASCENSION TO COUNTRY music superstar is a classic Cinderella story. Born in 1970 to a poor family in the small town of Wellsville, Kansas (with a population of about 1,600 at the time), Wright practiced singing country songs while chopping and stacking firewood with her siblings. Her grandmother would send her audio recordings of the Grand Ole Opry. Saturday nights consisted of family and friends gathering in the living room to sing together.

Wright began to climb up a ladder of success. Her early performances were at parties, nursing homes, and "clubs and honky-tonks at age 11." At 17, still in high school, she landed a gig as a cast member in the *Ozark Jubilee* show in Branson, Missouri, a Southern tourist destination. After that, she landed a spot in the Opryland USA revue show *Country Music USA*, in Nashville, where she portrayed country comedian legend Minnie Pearl.

Wright signed a recording contract and released her first album, *Woman in the Moon*, in 1994 on Polydor Records. By her third album, *Let Me In*, she moved to MCA Nashville, and produced a Top 20 country hit, "Shut Up and Drive." It wasn't until her fourth album, 1999's *Single White Female*, that her career launched into star status. She started collecting awards by the armload from the Academy of Country Music and Country Music Television and the Country Music Association Awards.

In 2001, Wright was still riding the crest of that wave. That year she was voted by *People* magazine as one of the "50 Most Beautiful People of the Year," and she released her third (and last album) with MCA, *Never Love You Enough*. Often noted as being a kind-hearted and generous person, Wright founded a charity called Reading, Writing, and Rhythm, devoted to music education. The foundation helps provide musical instruments and other equipment to schools in need. Wright was honored for her contributions in 2002 by the National Association for Music Education. By all appearances, it was a great time to be Chely Wright.

WRIGHT'S JUNE 12, 2001 fan club party was at the Wildhorse Saloon in downtown Nashville, an evening filled with performances by Wright and her country music co-stars. Later in the evening, an auction to benefit Reading, Writing, and Rhythm took place with items like a guided tour of the Country Music Hall of Fame by Wright (which sold for $2,000) and a pair of orange boxer shorts worn by country star Darryl Worley (which managed to fetch $550). But the most coveted item was the dinner date evening.

Essentially homeless and alone, thoughts of Wright were a welcome distraction in Richard's life, and so he navigated his RV toward Nashville.

"Chely initially met the fans one-on-one, to sign autographs. A little 'something' passed between us as we shook hands, and I was smitten." Richard wrote. Next, he recalls, there was a buffet dinner for the fans and Chely performed, joined by fellow country stars like Brad Paisley, Richard Marx, and Rascal Flatts. Wright was romantically linked to Paisley at the time. The two had met in 1999 and recorded a duet together in 2000, "Hard to Be a Husband, Hard to Be a Wife." They began a short on-again, off-again frustrating relationship.

"There was an awkward tension between Chely and Brad Paisley. Word on the floor was that they had broken up a month or two before. Had a window of opportunity opened up for me?" Richard wrote on the duet performance that evening.

After the country stars performed, the charity auction began. Bidding on dinner with Chely Wright shot up to $5,000, then slowed as it approached $10,000.

"Something inside me said, 'don't stop!' I finally topped the bidding out at $14,500," Richard says.

The auctioneer sent an assistant to get Richard's personal information, and the house lights came up. "Everyone around me was gawking at me like I was a rock star," Richard says. "Two or three guys near me shook my hand. It was kind of cool, but a little embarrassing." Richard met Chely Wright's fan club president, Chuck Walter, and was hustled backstage to talk to Country Music Television.

"They stared at me like I was a zoo animal," Richard says of the CMT crew. "I can't remember everything that was said in the interview, but I believe the term 'Chely's #1 fan' was mentioned."

Richard didn't get to speak to Wright that night. He talked to Chuck Walter and arranged to do a money transfer the next day.

IT TOOK A COUPLE of days to set up the date. Richard parked and set up at an RV park and waited.

"I used that time to buy a wooden plaque, paint it, and lay out a romantic poem I had written in sticker letters. I decided to wear my Marine Corps dress blues uniform on the date. I might only get one chance to impress Chely, so I was going to make it count."

Finally, after much anticipation, the big night arrived. A limo swung through the RV park and picked up Richard around 7 p.m. Inside the limo were fan club president Chuck Walter, Wright's publicist Shane Tarlton, and Chely herself.

"(She) was wearing a black cocktail dress, slightly above the knee. For some odd reason, she seemed a little thinner than before and visibly tired. At the time,

I thought this was due to her hectic schedule."

Wright's schedule that week was indeed hectic. She was participating in several events centered around Nashville that featured country stars called "Fan Fair Week." Besides her charity show and auction, the next day she presented at another charity event for Gilda's Club at the Country Music Hall of Fame, then walked across the street to present an award at the TNN and CMT Country Weekly Music Awards. The day after that, she played in the City of Hope charity softball game, and all this before getting ready to kick off a 30-city tour. Wright was also harboring a gnawing secret about her life, weighing down heavily on her, but few people knew about it. It would come out later. Years afterward, Richard would form his own elaborate theory as to Wright's tired appearance.

At first, Richard says that the date went well. Wright was "thrilled" with his uniform, telling him that her brother was also a Marine.

"To my surprise, Chely even suggested that it might be cool if I met him sometime. At that point, I thought, 'this is more than just a celebrity making small talk with a fan. She genuinely likes me!'"

A police report notes:

The dinner is very impersonal so that the winner won't get the wrong idea. [Chely Wright Fan Club representative Mark Jones] mentioned that Chely is a people person, he described her personality as making people feel comfortable around her, she is very unassuming. Richard McCaslin was the winning bidder last October [sic] 2001. McCaslin had dinner with Chely Wright. Jones said he thought McCaslin thought the dinner was more than a charity event.

As they talked in the back of the limo, Wright threw Richard a curveball when she asked if his parents were still alive. After a stunned silence, their deaths still raw in his mind, he answered, "No." The conversation returned to normal. They talked about their shared experience in theme parks. Wright had portrayed Minnie Pearl at Opryland and Richard had been Batman at Six Flags. They spoke of workout habits and music.

"Then she said something that caused me to seriously reconsider my Bohemian Grove plans. Chely suggested that she might be able to put me in one of her upcoming videos. The look in her eye and the tone in her voice told me that she wanted me to hang around Nashville for a while... and not just for work," Richard wrote of his interpretation of the moment.

The limo arrived at the dinner destination: Ruth's Chris Steak House.

"I offered Chely my arm, and she eagerly took it." They walked in, followed by Wright's fan club president and publicist.

"CHELY CLAIMS TO HAVE been a vegetarian since 1999, but she wasn't a vegan that night... although we did share a side dish of peas. Chely took three or four bites of her meat, then offered me the rest. You better believe I ate it. I knew a girlfriend/boyfriend bonding moment when I saw it," Richard recalled.

After finishing the steak, the entourage headed back out to Chely's limo.

"As we were leaving, Chely latched onto my arm and snuggled up to me. That was the proudest moment of my life! Outside the restaurant, we ran into one of her old producers. She introduced me to him like I was actually somebody." Richard was in seventh heaven.

"Once we were back in the limo, I gave Chely the flat gift box. She asked, 'Is it lingerie?' I wasn't expecting this, and all I could say was, 'No.' Chely then asked if she could open it. I was already blushing, and the poem was kind of sappy, so I said, 'Wait 'til you get home.'"

"This seemed to cool her jets considerably." Richard describes the rest of the trip back to his RV park as "uneventful" and that Chely appeared "distracted."

"I could feel my chances with her slipping away, but I didn't know why," Richard admits.

Wright casually put down the padded armrest between them.

"I looked up at Chely as if to say, 'What's up with this?' She didn't respond."

As they approached their destination, Richard asked if he would see her again.

"Chely hesitated, then to my surprise, she answered, 'yes.' She instructed (Walter) and (Tarlton) to secure a ticket and backstage pass for the next night's show. Our eyes met, and I decided to test her. I leaned in a little; stopping at the armrest. Chely hesitated again, then reached over and gave me an awkward hug. I said, 'goodnight' and got out of the car."

THE NEXT DAY, a hopeful Richard showed up at the convention center where Chely was performing. He wandered the center until he found Walter and Tarlton and asked for his backstage pass.

"(Walter) coldly responded, 'we didn't bring it.' Both of them simply looked away from me. I was being blown off, but I didn't know if it was their idea or Chely's. She arrived shortly afterward, but dozens of people were already following her to the convention booth, and dozens more were on the way."

Richard looked on helplessly as Chely and her growing crowd of fans blew past him in the hallway.

"Even if I could speak to her, I wasn't sure how she would react. Eventually, I decided to go back to the RV park and figure out what to do next."

The next few days must have been a depressing stretch for Richard, feeling rejected and alone in an RV park somewhere in Nashville, and this awful feeling peaked four days after his date with Chely Wright, on his 37th birthday.

"I developed severe stomach cramps. I tried to tough it out for a couple hours, but it got worse. Finally, I drove myself to the hospital; throwing up in the rental car once. It turned out that what I thought was food poisoning was actually a nervous breakdown." The doctor prescribed some pills.

Recovering in his RV, Richard decided he would attempt to see Wright again. One more chance. He chose to attend an upcoming concert on her tour, about two weeks away at Dollywood. Richard drove to Zanesville, "messed around a while, then headed south again to Pigeon Forge, Tennessee for Wright's show on July 7." He bought a seat in the fifth row, to the right of the stage.

"McCaslin then wrote a letter to Ms. Wright informing her that he would be attending the concert and advising of his seating information," Richard's Secret Service file reports.

He brought along a note he hoped to slip to Wright that read "Remember me, Chely" with his name and number on it "and folded his old Marine Corps dog tags into it," according to his Secret Service file.

At the Dollywood Celebrity Theater and Entertainment Park, Richard watched the show, and, he says, Chely saw him. "Chely didn't look directly at me until the last song. I was shocked when she glared at me like I kicked her dog!"

Richard managed to get his note into the hands of one of Wright's band members but doesn't know if she ever received it. The summer encampment at the Bohemian Grove was a week away. Richard was lovesick and felt defeat across the board. His parents were gone, his creative endeavors hadn't come to fruition, and his fairytale fantasy of a Chely McCaslin hadn't happily ever happened.

"Heartbroken, I drove the RV to Monte Rio, California," he wrote.

IN JULY 2001, RICHARD spied on club members entering the Bohemian Grove from a distance. He saw that security was tight.

"As stupid as this sounds, I was worried that if I were killed and the story got national media coverage, Chely might see it on TV and wonder if I had committed 'suicide by cop.' I didn't want her to live with the guilt and I wasn't ready to die just yet."

Richard scrapped the mission and headed back to Austin.

IN AUSTIN, RICHARD SAYS he tried writing Chely "a couple times" through her fan club, but his Secret Service file reports it was more obsessive than that:

"[Redacted] stated that McCaslin sent two (2) letters to Ms. Wright via the Fan Club that were forwarded on to Ms. Wright. McCaslin then sent additional letters; however, they were becoming too personal and were not forwarded to Ms. Wright. The Fan Club then put McCaslin on an informal list of people considered to be a threat to Ms. Wright. According to [redacted], the Fan Club sent McCaslin letters explaining the type of letters he was sending were not appropriate and would not be forwarded to Ms. Wright. [Redacted] advised McCaslin was angry with the Fan Club for not forwarding his mail."

But he kept trying. The Secret Service report continues by saying that in October 2001 Richard sent Wright a birthday present of "some old cassette tapes he had."

Desperate, Richard remembered talking about Wright's brother, stationed with the Marine Corps in Yuma, Arizona. He sent him "a letter and videotape of some of his previous stunt work," asking him to forward it to Wright. The Secret Service reports that "Ms. Wright's brother informed the Yuma Police Department, who contacted McCaslin regarding the package. McCaslin stated that the Yuma Police Officer that contacted him accused him of stalking Ms. Wright and advised him to discontinue his actions."

A Secret Service agent followed up in Yuma, looking for a criminal record, but found nothing, suggesting that Richard was let off with a warning.

It looks like that's the point Richard finally gave up on trying to contact Wright (at least for the time being).

The Secret Service report notes that "McCaslin said he is 'angry about the situation,' but there is not much he can do about it. McCaslin stated he would like a second chance. McCaslin stated that if Ms. Wright isn't interested in him, then he would like to be told in person. McCaslin stated he will do the 'honorable thing' and keep his distance from Ms. Wright."

Richard's obsession with Wright remains a difficult angle of his life for his few friends to come to terms with. Lon told me he found the situation "creepy" and added "that must have been terrifying for her." To me, the situation had hints of the current "involuntary celibate" or "incel" online subculture of men who espouse hate and violence over their inability to establish romantic or sexual relationships. I don't think Richard would have resorted to violence in this situation, but there is a sense that he felt entitled to have a relationship with Wright because he had bought a charity dinner with her.

AFTER 9/11, RICHARD STAGED his Phantom Patriot protests and began rethinking his mission.

"I had to return to the Bohemian Grove and finish what I started... whether it killed me or not," Richard decided.

On January 19, packed and ready to go, Richard spread his materials on the Bohemian Grove across his table for police to find.

"I got out the autographed photo of Chely and placed it on the other end of the table," Richard wrote. He placed a note on it that warned Wright not to "be corrupted by fame and fortune."

"I loaded my gear in the truck and headed for California," Richard wrote.

"He felt she would receive the letter in the event he was killed," the Secret Service report notes.

AFTER ENTERING THE GROVE, Richard got lost in the dark and broke into an empty cabin, where he sat awake, waiting for daybreak. Sitting there, shivering in the dark, Richard was devastated by emotional pain and close to ending his life.

"There is another factor in all this that I haven't discussed—guilt. I wasn't there when either one of my parents died, because I was pursuing my stupid show business career," Richard wrote to Lon from prison. "A part of me felt I should end up in an institution just like they did—a fitting punishment. So I made it happen."

And Richard wrote to me about that lonely, dark night in the Grove:

"The weight of the past few years bore down on me; the death of my parents, the loss of my childhood home and my lost opportunity with Chely. Now it looked like I might not accomplish anything in the Grove. I seriously considered suicide, but then I realized how cowardly it would look. I could at least find the owl idol in the morning and destroy it. I'd probably have the opportunity to die with some dignity in a gun battle with the cops later."

Richard had no luck destroying the Great Owl of Bohemia but quickly found himself set up for the gun battle that could have rapidly closed the book on his story.

He stood there in the middle of the forest road, ready to shoot. But here, the thought of Chely Wright saved his life.

"It would have been so easy to just 'go out in a blaze of glory.' However, a totally ridiculous notion popped into my head. Was I going to throw away any chance, no matter how remote, of ever seeing Chely again? No!"

From a police report:

He let out a visible sigh and lowered his head, he then lowered his rifle to the ground and removed his black satchel from his shoulder and placed it on the ground. He began to remove a sidearm from a holster. I ordered him not to draw the weapon. He complied with my directions, ultimately lying prone on the roadway.

"I think it's pretty lucky no one got hurt," says Jeff Mitchell, who works at the Sonoma County Public Defender's office. He would shortly be handling one of the strangest cases of his career. "There was a period of time he wasn't following their commands. He finally did. I think it really showed restraint on the police not shooting him."

The police rushed forward to arrest Richard. He was handcuffed and stuffed into the back of one of the patrol cars, then brought to the Sonoma County Jail in Santa Rosa.

"I was processed, fingerprinted, and my mugshot taken with a biometrics camera," Richard wrote. "I now belonged to Big Brother."

CHAPTER SEVEN

THE PEOPLE VS. RICHARD MCCASLIN

J eff Mitchell, public defender, has had some wild days in court. In January of 2007, he found himself in the unusual position of having to repeatedly punch his client in the face when the defendant decided to wrestle a court bailiff. Mitchell saw him going for the bailiff's gun and hit him until a Deputy Sheriff subdued the criminal with a Taser. But nothing will ever be as strange as his case defending Richard McCaslin.

"I kind of seek out unusual cases. I first heard about the case on the news, and then when I came into the office, I requested it," Mitchell told me in a phone interview from his office in Sonoma County. "I had heard of the Bohemian Grove, but I didn't know much about it."

MEANWHILE, AFTER SPENDING SEVERAL hours in a holding cell, Richard was placed in a small observation room with padded walls to spend the night. There was a small, rectangular window in the door and no furniture. Richard was issued a "paper hospital robe, a ratty blanket, and a thin sleeping mat." There wasn't a toilet, just a drain hole in the floor to urinate into. He was moved to a more standard cell the next day and kept in what he calls the "psycho ward" for two weeks.

He didn't spend this time completely alone. After a period of no personal conversations with anyone, he now found himself and his ideas the center of attention. He was visited by a parade of interrogators, starting with Sonoma County detectives. Then came "several shrinks" who interviewed him on his medical history. Was he aware of any mental illness in his family history? No. Was he currently taking any medications? No. Did he abuse drugs or alcohol? No. Did he have a previous criminal history? No.

The psychiatrists wrote down that they thought he should be "tentatively diagnosed with delusional disorder and adjustment disorder," according to a court document.

His next visitors were the Secret Service. The two agents asked him the details on his infiltration of the Grove.

"If Bush isn't a Bohemian Club member, then why are you interrogating me?" Richard asked them. But the Secret Service was also interested in Richard's symbolic appearances at the White House and on the Texas ranch of "POTUS Bush" (as he's referred to in Secret Service reports). Richard says he answered their questions and explained his motives truthfully. They shook his hand, wished him luck, and went on their way, but back at Secret Service offices, a large-scale investigation began. They examined his debit card transactions, following his movement across the country with rental cars and hotel rooms, and noted his purchase record at an Austin gun store. Agents were sent out to every city he had stepped foot in, to check local jail and mental hospital records (they all came back "negative") and interviewed family members and known associates.

To Richard's surprise, the Secret Service soon returned to interview him for a second round of questioning. This time, they weren't interested in talking about his raid on the Bohemian Grove, but in his contact with Chely Wright.

"They grilled me for a good hour about my date with Chely. I asked them what business it was of theirs, but they never gave me a straight answer," Richard recalled.

ABOVE: Richard after his arrest.

SHORTLY AFTER HIS ARREST, Richard had an arraignment. He was charged with five felonies and two enhancements. They were:

Arson: Structure

Arson: Property

Burglary

Exhibiting a Firearm to Police

Possession of a Billy Club

A. Being Armed During the Crime

B. Wearing a Kevlar Vest During the Crime

Richard believes count five is a bit of a stretch—he did have a billy club, but it was in his truck at the time of his arrest.

"It's just a stick," he adds. "Bail was set at half a million dollars, which was a joke since the authorities had frozen all my assets so that I couldn't post bail, or hire my own lawyer. This was a violation of the 8th amendment of the U.S. Constitution," Richard wrote. He was moved to Mental Health "R" Module in Sonoma County Jail.

Richard was offered a plea deal—plead guilty to the arson charges and get the other charges dropped—but Richard rejected the offer, confident he would be found not guilty by reason of necessity. A trial date for Richard's case was set for April 9, 2002.

WHILE HE WAITED, RICHARD hoped for a media storm to roll in and give his story exposure. This would be his saving grace, he figured. The sacrifice of his freedom would be worth it when the Bohemian Grove would become the hot news topic of the day, leading to the disclosure of the evil activities that happened there, and the lid would be blown off the society, once and for all. The Secret Service report notes that Richard had a great hope for "notoriety" and even that he might make "monetary gain from book deals and media interviews."

Right before his raid, according to the Secret Service report, he had mailed letters to then-FOX News personality Bill O'Reilly, *The Free American* patriot magazine, and local San Francisco television and radio news stations.

From my interviews with Richard, I got the impression that monetary gain was not a motivating factor as much as "notoriety." But that fame he hoped for didn't happen.

The story didn't get traction beyond a few short articles in local press in Northern California. Not surprisingly, Richard attributes this to conspiracy.

"The Bohemians used their clout to block national media coverage," he wrote. Richard believes one of the few journalists reporting on the story was paid off with a job promotion, not for her hard work, pluck, and gumption, but a kickback for "forgetting" his story. Cecilia Vega is an award-winning (including a 2010 Emmy) journalist who used to write for the *Press-Democrat* and the *San Francisco Chronicle* before moving on to television news with ABC. She went on to be an anchor for *World News Tonight* on ABC, and currently is the network's senior White House correspondent.

When I e-mailed her to ask about her reporting, she replied that she didn't recall the case.

"Sorry, I don't remember anything about that story (I don't even remember covering the event, let alone the subject). Apologies... that was many moons and many journalism jobs ago," Vega messaged me.

"That's a lousy thing to say about the guy who (indirectly) gave her the biggest break of her career," Richard said when I told him about this response. "I've always felt the Bohemian Club bribed or threatened her to drop my story. Vega's been reaping of her choice ever since."

I didn't take Richard seriously, although a heavily armed, skull-masked man raiding the Bohemian Grove was a memorable story.

"Sadly, Vega isn't just a 'bad apple,'" Richard continued. "Almost all 'journalists' (newsreaders/actors) are forced to lie on a daily basis to keep their jobs. The higher they rise in the ranks, the bigger the lies they have to tell... I'm sure Vega e-mailed her Boho 'handlers' and let them know about your e-mail."

IN READING THROUGH THE letters Richard wrote Lon from prison over the years, there is a consistent desperation for media attention. He asked Lon to send his story to a wide range of outlets, from mainstream to the obscure. There was a letter he wanted Lon to forward to Ira Glass of *This American Life,* and he repeatedly asked Lon to get the comic version of his life to two Austin filmmakers he thought would be interested in a Phantom Patriot movie: Richard Linklater, director of *Slacker,* who had cast Alex Jones in a bit role as a street preacher in *A Scanner Darkly* (2006); and Robert Rodriguez, director of comic book movie *Sin City* (Richard hoped he had gotten his foot in the door by being an extra on Rodriguez's movie *Spy Kids*).

Richard continued to hope that his story was out there and requested Lon to look up media watchdog site Project Censored to see if they had shared any articles on him, and in another letter asked if Snopes had reported on him as an urban legend. In 2006 he wrote to Lon excitedly telling him he thought the movie version of Alan Moore's vigilante graphic novel *V for Vendetta* would "reawaken America's interest in the Phantom Patriot story." A cartoonist from

Nebraska named Neal Obermeyer contacted Richard in prison, telling him he was hoping to put together a documentary on Real-Life Superheroes, including a segment on Richard.

"This is it! This is the opportunity I've been waiting for. I knew that someday, someone in the media would take me seriously," Richard wrote Lon. But Obermeyer's documentary never panned out and no other media or movie directors picked up the story.

DESPITE THE SNUBS, RICHARD'S story was picked up by one unlikely messenger: Les Claypool.

Claypool is famous for his mind-bending bass playing, which developed into a signature sound of slaps and twangs with his alternative/prog-rock band Primus, as well as other projects like Oysterhead, and his collaboration with Sean Lennon, The Claypool Lennon Delirium. Claypool lives close to the Bohemian Grove in nearby Occidental, where he has property he's dubbed "Rancho Relaxo" that includes his house and home recording studio. It's there that he turned a local news bit into a song titled "Phantom Patriot," track 6 of his 2006 solo album *Of Whales and Woe*.

Delivered with Claypool's signature bouncy bass, the song explains Richard's raid on the Grove in simplest terms with a dramatic, rousing chorus of *"the Phan-tom Paaaatrioottttt."*

After months of trying to get Claypool on the line, his publicists finally arranged ten minutes of phone time for me in January 2016, while Primus was on the road with Tool in Texas. It was an exciting moment for me, as someone who flipped cassettes of Primus albums like *Sailing the Seas of Cheese* and *Pork Soda* frequently on my boombox in the '90s. But Claypool was cautious about the subject of our interview.

"Is he... is he a stable individual, would you say? I don't want to get on the bad side of someone who isn't necessarily stable," is one of the first things Claypool says to me. I then found myself in the odd position of trying to assure Les Claypool that I didn't believe he was in danger of being stalked and murdered by the Phantom Patriot.

Living as close as he does to the Bohemian Grove, Claypool was familiar with all the lore.

"I've had a lot of friends who have worked there over the years, and there's all this mystery of what happens in the Grove with the Bohemian Club, it's a collection of the elite as well as a bunch of artists," Claypool explained. "Actually, my old music teacher was a trombonist for the Bohemian Club way back in the day. But there is this mystery, and a bit of *conspira-noia* as to what goes on there and some of it is fairly extreme."

Writing the song, Claypool says, was as simple as an oddball story catching his eye.

"I was flipping through the newspaper and read about the Phantom Patriot, and it struck a chord with me because it was pretty hilarious that this guy went in to challenge these, uh... mysterious forces and he ended up going the wrong time of the year, and there was nobody there.

"The way I approach the things that I do, my craft, is various experiences will strike me a certain way, and they inspire some kind of creativity. Same with this Phantom Patriot thing. I have no intent or agenda, I thought it was an interesting story, and I wanted to convey it with music. We haven't played it in a while because I haven't had that band, but it was an enjoyable song to play."

An animated music video for the "Phantom Patriot" song was released. It depicts an inept commodore struggling with a gang of anthropomorphic cannonballs aboard his ship. The wily cannonballs manage to dupe the commodore, who accidentally blasts a hole in his hull. The cannonballs escape with the rescue boat, cheering and drifting away as the commodore goes down with the ship.

At first, Richard was quite flattered that Claypool had written the ballad, declaring to me that it was a "modern-day folk song." But his attitude darkened as he began to connect Claypool to the ever-growing web of conspiracy.

"Claypool definitely made this song and video to mock me, probably as a favor to his Bohemian Club member buddies in the Grateful Dead," Richard wrote. "They were inducted into the Bohemian Club during the 2002 summer encampment. So much for the 'counterculture'!"

Although it sounds odd, two members of the Grateful Dead, Bob Weir, and Mickey Hart, did indeed become Bohemian Club members, documented by the Bohemian Grove Action Network.

"I'd like to think Jerry Garcia would have never done that," BGAN founder Mary Moore lamented.

Hart stays at Hill Billies Camp, and Weir is a member of Rattlers Camp. Weir spoke candidly about the Grove during a video interview he did to promote HeadCount, a group that registers voters at concerts.

"I don't talk about the Bohemian Grove much, because it's a place where people go to get away from the spotlight," Weir responded to a question during the interview that came in via Twitter. He fondly described the Grove as a social setting. "I enjoy having a chance to get together with those guys, knock a couple back, and talk it down," he explained.

"The stuff you hear in the rumor mill, while entertaining, I've never caught any virginal sacrifices," Weir says, while his show hosts and fellow guests laugh.

As for the Claypool and Grateful Dead alliance against him, Richard explains:

"They couldn't resist rubbing my failure in my face, but they couldn't risk turning me into a folk hero with a straightforward video. Claypool may have been concerned that I might sue him for copyright infringement or demand residuals. The Grateful Dead probably didn't like the fact that the Phantom Patriot somewhat resembled their album cover mascot."

I was confused about why Richard would think the "Phantom Patriot" music video with the cartoon commodore and cannonballs had anything to do with him but was quickly learning that Richard sees a deep symbolism in many things.

For example, Richard would later note in a letter to me that he went to see a movie (he treated himself to superhero movies when they were released in theaters), where he witnessed a preview for *Legend of the Guardians: The Owls of Ga'hoole*, a CGI fantasy adventure featuring a group of talking owls.

"There's something sinister about the massive publicity for this 'Owls of Ga'hoole' movie," Richard wrote. I could imagine him sitting by himself in the theater, his hand halfway in a bucket of popcorn, staring at the screen in stunned alarm through his 3-D glasses as talking CGI owls swooshed out of the screen directly at his face.

On a second look at the Claypool video, Richard found a hidden story.

"Despite appearances, the Les Claypool video *is* about me. I had to watch it several times, but I finally figured out the weird symbolism (mostly)," Richard wrote to me. "The bumbling sea captain is me. The cannonball creatures are the Bohemians. The ocean might represent the grove. The sea captain fails to shoot the cannonballs but ends up sinking his own ship. The happy little cannonballs escape in a rowboat labeled 'HMS Pandora.' Translation: I failed to shoot/stop the Bohemians from committing their crimes. They help the prosecution to throw me into prison. The Bohos are then free to continue causing trouble for the world."

When I run this theory past Claypool, he is stupefied, and a bit freaked out.

"That video, it was an animated short I had found online, and I liked it, and it fit with the song really well, I just took the two and put them together. I also did that with another song. My son, especially when he was younger, was a huge animation fan. He would watch all this crazy animation on his computer when he was a kid, and he would turn me on to some of it," Claypool explains. "The one for 'Phantom Patriot' just fit perfectly with that song, so it wasn't created with him in mind at all, it was just a good fit, kind of like when people watch the *Wizard of Oz* with *Dark Side of the Moon*—just a happy coincidence."

CALLING IN THE HOLLYWOOD BUDDIES

BESIDES LES CLAYPOOL, ANOTHER person to take a run at the Bohemian Grove story was comedian Harry Shearer, well-known for his voice work as various characters on *The Simpsons* and roles in comedies like *This is Spinal Tap* and *A Mighty Wind*. Shearer's directorial debut, *Teddy Bear's Picnic*, was released on March 29, 2002. Richard had been in prison for just a couple of months. The movie is a direct satire of the Bohemian Grove, where Shearer says he was once a visitor. He explained his encounter with the publication *Tastes Like Chicken* in 2002:

> I did an awful lot of research before writing the script. Then, coincidentally, after writing the script, I was invited to the place itself. I got to see the way the place was laid out, how stuff looked, and how people acted. I think I was pretty close to the mark.

Teddy Bear's Picnic features a group of the world's most powerful men (played by comedians like Fred Willard, Michael McKean, George Wendt, Kenneth Mars, and Shearer himself) retreating to "Zambezi Glen," where they witness an "Extinguishing of Time" ceremony in front of the statue of a giant pelican. A couple of disgruntled employees sneak in a video camera and tape the club's antics, including the men dressing in drag and doing a can-can dance.[3]

Richard believes the timing of this comedy wasn't coincidental, as he explained in a letter.

> "You may have seen the Simpsons episode where Mr. Burns attends a 'summer retreat for billionaires.' I've mentioned that Harry Shearer, the voice of Mr. Burns, is a Boho in real life. He was also the producer of 'Teddy Bear's Picnic.' It's a small world, after all.
>
> It became obvious to me that this movie was slapped together on short notice to confuse the public (at least in the Bay Area) about what really happened in the Grove. I guess I should feel flattered. I stirred up enough rumor and controversy about the Bohos that they had to call in their Hollywood buddies (at the last minute) to help them with damage control."

---

3   A more recent parody of the Bohemian Grove took place in season five, episode eight of *House of Cards* in 2017. President Frank Underwood visits the "Elysian Fields," where a ceremony takes place in front of the statue of a giant crow, and the motto is "buzzing bees here not sting."

This is an example of where a theory of Richard's is not only implausible but impossible. Shearer did shoot the film in three weeks, but Richard's timeline is highly flawed. The film was widely released just over two months after his raid; however, it had been in production long before then and screened at the U.S. Comedy Arts Festival, the USA Film Festival, and the St. Louis International Film Festival in 2001, *before* Richard's arrest.

The other issue is that "calling in their Hollywood buddies" seemed not to be a great strategy in this case: *Teddy Bear's Picnic* was an absolute bomb by Hollywood standards—it grossed just $28,149 at the box office in a limited release. Additionally, the alleged Bohemian Grove media stranglehold seemed to be no help promoting the film; it was slammed in a chorus of negative reviews.

"Tiresomely one note," said *Variety*. "The satire is unfocused, while the story goes nowhere," the *San Francisco Chronicle* opined. "Unfocused and underdeveloped," said the *New York Times*. "Supremely unfunny," according to the *Hollywood Reporter*. And the *San Francisco Examiner* pulled no punches in calling it "an ugly, pointless, stupid movie."

You would think an all-powerful organization like the Bohemian Club could use its wide-ranging influence to cook up a movie that would be seen by more of the general public.

UNLIKE CLAYPOOL AND SHEARER, the Bohemian Club was not saying "har-de-har-har."

During this period of various visits from psychiatrists, local reporters, detectives, and Secret Service, Richard did experience an actual Bohemian Club conspiracy. On two occasions, a man visited Richard in jail. He flashed Sheriff's Department officials a Secret Service badge and "whispered he was an agent," according to Cecilia Vega's *Sonoma Press-Democrat* report (Richard's theory being of course that this was written before Vega had been "bribed or threatened"), then sat down and grilled Richard on the details of his raid. This Secret Service agent was retired and worked for the security detail of the Bohemian Grove, who was conducting its own probe into the incident.

"Sheriff's officials said the Grove security man, identified as Martin Allen, misrepresented himself to gain privileged access to McCaslin in the county jail," Vega reported. Later, the article quotes assistant Sheriff Mike Costa as saying that Allen "took advantage of all the resources available to him to accomplish his mission, which was to see Mr. McCaslin for longer than the 30 minutes granted to him as a civilian." Costa went on to say that Allen's "visiting privileges have been revoked."

But by then, Allen had questioned Richard for hours, asking for every detail on how he had gotten into the Grove and what he had seen inside.

LON, MEANWHILE, WAS SURPRISED to find out what had happened to his stuntman classmate and friend.

"I think I got a call from the Secret Service first. I know I got a call from the local sheriff, a local detective, and the Secret Service. I was on my way up to Vallejo to direct a show. Eventually, I was able to talk to Richard and then get up there to see him. He was still in County, still in the psych ward."

Lon grabbed a phone handset and talked to Richard through a thick panel of glass.

"He told me what had happened and his motivation, but he was a little tight-lipped. I said, 'Regardless of what happened, you're here. So, what's the next thing?'" Richard granted Lon power of attorney so he could help sort out his finances. Lon set to work, helping to figure out what to do with Richard's property.

"I got the paperwork to get his truck out of impound, and I got it the day before the tow truck guy was going to impound it, put it up for auction, buy it, and give it to his son." Lon tried to get Richard's few valued possessions—his collection of comic books and swords, photos, art—from his apartment in Carson City. He tried to get the items in exchange for rent owed and "made many generous offers" but found that the landlords had probably sold them all, mad they had suddenly lost a tenant. Lon ended up taking them to court. He stayed in contact with public defender Jeff Mitchell, "trying to keep him thinking on the case," and later helped with filing appeals. He used Richard's account to buy items he wanted for his prison time, and handled payments Richard wanted to send to people.

I asked Lon why he would bother with all that work and why he didn't say "good luck" and leave Richard to his own devices in prison.

"He was a good guy and needed someone to look after him," Lon said. "I talked to his mom, probably shortly before she died. She wanted to be sure that he had friends, she was worried, and I'm not sure he had a lot of friends. He had some friends down in Houston, and in talking to them, it wasn't clear if they were tight."

ALTHOUGH LON WAS WILLING to offer support, a key person in the motivation for the Bohemian Grove raid, Alex Jones, was not.

"I thought it was irresponsible that he offered no support or didn't accept any responsibility," Lon says. Jones had given Richard motivation, fired him up, and even provided driving instructions to get to the Grove, but acted surprised that anyone had taken him seriously when confronted with Richard's actions.

"I think it's horrible... sounds completely insane," he told the *Press-Democrat*, adding he was "shocked."

"I talked to Alex Jones, I called him," Jeff Mitchell told me while describing how he prepared for the case. He was curious if Jones had produced any other media on the Bohemian Grove that Richard might have seen. "He didn't want to talk very much. He was kind of nervous about fallout, maybe he can be held responsible in some way, I think he was worried about that. He didn't want to have anything to do with the case, so our conversation was pretty brief."

This would become a regular routine for Alex Jones—he beats the war drum but ducks for cover when people take him seriously, and the shit hits the fan.

Mitchell remains convinced that the *Dark Secrets* video is a vital part of the story.

"Based on that tape, I saw the progression of his thought process," Mitchell explained. "The way he explained it was, the tape not so much changed him as evolved him into more of an anti-government Constitutionalist. I saw how he got there, I didn't need to embrace those views to defend him, but I could see how he progressed and got to that point."

COURT CASE #SCR-31916, *THE People vs. Richard McCaslin* began with jury selection on April 8 (potential jurors were asked things like "do you believe in Government conspiracy?"), and the trial started the next day.

The case was presided by Judge Elliot Lee Daum, who Richard says "had 'Bohemian tool' written all over him."

Prosecutor Charles Arden spent the next few days offering and receiving into evidence photos of the crime scene, a map, and Richard's weapons and Phantom Patriot costume as exhibits. He called to the witness stand a parade of everyone Richard had encountered: Grove security and maintenance people, arresting officers, and detectives.

A transcript of the trial shows that prosecutor Charles Arden often found himself on a merry-go-round trying to examine Richard, as in this exchange, after he introduces a picture of Richard's weapons into evidence:

> Q: Would you consider that a lot of arms?
> A: That's a subjective opinion.
> Q: I'm asking you. Do you consider that a lot of arms?
> A: To the average person.

Or in this exchange in which Arden asks about the police response at the Grove:

> Q: These police officers that came acted very appropriately according to you, right?
> A: Yes.
> Q: Even meeting up with this horrifying situation created by you, right?
> A: Your word would be horrifying.
> Q: What would your words be?
> A: Unusual.
> Q: How unusual?
> A: Very unusual.

Mitchell had put together the best case he could. He even had a chance to visit the Bohemian Grove.

"In preparation of criminal cases, it's really common to go to the crime scene, it's just something you usually do, so I sought to go there so I'd have a better idea of how the events unfolded. Since it was a private club, I had an agreement with them that what I saw I would only use in preparation for the case, so I have to honor that agreement. I can tell you I didn't see anything unusual," but Mitchell adds that what he got to see was "very limited to the areas pertaining to Richard's activities in the case, where he encountered people and where he lit the fire."

The next frustrating development in the case was that the court barred introducing Alex Jones' *Dark Secrets: Inside Bohemian Grove* video into the trial as evidence.

"Our defense was going to be based on that video made by Alex Jones, that he reasonably believed that he needed to go in there to stop a criminal activity that he believed was going on. It's a common necessity defense, that the greater harm of what he believed was happening in the Grove necessitated him going in and breaking the law. I knew that it would be difficult to put on as a defense. One of the difficulties of putting on such a defense is you have to be able to show there is some significant imminent harm that is going to happen to someone. We didn't have evidence of that; we had his belief based on the video. I had the court review the video, the court watched it, and then they denied us putting that on his defense. In the appellate decision, the appellate court addressed that, and they agreed with the trial court. They felt under the law, the tape was properly excluded, and that defense was not allowed."

"Frankly I didn't allow the jury to see that tape because I found the tape to be not only of such poor quality in terms of its production value, to say the least, but the message that it put out and the effort to try to foment and agitate where there was nothing to agitate about," Judge Daum said in his sentencing decision, adding that *Dark Secrets* was a "waste of time" and a "piece of trash."

On April 15, at 3:41 p.m., the day ended with closing arguments from Charles Arden on behalf of the People and from Jeff Mitchell in Richard's defense.

"ON THE ONE HAND I think he hoped the jury would validate and side with him, but on the other hand, he also expressed to me that he didn't think he was going to walk out of there," Mitchell explained. I think he saw both sides of it. In his statements to the police, he admitted he had done everything. The whole issue wasn't who did it or what was done; it was why he did it. There was a hope that he would prevail, and the jurors would see his side."

Richard was allowed to address the court. He said that the court had tried to say he was crazy, but he remained convinced about the Bohemian Grove. "Prove me wrong. Get an investigation in there," he told Judge Daum. "It all boils down to if you want to know the truth or not."

He added that he had no plans to attempt something like his Bohemian Grove raid again.

"This was a one-time deal. Honestly, it's my opinion that this country isn't worth fighting for anymore," Richard said.

On day six of the trial, April 16, the jury commenced deliberations at 10 a.m. and returned to the courtroom an hour and five minutes later. The verdict was that they had unanimously found Richard "guilty" on all five felony counts and enhancements.

TO ADD TO RICHARD'S bad news, his chances of a media blitz faded away. Court TV and other national media milled around outside of the courtroom, waiting to interview Jeff Mitchell on Richard's case. However, the trial was happening at the same time as another case in the courthouse. Reverend Donald Kimball was a Roman Catholic priest on trial for allegations of raping and molesting teenage girls. He would also be charged with felony assault and vandalism for an incident during the trial in which he attacked a photographer for the *San Francisco Chronicle*. It was a high-profile case—Connie Chung had interviewed him for CNN—and when a break in the case happened, the assembled media personnel took off down the hall to get to the other side of the courtroom. Richard's case was left in the dust, and he attributes this, again, to conspiracy.

"It is my belief that the Bohemian Club used their considerable influence to manipulate Kimball's case into a national media circus," Richard wrote. "This tactic served two purposes. First and most importantly, it pushed the Phantom Patriot story into obscurity. Second, it was another opportunity to embarrass organized religion in general and the Catholic Church in particular. An anti-Christian cult, like the Bohemian Club, would enjoy this immensely."

RICHARD'S "SONOMA COUNTY FELONY Presentence Report," dated May 7, 2002, listed several factors to consider while determining his sentence. They listed "Favorable Factors" like no prior record or evidence of substance abuse. "Imprisonment could have a detrimental effect on the defendant," they conclude.

"Unfavorable Factors" stretches to four paragraphs and includes this statement:

> The defendant is an intelligent and engaging person, with an air of sadness about him. Prior to this offense, his life appears to have largely been reflective of an inability to realize his goals, and a difficulty connecting with others. Currently, he remains absolutely convinced of his beliefs, and there is nothing to indicate that he is likely to move from that stance. He believes there is both historical precedent and biblical example for his actions. He has no regrets for his conduct, and states that his "conscience is clear." He also states that although he is disappointed in the lack of support he has received for his position, he does not plan on repeating this kind of behavior in the future.

The report goes on to say that Richard "remains entrenched in his delusional [Richard adds quote marks around this last word with pen before mailing the paper to me] beliefs and is not open to conceding that he may be in error." Because of this, they say, "He is felt to be absolutely unsuitable for release into the community. We have no faith that the defendant will just quietly return to his home in Texas and put this behind him... Although the defendant presents as a mild-mannered personality, he has shown without a doubt that he presents an extreme danger to anyone he chooses to target. In this offense, he was fully prepared to die, and to take as many others with him as he could [Richard crosses this last line out with pen], in the name of his 'convictions.'" [Richard crosses out the quote marks around the word "convictions."]

The report notes that Richard had one incident in a section titled "In-Custody Behavior."

On February 11, 2002, correctional officers found poems, which were handed over to the Secret Service, and their report mentions being given a poem titled "Warlocks of Washington," that names Bush, Cheney, Powell, Rumsfeld, and Ashcroft by last name with the final line reading "the Warlocks of Washington must fall." Another poem, "The Trial for the Truth," was "about himself, 'the Phantom Patriot,' and the upcoming judicial proceedings."

The presentence report ends with a recommendation that parole be denied and that he be sentenced to nine years, eight months in state prison.

The Bohemian Club had not commented on the case, but they did send a letter to Judge Daum dated May 7, 2002. They mentioned how much the incident had frightened their employees and noted correctly that "Mr. McCaslin did not indicate, and has never indicated, remorse for his actions. He testified that he thought his conduct, including killing, was justified because of his bizarre claims about criminal activity in the Grove," and that the circumstances combine "to warrant an enhanced sentence of Mr. McCaslin, which is needed to protect the community."

Richard's sentencing took place on May 14. Judge Daum threw the book at him and sentenced him to 11 years, eight months in state prison.

JEFF MITCHELL AND LES Claypool had one last encounter with the Phantom Patriot, together.

"His case was long over, the appeal was done, it was probably a year or two since his case was done, and I was just clearing out papers that had come into my inbox and I happened to see one, Richard McCaslin something," Mitchell recalled. "It was a notice of disposition of exhibits in the case since all the appellate periods had run. They were going to destroy the exhibits, and I thought 'that uniform is going to be destroyed, that would be kind of an interesting thing to have,' so I talked to my boss and I said I want to see if the district attorney would agree to let me have it. He said 'you can ask to have it, but don't ask for the matching bulletproof vest,'" Mitchell laughed.

"I talked to the D.A., and he agreed, with the stipulation I wouldn't display it publicly and wear it out or give it back to Richard or anything like that. I could have it just for my personal use in my office."

Enter Les Claypool.

"I knew he had written a song called 'Phantom Patriot' because my younger sister is a big Primus fan. I knew about it, then one day I was going through the calendars at court, looking at what cases were coming through, and the name 'Les Claypool' caught my eye."

Claypool, Mitchell recalls, was in for a misdemeanor for "some minor fish and game violation, fishing in the Russian River with a barbed hook. I thought, wow, I've never heard of anyone else named Les Claypool, so I went up to court and checked around, and it was him, so I said, 'if you want, I'll represent you.' We got the fine reduced and secured his ticket. I told him I represented Richard, and I told him I had Richard's uniform. I said, if you want to check it out, come into my office, and I'll get it."

"I was actually really impressed. I thought it was well-made," Claypool recalled in my phone conversation with him. "It was kind of cool."

I asked Claypool for any final thoughts on the Phantom Patriot.

"I hope he can move through life and conquer his demons. I don't actually... like I said this is a little touchy for me; I'm sort of surprised I'm doing this interview, 'cause it does make me a little nervous, especially hearing he is so sensitive to things that he is offended by animated videos. I don't need that in my life. I mean, I'm just a bass player raising a couple kids."

RICHARD SERVED HIS FIRST 90 days in San Quentin State Prison. Opened in 1852, San Quentin is so big it has its own zip code, and is home to the largest death row in the United States. It's been home to a long list of notorious criminals and immortalized in pop culture like Johnny Cash's live album recording a performance at the prison.

"San Quentin," Cash sings to the prisoners, who explode in cheers, "may you rot and burn in hell." Richard was held here in a crowded cell.

"San Quentin is old, very old. They've been talking about tearing it down for years. Some of the walls look like they're from the Civil War era," Richard says. "They consider it a transfer prison unless you're a lifer. You're not supposed to be there more than 90 days before you're transferred somewhere else. Of course, they take the maximum time to do the paperwork, so on my 90th day, I was transferred to Soledad."

Correctional Training Facility, commonly known as Soledad State Prison, is located five miles north of Soledad, California, approximately 130 miles south of San Francisco. The overcrowded facility was opened in 1946 and can hold up to 3,312 prisoners, but as of a 2012 census, it was close to double the capacity with 5,636 inmates. This was where Richard would spend the next six years, assigned prison number T54990.

He was escorted to his cell and standing in front of the cell door with his personal effects in his arms, and he was asked one blunt question by his new cellmate, Joe [I'm redacting his last name]:

"How long do you have?"

RICHARD WOULD SPEND ABOUT the first three years of his sentence sharing a cell that he describes as being the size of an average bathroom with his "cellie" Joe.

"We had a good many things in common," Richard told me, describing Joe. "He was ex-Army; I was an ex-Marine. Joe was a Midwesterner, from Detroit, and was about my age, a year or two older. He was a lifer," Richard explained. "He didn't talk much about his prison history, but he had been in at least ten years by then. The building I was in was about a third to half lifers. You had four types in there. The lifers, I realized, weren't exactly career criminals, they were guys that had screwed up really bad once or got caught once. Then there were gangbangers, illegal immigrants, and mentally ill guys, the worst of the mentally ill were in a separate yard."

Joe was serving a life sentence for killing his wife, according to Richard.

"He had physically caught her with another guy," Richard says. "I thought that was a soap opera thing, but I guess guys actually walk in on their wife with another guy."

After speaking with Richard, I looked up Joe online in the California prison system and wrote to him in 2015 and '16. I found he had been transferred to Avenal State Prison, about halfway between San Francisco and Los Angeles.

"I didn't think he was strange at all," Joe wrote about Richard. "He carried himself like an adult, had good manners. We got along well, with no trouble. We talked and enjoyed a lot of the same TV shows. But the best way to do time with other people is to have some conversation but don't just talk and talk to hear yourself speak. A lot of people in prison talk and talk and talk and never shut up, and they don't have anything to say. And the biggest reason is they are afraid to be alone in their own head!"

"IT'S STRANGE HOW YOU get used to it," Richard says. "You develop a system where only one guy is on the floor at a time. You put up a sheet when you use the bathroom, all kinds of odd things you learn to do. You make strings out of torn-up sheets, intertwine them to make rope. You're better off washing and drying your own T-shirts and underwear because if you have new ones and you send them out to prison laundry, you might not get them back."

Richard had Lon place an order and furnished Joe and himself with a TV.

"You could buy a TV from the prison store, 100 bucks," Richard explained. "All the appliances were made with clear plastic so you couldn't hide contraband in it. Joe didn't have a TV, his mom hadn't sent him money for a while. He had a radio, but I said, I'm not doing time without a TV. We set up a little shelf for it."

I asked Joe if he and Richard had favorite TV shows they would watch.

"There are not a lot of TV stations in most prisons, usually around 6–7 TV stations. Not 175 like everyone else in the world gets! Ha ha. Well, let me see? We used to watch NFL Sunday, *Austin City Limits*, country music videos, and we used to watch that guy that paints on PBS, he had a big afro and beard, white guy [*The Joy of Painting with Bob Ross*]. We also used to watch this kind of cartoon called *Teletubbies*, it was kinda strange but also interesting enough. Other PBS shows, nature and science stuff. *Wheel of Fortune* and *Jeopardy*."

"Joe and I enjoyed your appearance on *CSI*," Richard wrote to Lon after he guest-starred on the show in 2003.

Joe also told me the story of how he and Richard got a new cellie named Buddy, a mouse caught in one of the education department classrooms. Joe brought Buddy back to the cell to meet Richard. They kept him in a plastic container at first, but he was so tame and calm, they soon let him wander free, building him a small box home with a hole in it and a braided rope to climb up near their TV.

"He always climbed up on my leg and sat there on my lap," Joe wrote. "He would run up my arm and sit on my shoulder while we watched TV. He was quite playful and stayed right next to us all the time. We fed him mostly nuts, crackers, a little lettuce. But he loved puddings! Chocolate pudding became his favorite."

Buddy hung around about a year with Joe and Richard before he disappeared, Joe said.

AFTER A COUPLE OF years, Richard transferred out of his cell with Joe.

"You start with a certain amount of points, based on what your felonies are. If you don't get in trouble, your points reduce. After they reduce to a certain level, they move you to a different yard, and you get a few more privileges and all that," Richard said. He left his TV to Joe, who traded a footlocker in exchange. He says it was somewhat of a lateral move—he switched from a cramped cell to an overcrowded dorm room.

"To be honest, I was better off with Joe, because they put me in a dorm where the capacity was double what it was supposed to be. It wasn't to code at all. One year the feds came in to inspect and what they did was move some of the bunks to the gymnasium before the inspection so they would pass occupancy."

RICHARD DID SEE CHELY Wright again. But it was in the form of a dog-eared copy of *For Him Magazine*. Wright's image had been toned down early in her career, but the *FHM* shoot was all black leather and lacy things. Richard looked at these photos under the harsh lights of Soledad.

"It was surreal to see Chely in a magazine and remember how we talked and laughed in the limo," Richard wrote.

"I CAME CLOSE TO a couple fights in there, always stupid stuff. I worked as what they called a porter or a janitor," Richard told me. His new job paid about $20 a month. "There were guys who always wanted a favor, wanted to get stuff you could get as a janitor. It's a dog-eat-dog world for scraps in there."

A memorable moment was witnessing a prison riot.

"I was in my dorm, sitting on my bunk drawing comics and it went off," Richard remembers. "Usually with riots, it's somebody who didn't pay a drug debt, can't pay it, go to their homies for help. Very few guys in prison handle their own problems, they go to their homies, and it turns into a group argument."

As the riot broke out, an alarm went off, indicating everyone was on "lock-down."

"Old scores were being settled all over the dorm. I wasn't affiliated with anyone like the skinheads or anyone. They respected me, I was older than most of them. They called me an 'O.G.' They'll say that means 'Original Gangster,' but I think it meant 'Old Guy.' They knew I was an ex-Marine who had done something funky to stick it to the man, so they respected that and didn't pressure me to join."

Richard watched the riot from his bunk and from the window he saw "there were probably over 300 guys in the yard, it looked like everybody was fighting everybody else." Rocks and debris were thrown as guards teargassed the yard. He says the prison was intentionally vague of the damage the riot caused. "It's not like they put it on the bulletin board. The rumor was one guy got stabbed to death, and a couple more broke arms or legs getting pushed over the second-floor rails. By prison standards, that's pretty tame."

After the riot was contained, the prisoners were all moved to the prison yard, where they sat cross-legged, hands cuffed with zip ties.

"You're all sitting out there for hours like you're in a fricking Nazi concentration camp while they go through all the bunks and lockers. The riot went off in the afternoon, 2 or 3, and we were out there until after sunset, 10 or 11 at night."

Prison was a harsh environment for Richard, who had never been to jail before, never even really been exposed to a criminal element. Now stuck in an overcrowded prison, Richard wanted to escape into the fantasy world of comic books and conspiracy theories again.

ABOVE: Cover of *Prison Penned Comics,* 2008,
Richard McCaslin.

CHAPTER EIGHT

IT'S CALLED ART THERAPY!

T o make prison life even worse, Richard discovered his precious comic books were forbidden as reading material because they were not considered "educational" in nature.

"They had a rule, at least in California prisons, which quit allowing comics to be shipped in sometime in the '90s. Periodicals had to be mostly text so that they'd be 'educational.' The hypocrisy of it was they'd allow guys subscriptions to magazines like *Maxim* and *FHM*, yeah, they're educational, OK. There were some old comics in there from the '80s that guys kept and would trade."

Eventually, he was able to get a subscription to *Wizard* magazine after pleading his case with prison officials, explaining that it wasn't a comic book, but a magazine devoted to news of the comic industry.

"They held my first issue about three months deciding if they were going to let me have it or not," Richard says. After they forked it over, Richard soon found that his stack of *Wizard* back issues and his creative art ability became a commodity for him.

"Once I had them a couple months, I would trade them for food or whatever to the guys that did tattoos—they'd trace the pictures and use them as patterns, or use them to make birthday cards for their kids, tracing Batman or Spider-Man," Richard told me in an interview. "I made a little money doing that, drawing cards for guys. I don't remember what the going rate was. One of the big currencies was Top Ramen, and guys would buy those by the caseload at the prison store. I wasn't a fan—the salt content alone will kill you—but Joe ate one every day. I don't know how he kept from dying from a heart attack." Richard added that other popular trade items were Sriracha and peanut butter packets. Food was valued in prison because good food was rare. Richard says he lost 15 pounds off his lean frame while in Soledad, his least favorite memory being the prison bologna.

"True mystery meat," he said. "We had stray cats that would come around the yard to be fed. They would not touch the bologna."

Another currency, but one Richard didn't truck in, was Pruno.

"Toilet wine," Richard said with a laugh. "They wouldn't give you much juice, because guys would turn it into Pruno. They'd ferment it three days in the toilet, they'd steal yeast from the kitchen, that's what they call the 'kicker,' they'd put in a plastic bag, and they'd hide it in the ceiling tiles of the dorm. They'd let it sit up there at least three days, then drink what I'd call furniture polish. No matter how many times the guards went around and found these bags, the dorm always smelt like Pruno. Always."

ALTHOUGH COMIC BOOKS WEREN'T allowed in, there was no rule about creating them. Richard was approved art supplies like paper and colored pencils, and filled his spare time drawing. He began work on a major project: his graphic novel-length comic book titled *Prison Penned Comics*. The first major story in the book is an autobiographical comic, "Phantom Patriot: The Skeleton in America's Closet," which details his motivations and raid on the Bohemian Grove, and his court date. The comic storyline is accurate about how the events went down but filtered with his own spin.

Richard joined the prison art program and began creating his comic using available supplies, and would spend time drawing on a clipboard in his bunk. He scoured the prison's magazines and books for visual references and sent Lon a long list of pictures he was looking for. He made do with what he had. One panel shows a skyline of Austin, which Richard created by speed-sketching during the opening credits of PBS' *Austin City Limits*. Richard was hoping this autobiography would finally get his story attention. As he started the project in 2005, he wrote to Lon that the book "could become one of the most unique comic books/graphic novels in the artform. I can't remember seeing or hearing about any comic book based on a true story that was actually written and drawn by the vigilante himself. Also, there may be comics about prison, from time to time, but how many of them are actually created there?"

The second major story in *Prison Penned Comics*, "Agent of Armageddon," is a wild, trippy fictional story starring himself, drawn during his last year in prison. Richard made a drastic (but short-lived) life change—he converted to become a Jehovah's Witness. He decided it was time to adopt a new superhero persona to reflect this metamorphosis, and from the confines of Soledad came up with a Jehovah's Witness superhero persona on paper: The Revelator.

"Prison is where they get a lot of guys," Richard would later tell me, shaking his head remembering his conversion. "They had weekly meetings, and I went to one because I was curious."

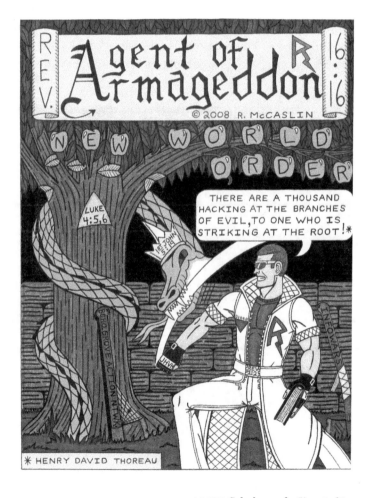

ABOVE: Splash page for "Agent of Armageddon," *Prison Penned Comics*, 2008, Richard McCaslin.

This new character wore white-rimmed sunglasses, a popped collar on a shirt with a purple triangle (the symbol Nazis marked Jehovah's Witnesses with), and held a Bible. The Revelator looks like a cross between a street-corner preacher and a keyboardist for an '80s New Wave band.

"This issue is what I'm sure most psychologists would call my 'apocalyptic revenge fantasy against the Bohemian Club,'" Richard told me about the "Agent of Armageddon" comic. "Hey... I had to work through the anger and frustration of being locked up for taking on the mission of going after the *real* 'Lex Luthors' and 'Norman Osborns'[4] of this world! It's called art therapy!"

The comic starts with Richard drifting off in his bunk in Soledad. Waking up, he finds himself in the prison yard, surrounded by folk heroes Uncle Sam, Pecos Bill, John Henry, and Paul Bunyan. Also present in the roll call is the grinning, empty-eyed Phantom Patriot, who has been embraced into the league of American folk heroes. These assembled heroes offer Richard encouraging words to keep him going when he complains about the treatment his legacy has received.

4 If you aren't a comic book fan, Lex Luthor is the archnemesis of Superman; Norman Osborn is the
   wealthy scientist who becomes the Green Goblin villain in the Spider-Man stories.

116

"You've put your ax to a pretty big tree! It's going to take a while to chop it down," Paul Bunyan tells Richard, paraphrasing Matthew 3:10.

"What my 'folktale fraternity' is getting at, is this, Rich," the Phantom Patriot says, putting a consoling hand on cartoon Richard's shoulder. "I lost the 'Battle of Bohemia,' but you must press on!"

Next, Richard is visited by a glowing angel, Regnessem (read it backward) who tells Richard he has been chosen to be THE REVELATOR.

Perhaps the most "art therapy" or "revenge fantasy" scene, depending on how you look at it, is Regnessem's and The Revelator's wild flaming chariot ride through the Bohemian Grove. Here, the story does not end with Richard face down on the asphalt, handcuffs clipped on his wrists and four cop knees in his back. Instead, Richard and his angel find Bohos in the midst of sacrificing a baby to the Great Owl of Bohemia. The Revelator and Regnessem's chariot obliterates the security guards with holy fire, as Revelator shouts "Woe to the wicked!" They then confront the monk-robe-clad Bohemians. Their leader's name is Illuminus

and he wears a giant eyeball on his head, a villain Richard would go on to use in several future projects as his archenemy representing the New World Order.

Richard punches him, shattering his eyeball mask, then pins his neck underneath a rope wrapped around the Great Owl. Richard saves the baby while Regnessem lifts the 40-foot statue out of the ground, flies into the air, and hurls it (struggling Illuminus and all) into the Pacific Ocean.

With that all wrapped up, the duo then speeds to Washington, D.C., to take on an assembly of political dynasties at the White House. Assembled in the White House's Situation Room are George and Laura Bush and Al and Tipper Gore, two sides of the same coin. All four have the mark of the beast, 666, burnt onto their foreheads. The Revelator soon encounters a trio of false superheroes who serve as White House protectors—Magistrate, Babylon, and Plutocrat, representatives of corrupt government, false religion, and greedy corporations, respectively.

"These so-called 'superheroes' represent your current world system. They will ridicule your stand for truth," Regnessem warns. Richard beats them all.

Richard helps fight in a just battle, and soon the armies of heaven join him on Earth in a battle of Armageddon, attacking the legions of hell and the corrupt United Nations army. The angel Michael leads the fight. After Satan, depicted as a multi-headed dragon, is hurled back to the depths of hell, Richard asks Michael if he will see his parents in the resurrection.

"Richard, they are in Jehovah's memory," Michael informs him, as his parents appear in a vision, surrounded by a holy light. Richard has a tear streaming down his face.

So there it is, neatly wrapped up in a 33-page comic: Richard finally saves a baby from sacrifice at the Bohemian Grove and destroys the Great Owl statue, Satan is defeated, the corrupt White House is overthrown, and he gets to see his parents one last time.

At the end of the comic, Richard wakes up in his bunk in Soledad. A note is next to him that reads "Keep looking, keep awake; for you do not know when the appointed time is!—Mark 13:33" Signed: "JC."

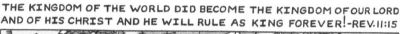

THE PSYCHOLOGY OF CONSPIRACY

RICHARD CALLS HIS WORK "art therapy." Court-appointed psychologists said he was "delusional."

In their psychological profile of Richard, the Secret Service reported that his "psycho-environmental stressors" were rated as "severe" and listed his psychological abuse by his father, poor self-image, shyness, awkwardness toward women, unhappiness with his time in the Marines, lack of satisfying employment, the death of his parents, his "unsuccessful reconnaissance foray to the Bohemian Grove" and his failure to establish "a mutually satisfying personal relationship with a country singer on whom he had a crush," as well as his legal difficulties, as impacting his mental state. The Secret Service psychologist lists in his report insight on the Phantom Patriot and the Bohemian Grove raid:

"Having grown up with an over-controlling and physically abusive father, it is perhaps not particularly surprising that Mr. McCaslin should want to come to rescue or otherwise intervene in the case of children whom he saw as enslaved or physically abused by those who are older or more powerful than they are. This seems to have made him, then, particularly vulnerable to the message of radio commentator Alex Jones about the Bohemian Grove and the supposed videotaping of child sacrifice and child slavery rituals at that location."

The psychologist also notes that the Phantom Patriot and other superhero personas might have derived from Richard's shyness and feelings of inadequacy with women.

"Mr. McCaslin's report of going into the darkness of the night with his skeleton mask and in the garb of the 'Phantom Patriot' is reminiscent of schoolboy rescue fantasies for young damsels whom he felt too shy to approach, but with whom he was utterly fascinated," the report notes.

The report indicates that the psychologist did not feel Richard was an excessively violent individual and noted he had been able to channel his energy into things like high school football and joining the Marines, but didn't eliminate him as a potential threat.

"While Mr. McCaslin does not single out President Bush as being even a leader at this perceived evil band at the Bohemian Grove," the Secret Service psychologist noted, and someone at the Secret Service reading the report highlighted the rest of the sentence, "he is quite clear he would kill anyone, including President Bush if he were to verify his suspicions that President Bush (or anyone else) is actively involved with the enslavement or murder of children."

I WANTED TO GET more insight into how conspiracists think, and I knew someone who would be uniquely qualified to talk about Richard, as well as offer insight on similar attributes that conspiracy theorists might share.

Dr. Daniel White has a Bachelor of Science and two Ph.D.s in Psychology and Biological Anthropology. I first met him online when he was working on his Psychology Ph.D. at the University of Sydney and working on his final paper (along with five other authors) about the psychology of Real-Life Superheroes. It was published in 2016 and titled "Look Up in the Sky: Latent Content Analysis of the Real-Life Superhero Community."

"The objective was to identify how it was possible for individuals to act in what was technically an anti-social way—for example, violating social norms by expressing extreme altruism—literally what made these individuals go above and beyond what a normal person would do," Dr. White says on the paper. "I suspect that while many RLSH would not consider themselves anti-social, they would definitely say they are not your ordinary citizen, for pro-social goals (helping other people). In other words, how do you get pro-social anti-social behavior?"

Dr. White's examinations of conspiracy theories have tied into his study of subcultures, and he told me he used conspiracy theories in the classroom to teach aspects of social psychology.

To help understand the id of a conspiracy theorist, I asked Dr. White what studies have shown about their personalities.

"There has been quite a bit of research into the personality of someone who believes conspiracy theories, ranging from high levels of paranoia, proneness to cognitive fallacies (such as conjunction fallacy) or even a higher tolerance for cognitive dissonance, high levels of narcissism (after all the idea that the government is spending millions spying on yourself requires a certain level of perceived self-worth), a tendency toward teleological explanations," Dr. White explains. Teleology refers to the purpose of something's end game: an acorn wants to become an oak tree, for example.

"There was a recent study published (in the *Journal of Individual Differences*) that suggests that individuals who believe in conspiracies have a lot in common with personality traits found in the schizotypy constellation; i.e. have low levels of trust, eccentric in terms of ideology, and have a higher likelihood of having unusual perceptual experiences," Dr. White continued. "The study also said there was a strong need to feel important or unique, which might be expressed as narcissism."

Dr. White said that he's attended several conspiracy-themed talks and group meetings and believed everything he laid out "does sound like a very good fit." All of what Dr. White has told me also seems to match Richard.

He mentions the study also found conspiracists "infer meaning where others do not" and that "they consider the world a much more dangerous place than it really is."

But Dr. White also thinks there's an essential aspect to conspiracy theorists not mentioned—a curious, truth-seeking mind.

"I'm more inclined towards a description featured in a recent Netflix documentary, *Behind the Curve* [about people who believe the earth is flat], in it a scientist suggests a conspiracy theorist should be considered as someone who questions (similar to a scientist—I wonder how many scientists would appear to express traits similar to those found in the schizotypy constellation) and trying to make sense of the world, who doesn't take the 'because that's how it is' approach and wants to know more, but simply doesn't have the training or tools to explore their area of interest correctly."

Dr. White feels the lack of skills needed to critically examine sources is the first of three reasons people believe poorly sourced, and logical fallacy-filled theories.

"Secondly, we are so used to following authority figures or perceived authority figures, that as soon as someone claims to be one, we immediately believe them. 'Ufologist' sounds way more impressive than 'nutjob with an aluminum foil hat' after all," Dr. White says. "Those 'selling' conspiracy theories are better at selling themselves as experts than their mainstream alternatives, as well as what their 'research' finds. Science is very self-doubting in its presentation; usually, a finding is put forward as something along the lines of 'based on our findings we can predict that the most likely explanation is …. however here are the limitations of our study.' Compare that to 'the government is tracking you through your mobile phone, this is a fact, and I have absolute proof of it.'"

The third and last factor Dr. White suggests is that a lot of conspiracy fits on our outlook on the world.

"(Conspiracy) often fits with preconceived notions of the world—no matter who we are or what our beliefs are—we always find first and foremost evidence to support our preconceived notions—and conversely we have a huge tendency to disregard information that disagrees with what we believe."

Dr. White's last statement made me realize how many people hold some conspiracy beliefs. It might not be extreme, like 9/11 false flags or fake moon landings, but everyday workplace theories of co-workers secretly conspiring against one another and keeping secrets.

HOW MANY PEOPLE OUT there are true conspiracy believers? Polls tend to vary, but many of them point to a significant part of the population who believes in at least one conspiracy. Chapman University's 2016 3rd Annual Survey of American Fears found that when participants were asked if the government was concealing what it knew, 54.3 percent said "agree" or "strongly agree" when that statement was applied to the 9/11 attacks, 49.6 percent answered similarly to the JFK assassination, 42.6 believing there was an alien encounters cover-up, and 30.2 percent believing there was a conspiracy about Obama's birth certificate. Interestingly, one-third of the people polled also thought there was a cover-up of the "North Dakota Crash." If you're not familiar with that theory, it's because the pollsters made it up to see how people would respond to a nonexistent conspiracy.

A 2018 Monmouth University poll showed that 27 percent of people said a Deep State shadow government secretly running things "definitely existed," with a 47 percent saying it "probably exists," though they struggled to define what the Deep State was.

These numbers in the polls seem to indicate the theories have become more popular, but an approaching conspiracy Dark Age is something that's been heralded for decades. As Elizabeth Kolbert wrote in a 2019 *New Yorker* article ("What's New About Conspiracy Theories?") the theme repeats itself often:

"'It's official: America is becoming a conspiratocracy,' the *Daily News* announced in 2011. 'Are we living in the Golden Age of conspiracy?' the *Boston Globe* wondered in 2004. 'It's the dawn of a new age of conspiracy theory,' the *Washington Post* declared in 1994.

"I have to wonder if it has become more popular or if it has always been there. After all distrust of the government is not a new thing and choosing alternative medicine over mainstream has always been around," Dr. White says. "Certainly, it seems 'louder' now, but perhaps that is just a consequence of the more connected world we live in. I would agree that it does seem to be becoming a more popular way of thinking. There could be many factors—life is faster, perceived as more chaotic than ever before, there seem to be so many factors affecting every person—perhaps with so much information, it is easier to infer meaning when there is none. Maybe the reason is that modern society provides too much information and not enough tools to understand it."

THE FUSION MINDSET

IN THE CASE OF extreme conspiracists like Richard, there is something stronger at work than run-of-the-mill cognitive dissonance. A 2019 article for *The Atlantic* by James Hamblin talks about something called "identity fusion." This term describes when people strive to "create a world in which their ideas of themselves make sense." Creating this world gives us "a sense of order, even if it means doing things the rest of the world would see as counterproductive," Hamblin writes.

Counterproductive things a person might do to stay in this identity include self-sabotaging relationships and acting against their self-interests to maintain their beliefs about themselves.

"Fundamentally, fusion is an opportunity to realign the sense of self. It creates new systems by which people can value themselves," Hamblin reports. "A life that consists of living up to negative ideas about yourself does not end well. Nor does a life marked by failing to live up to a positive self-vision. But adopting the values of someone who is doing well is an escape."

This is where a charismatic leader comes in, someone to fuse identities with. It could be a cult leader like Jim Jones, but it could also be a self-described vocal "truth seeker" like Alex Jones or a personality like Donald Trump. These people loudly enter a person's life, grab their attention like glue, and transform them. This new identity taken on as one's own becomes unshakable. A person who puts on a MAGA hat and becomes an InfoWars devotee is rarely going back. Identity fusion is a rejection of anything that conflicts with this new reality.

"As opposed to cognitive dissonance—the psychological unease that drives people to alter their interpretation of the world to create a sense of consistency—self-verification says that we try to bring reality into harmony with our long-standing beliefs about ourselves," Hamblin writes. "Once you step inside the fusion mindset, there is no contradiction."

IN 2005, RICHARD RECEIVED what might have been his first good news in a long time.

"Judge Daum had illegally over-sentenced me," Richard wrote. His new release date was in 2008, for a total of six years in prison, followed by three years parole. He wrote to Lon a couple of months before his release, telling him he was looking forward to getting a hotel room when he got out, so he could have his own space.

"I'm just sick and tired of smelling armpits, a-holes and cigarette smoke!" Richard wrote.

Richard was released from Soledad on May 19, 2008. He was a free man. He spent "about half the day" waiting for paperwork to be filled out, then had a prison guard escort him to a bus station in "a little town, I can't remember the name." The guard waited until Richard got on a bus out of there.

"It's funny now when you look back at it, but not when you're living it. I guess you can get used to anything, and you get in a routine. I sure wouldn't want to go back," Richard told me. "If something happened and the cops caught me, they'd have to shoot me, because I would not go back there. I was making a statement the first time I went to prison. Anything past that is a waste of time, a waste of life. I remember the first time I drove past San Quentin and Soledad, and it felt weird, you look over and say, 'I spent several years of my life in there, and now I can drive right on by it.'"

CHAPTER NINE

REPTOID ROYALTY

I n February 2014, I spent four days at the International UFO Congress, the largest annual meeting devoted to all forms of UFO research, which was held at a hotel and casino in the desert outside of Phoenix in Fountain Hills, Arizona. I was there to work on a book about paranormal investigators, but I thought about Richard while there. Government conspiracy and ufology go hand in hand, and I heard speakers talk on the secret UFO storage area the government had maintained at Ohio's Wright-Patterson Air Force Base, and debates on whether we would ever get disclosure on what U.S. intelligence knew about visitors from outer space.

One of the features of the International UFO Congress was a daily "experiencer session," a sort of group therapy meeting for those who claimed they were abducted or had other encounters with extraterrestrials. In addition to the mistrust of the government, there were several theories bouncing around the conference about what the intent of alien visitors might be. These theories ranged from friendly "space brothers" ushering in a new era of peace to a hostile takeover.

Fear of alien invaders has been with us for a long time. On October 30, 1938, there was a public panic when radio listeners tuned to a mock radio report of Martians landing when Orson Welles and his Mercury Theatre on the Air performed a dramatization of H.G. Wells' *The War of the Worlds*. Portrayals of an invasion have perennially played to our fears ever since, in scenes like the White House being blown up by alien technology in 1996's *Independence Day* or visions of an extraterrestrial police state dystopia in 2019's *Captive State*.

Real-life fears of alien abduction began to spread in the early 1960s with cases like Betty and Barney Hill, who claimed to have been kidnapped from rural New Hampshire by aliens from the Zeta Reticuli system. Since then many have claimed they've been part of strange and frightening alien experimentations. The villains in these stories include a range of different races of aliens, and none is more terrifying than a shape-shifting, blood-drinking, scaly race known as the Reptilians.

REDWOOD CITY

RICHARD WASN'T COMPLETELY FREE when released from Soledad—he still had three years of parole to serve.

"They screwed me over on my parole because I requested to be sent to Los Angeles County, where Lon lived. About three weeks before it was time for me to leave, they called me in and said, 'we weren't able to do it, we're sending you back to Sonoma County, and there's nothing you can do about it,'" Richard says, noting it was a strange plan as Sonoma County was home to the Bohemian Grove, the scene of the crime. Richard got on a bus to Santa Rosa with his $200 gate money given to prisoners on their way out.

Richard found a hotel in Santa Rosa and called Lon, who shipped him a debit card so he could access his money. The Santa Rosa police showed up a week later, confident Richard had snuck back up to take another run at the Bohemian Grove. After showing them paperwork, he was sent to the Santa Rosa parole offices, who determined he wasn't supposed to be in Sonoma County after all and gave him 24 hours to report to Redwood City, a city of about 77,000 people 27 miles south of San Francisco in San Mateo County. Failure to do so would land him back in prison, so Richard packed his few belongings and got on the bus immediately. The police were there to make sure he got on board.

Richard was still on parole and living in Redwood City when he first contacted me in 2010. He described the city as "tolerable" but had no plans to stick around after his parole was up. "The weather is great, but the rent is sky high," he says of the Bay Area. "I'd never be able to afford and maintain my own home in a decent area."

Richard found an apartment and began checking in with his parole officer, John Alvarez.

Richard had put down a decent amount of money to get his 94-page color *Prison Penned Comics* printed, and perhaps trying to convert Alvarez from skeptic to believer, Richard gave him a copy.

"Have you been looking for Real-Life action and relevance in your comic book reading?" asks cartoon Richard on the cover of the book, wearing his prison jumpsuit and handcuffs, flanked by the Phantom Patriot and The Revelator, both with arms crossed across their chests. "...then check out my journey through Bohemian Grove, into the Soledad State Pen and beyond!"

However, flipping to the inside front cover, Alvarez was not at all amused to find two full-color photos of Richard dressed as the Phantom Patriot, carrying his Crossfire MK-1 in one picture and his Glock and ninja sword in the other. The images were taken in 2001, before Richard's arrest, but Alvarez had no context and jumped to the conclusion that the photos had been recently shot and that Richard was currently armed, costumed, and in serious violation of the law.

He assembled a team to raid Richard's apartment immediately after Richard left the parole office.

"I get a knock on the door, open it, and there's a gun in my face," Richard told me, shaking his head at the memory. "My parole officer has three backups, a bomb-sniffing dog, all this stuff. They go through my apartment, tear it all up. They took the stove door off the hinges; I don't know what that was. He takes me to jail, and they dump me there, they're like 'well if we find out you're clean, we'll let you go at some point.' I said, 'you better have me out of here in 24 hours, or I will sue your ass for false arrest, and you know I have the money.' He gives me this look. Twenty-four hours later, he's back."

Richard was released, but a new set of parole conditions had been drafted. The list made it very clear they did not want another visit from the Phantom Patriot to happen. A document he was given titled "Special Conditions of Parole" laid down these five points:

> You will submit to anti-narcotic testing as directed by a Parole Agent.
> You will not be within 35 miles of Occidental, CA, Bohemian Grove.
> You or persons acting on your behalf will have no contact with the Bohemian Club in San Francisco, CA.
> You will not be within ¼ mile of the Bohemian Club in San Francisco, CA.

Map to be provided.

You will not possess or have access to costumes-clothing.

Alvarez's copy of Richard's comic book was turned over to the Secret Service.

AS FOR CHELY WRIGHT, Richard decided it was time to get her out of his head.

"I decided to go 'cold turkey' on all things Chely; music, videos, magazines, etc. I had to get on with my life." It would turn out his decision would be short-lived.

Richard signed up for a dating website and tried opening his mind to the concept, but not too much, as he told me in a letter from 2010.

> "I've tried Internet dating, but it's kind of pointless. I don't want to date women my age and no woman (of my choice) wants to date a 46-year-old ex-con. On the other hand, I haven't been trying that hard because I don't want to get stuck in California and the Bay Area in particular.
>
> I think my days of dating 'normal' women are long gone. I've tried dating online with no success. I decided to admit on my personality profile that I had been to prison for arson and weapons charges. All of the women who were brave enough, desperate enough or who were just scammers bailed on me shortly after I told them my last name. Google and Wikipedia are obviously to blame for that.
>
> However, I'm still picky about the women I choose to ask out...under 40, never married, no kids, no smokers, drinkers, or druggies, no religious affiliation (not anymore), pretty, with a decent body.[5]"

RICHARD, DESPITE HAVING a sizable amount of inheritance waiting for him when he was released, found part-time work, to make extra money and fill his time. He had a job delivering free glossy car-ad magazines around San Francisco until he was fired for having a fender-bender in the company van on one of the city's hilly streets. Richard then found a job delivering food for Boston Market. In his spare time, he became active in Redwood City's Kingdom Hall of Jehovah's Witnesses. He attended the local Kingdom Hall regularly, went to meetings, played flag football (and injured his knee in the process), and like all Jehovah's Witnesses, spent quite a few afternoons walking around to knock on doors and try to recruit new members.

---

5   Richard adds this footnote to his letter: "This list is just in case you know of any hot, young heroines who might team up with an 'old warhorse.'"

NINE HOURS WITH DAVID ICKE

RICHARD'S INTEREST IN CONSPIRACY was as intense as ever. But after Alex Jones declined to offer support and denounced his raid, Richard abandoned the theorist he had been so devoted to and tried to find someone new. He found the teachings of conspiracy guru David Icke.

Icke had a healthy, mainstream life up until a sudden snapping point. He had played professional football, but after he began suffering from arthritis, he took on a job as a BBC sportscaster. An interest in the plight of the environment led him to become a well-known spokesman for the British Green Party. In 1990, his life began to change drastically. A psychic told him he was a healer that would pass important messages on to the human race. In 1991, he held a press conference in which he announced he was "a son of the Godhead." He began to wear only turquoise-colored clothing for some time and predicted the world would end in 1997.

As his beliefs, a mix of New Age and conspiracy theory, developed, he began to prolifically churn out thick volumes of books and DVD sets on what would appear to be every random line of thinking that's entered his head. David Icke became a cottage industry, with his books often translated into other languages and going through multiple printings. He has also lectured extensively around the world, with his speeches often rambling on to over nine hours in a single day.

A free man, Richard was soon able to capture one of these marathon talks himself.

"I attended a David Icke event in San Rafael. The crowd was somewhere between two and three thousand people. This guy is for *real*; no teleprompter, no prepared speeches, no 'guru'-like behavior. From 10 a.m. to 9 p.m. (two breaks for meals), Icke presented a PowerPoint video program, based on his books. He doesn't mince

ABOVE: David Icke, 2013.
CREDIT: WIKIMEDIA COMMONS/TYLER MERBLER.

words. Icke isn't afraid to talk about aliens, other dimensions, Zionism, etc. He is passionate about exposing serial pedophiles, like George Bush Sr. At the same time, he can be quite funny; his speech is peppered with British slang."

Icke has many beliefs that would be considered fringe, but none is as infamous as the theory he has been the most major proponent of—that a race of malicious extraterrestrials called the Reptilians has infiltrated the leadership roles of the world. These reptile-like aliens are seven to 12 feet tall, but through shape-shifting and hologram technology they can disguise themselves as humans and have a slow-burning plot to enslave the entire human race as an inside job.

"The world is controlled today by the reptilian shape-shifters and their bloodlines," Icke writes. "Reptilian bloodlines are chosen to be U.S. Presidents, prime ministers, chancellors, and other world leaders. All of it has been planned for hundreds of years," Richard explained to me in a letter. He calls these Reptilian bloodline leaders "Reptoid Royalty."

To help me understand this theory better, Richard suggested I read a copy of Icke's book *Children of the Matrix* (subtitled: *How an interdimensional race has controlled the world for thousands of years—and still does*, 2001). My informal rule for writing this book was to always read anything Richard recommended, but I immediately regretted this decision after picking up Icke's 459-page-long Reptilian rant. Icke's style rambles from conspiracy to conspiracy, with lots of info on the Reptilians sounding like a mishmash pulp of sci-fi plots.

"The reptilians are a tall, mostly humanoid-type race, with snake-like eyes and skin and they are connected to the classic 'greys' with the big black 'eyes,' which have become the very symbol of the 'ET.' Often these various extraterrestrial factions battled for supremacy in the legendary 'wars of the gods,'" Icke writes in *Children of the Matrix*. He goes on to explain that people occasionally witness these power players slip from human to Reptilian form when you accidentally tune in to their fourth-dimension frequency. A telltale sign of a potential Reptilian is their cold, emotionless eyes, with slatted pupils. Icke suggests, "Next time you see Hillary Clinton, watch her eyes."

It's a theory so outlandish that other conspiracy theorists often ridicule it as being hogwash. On an episode of *Conspiracy Theory with Jesse Ventura*, Alex Jones tells conspiracy theorist and former wrestler and Minnesota Governor Ventura that Icke's theories have made him a "turd in the punchbowl." Ventura then sets up an interview with Icke and confronts him with an angry and awkward exchange in front of the cameras.

Gov. Ventura: All right, you got a big list of these world leaders and politicos that you say are these shape-shifting hybrids. Am I one?

David Icke: I... I have no idea.

Gov. Ventura: Well, you're telling me you can't answer anything, that I have to go sit through nine hours of your discussion to grasp what you're going to talk about. And then if I sit through this nine hours, will it then become clear to me?

David Icke (angry): It depends what you make of the information!

Gov. Ventura: You're deflecting from what you're saying and putting it back onto me.

David Icke (exasperated): Oh, dear!

Gov. Ventura: That I have to be open-minded enough to—

David Icke: No!

Gov. Ventura: —to accept everything that you talk about!

David Icke: What bloody rubbish!

Eventually, Icke has had enough with former Gov. Ventura, and the two conspiracy theorists part ways. "That guy can (censor beep) off," Icke says angrily to the camera, after storming out of the room.

ICKE IS THE MOST FAMOUS promoter of stories about an evil race of aliens invading the earth, but not the only one. A hidden underground base, supposedly in Dulce, New Mexico, is where theorists claim seven-foot-tall gray aliens do experiments on human guinea pigs and is the site of a battle between aliens and Delta Force, called the "Alien-Human Battle of Dulce." Sixty humans allegedly died in the war.

Others picked up Icke's concepts and came up with other details. A list circulating through forums related to aliens says that potential signs a person could be a Reptilian in disguise include things like "predominance of green or hazel eyes that change color like a chameleon," "low blood pressure," "keen sight and hearing," "true red or reddish hair," and a "love of space and science."

ICKE'S TEACHINGS HAD such a profound effect on Richard that he completely dropped all of his religious beliefs, turning his back on the scriptures that had inspired him so much previously.

"After reading David Icke's books, I decided to leave Christianity entirely. I would now categorize myself as 'spiritual, but not religious,'" Richard wrote. "Keep in mind that a couple years ago, I was a hardcore Christian/Jehovah's Witness who didn't really believe in any E.T.s. That's how thorough and compelling his research is. The evidence for the existence of Reptilians is everywhere—historical, religious, mythological, biological, and archeological. You just have to know where to look."

Richard told me in a letter that Icke's writing had also only strengthened his beliefs about the Bohemian Grove.

> My opinion of the Bohemian Grove has *not* changed. In fact, my belief in a "satanic" government conspiracy has only been strengthened by reading two David Icke books, *The David Icke Book to Global Conspiracy* and *Human Race, Get Off Your Knees—The Lion Sleeps No More*. He has done vastly more research on Bohemian Grove and the Illuminati than I have and can explain these subjects in much greater detail and clarity. Icke isn't hampered by false religious beliefs (like I have been for so long). I highly recommend his books and videos to everybody. He's not trying to save the world single-handedly; just show the rest of us what we need to do together to make that happen.

What I had trouble understanding was what this race of Reptilian aliens was waiting for, hiding out in our human bodies. What was the Reptilians' end game? The answer was quite complicated, I was informed. Richard wrote out a synopsis over several pages about the Reptilians bleeding the world dry of energy and eventually dominating the world, and told me about the surprising cast of politicians and celebrities who were Reptoid Royalty. My mind boggled as I read over it, and I was sad to see Richard's conspiracy had grown so big that it now included Marvel Comics head honcho Stan Lee, the man who had helped create so many of Richard's beloved comic book heroes. How could he have reached such a wild conclusion? He explained it to me in a letter, along with random statements in follow-up messages. You can find a chart documenting Richard's Reptilian conspiracy at the end of this chapter.

If, by the way, you think the Reptoid Royalty conspiracy is just something peddled by David Icke and eaten up by a few impressionable people like Richard, consider this: a poll on conspiracy belief by Public Policy Polling found that over 12.5 million Americans not only believe in Reptilians, but believe they have infiltrated our government at the highest levels.

As it turns out, belief in Reptilians can be a dangerous thing. In 2017, two former followers of an Ohio conspiracy guru named Sherry Shriner fell into an escalating Reptilian finger-pointing session. Shriner, who had an online cult following, preached a "heady stew of conspiracy theories, apocalyptic biblical interpretation, and warnings about 'reptilian' extraterrestrials living secretly as humans," similar in tone to Icke through online writings, video, and a podcast, according to the *Washington Post*.

Two of Shriner's followers, Steven Mineo and Barbara Rogers, who lived in the Poconos in Tobyhanna, Pennsylvania, had a falling-out with Shriner after she called out Rogers for being a Reptilian. Shriner's evidence was a social media post Rogers had made about her love for eating a rare steak tartare with minced garlic. Her tastes for undercooked meat pointed to a Reptilian bloodlust, Shriner informed her followers.

Mineo was extremely distraught about splitting ways with Shriner's group and suggested that Shriner herself was a Reptilian (conspiracy theorists often strike at those they don't like by accusing them of being Reptilians, Illuminati, undercover CIA agents, etc.)

On July 15, 2017, Rogers claimed that Mineo put a gun in her hands and held it there, lifting the weapon to his forehead, demanding that she shoot him, then squeezed her finger on the trigger, ending his life.

"I was not in control of the situation," Rogers told reporters. "I was not the dominating party in that situation."

Shriner died in 2018 of natural causes.

In June 2019 Rogers was convicted of third-degree murder and sentenced to 15 to 40 years in prison.

RELIGION WAS OVER FOR Richard. He decided to leave his Jehovah's Witness Kingdom Hall, but in true Richard fashion, he decided not to slip quietly out the back door.

"I quit in front of my whole congregation after learning that their founder, Charles Taze Russell, was a 33rd degree Freemason and Knights Templar—a major player for the Illuminati!" After informing the entire Kingdom Hall about their conspiracy connection, Richard turned his back and left what few friends he had made there behind.

Richard would soon be trying to deal with another group of people, one much different than the Jehovah's Witnesses. As if Reptilian aliens secretly dominating the human race wasn't an intense enough revelation, Richard had another surprise about the world he entered after prison—he was no longer alone in his costumed fantasies. An entire "movement" of people calling themselves "Real-Life Superheroes" had sprung up.

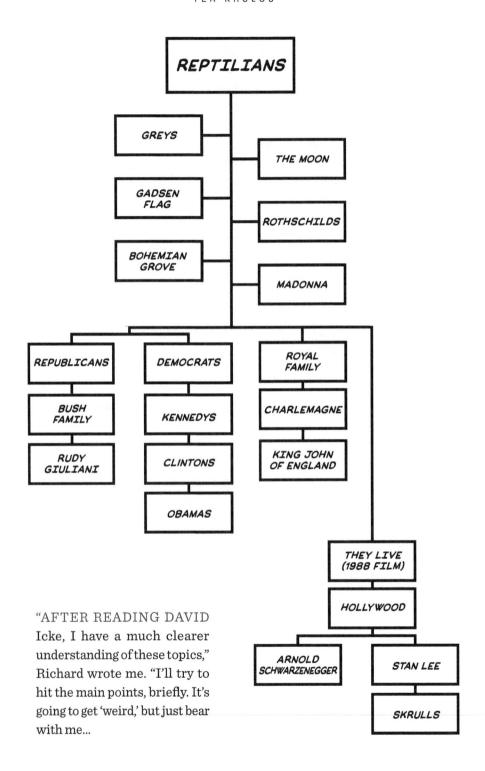

"AFTER READING DAVID Icke, I have a much clearer understanding of these topics," Richard wrote me. "I'll try to hit the main points, briefly. It's going to get 'weird,' but just bear with me...

1: "The ruling class Reptilians operate from the 4th dimension, just beyond human sight and visible light. They manipulate and control humanity through their reptilian/human hybrid bloodlines. These people have been kings, queens, pharaohs, czars, dictators, prime ministers and presidents throughout history."

2-10: "All American presidents (including Obama) are descended from King John of England, who was descended from Charlemagne. So much for Democracy! The 4-d Reptilians aren't compatible with our 3-d reality, so they have to possess the hybrids (the Bushes, the Clintons, the Obamas, the Kennedys, etc.)"

11. "The leading Reptilian family is the Rothschilds, from Frankfurt, Germany. They ultimately control all politics, religion, corporations, medicine, education, and the media through various secret societies (like the Bohemian Club)."

12. "Giuliani is a Reptilian hybrid and crossdressing freak, who had prior knowledge of the 9/11 attacks and used the recovery effort to bolster his own reputation."

13. "Heavy drinking and drug use makes people susceptible to 'demonic' (4-d Reptilian) influence and even possession... Bohemian Grove is the 'Woodstock' of the Establishment...with 'satanic' rituals and snake people!"

14. "Over the last few years Tea Party members and Constitutionalists have been flying the colonial Gadsen Flag (the yellow one with the snake on it) However, if you try to explain the Reptilian agenda to most of these people, they will either laugh in your face or want to hit you. Morons!"

15. "The Greys are the creatures that everybody thinks of whenever Area 51 is discussed. They are the genetically engineered, soulless, 'biological robot' servants and 'errand boys' of the Reptilians. It has been suggested their DNA was used to create the Asian race."

16. "There are colonies of Reptilians who live in our three-dimensional reality in underground cities here on earth and on the moon. The moon is actually a hollowed-out planetoid 'mother ship' that was put into orbit many millennia ago. From there, the Reptilians somehow broadcast a low vibrational 'program' which causes us to perceive reality through our 5 'physical' senses."

17. "The Reptilians control Hollywood and the music industry."

18. On the film *They Live*: "Corny but conceptually accurate."

19. "I didn't watch the Superbowl, but I saw clips of Madonna's performance on the news. From what little was shown, it definitely had a lot of pagan symbolism, which ultimately means Reptilian. I've read she is somehow related to the British royal family, which once again means Reptilian."

20. "Have you heard this crap about Arnold Schwartzenegger and Stan Lee collaborating on a new comic book and cartoon series called 'The Governator?'Arnold would almost have to be a Reptoid hybrid to marry into an Illuminati family like the Kennedys and produce children (bloodline purity)."

21. "I came across a YouTube video for a Hillary Clinton fundraiser. In it she personally thanks Stan Lee for his generous contribution. The Clintons are Reptoid hybrids. Bad associations, Stan!"

22. "Is Stan Lee a Reptoid hybrid? Who wrote all those *Skrull* stories back in the 60s? Takes one to know one?"

"...a lot of comic book fans would probably brand me as a heretic for sullying the reputation of their childhood idol. Heroes are supposed to follow the truth, no matter where it leads. Deal with it!" Richard concluded.

CHAPTER TEN

THE THOUGHTCRIME TOUR

O n May 19, 2011, Richard was finished with his parole and a free man. Less than 48 hours after his probation ended, Richard was on the road. He had been carefully working on a plan for months to do a coast-to-coast tour, staging a one-man peaceful protest in every state. After some debate, Richard decided that instead of relaunching his Phantom Patriot persona, he would create a new one. He invented a new costumed character named Thoughtcrime.

Richard viewed the tour as a chance to see America through his eyes, express his First Amendment rights and hopefully draw attention to a variety of issues—"TSA fascism," Masonry, the false flag attacks of 9/11, the country music industry's brainwashing tactics, the New World Order and their agenda, and of course, President Obama's Reptilian bloodline.

The Thoughtcrime persona was a tribute to George Orwell's classic tale of warning, *Nineteen Eighty-Four*. In that dystopian tale, people are hunted by the Thought Police for entertaining ideas that would potentially be dangerous to the government—*thoughtcrime*.

Richard's Thoughtcrime costume sported a long-sleeved shirt with a message scrolling down each sleeve. The left arm has an angry red circle with a slash through it above the word "POLITICS" and the right sleeve matches with the word "RELIGION." The chest bears the Thoughtcrime logo—a smiley face with an exclamation point floating above it. For accessories, he has a large red belt that reads "Freedom," red goggles, and a cap that reads "Thoughtcrime." He also added a backpack to stash his gear in with a Bohemian Club owl symbol on it next to the words "I survived Bohemian Grove." The look, with all of its labeling, is like an out-of-control editorial cartoon.

"It's ironic and 'subversive' without being creepy, like the Phantom Patriot costume. The prison stripes are an obvious reference to my past incarceration. If the media decides to acknowledge my existence, this subject will come up," Richard told me. "Now they've 'painted themselves into a corner.'"

Every decent superhero needs a vehicle, and so Richard bought a 2008 Chevy HHR panel minivan to serve as his Thoughtcrimemobile. He outfitted it with magnetic signs to display messages like "Freedom is the Right to Tell People What They Don't Want to Hear—George Orwell" and a detachable delivery-driver-style sign that lit up that read "Dare to Commit Thoughtcrime." With that out of the way, Richard began to try to figure out the logistics of his journey and told me about his considerations in a letter:

> I'm still hammering out my itinerary for the "Thoughtcrime Tour." There are a ton of things to consider. How much money am I willing to spend? How long am I ready to be unemployed and functionally homeless? When will I decide that the tour is finished and where will I choose to live after that?
>
> I have a decent inheritance and a small income from investments; so I'll be OK financially (if the economy and stock market don't completely collapse). I spent most of the summer of 2001 on the road (with an R.V.). I wouldn't live that long in an R.V. again. It gets tiresome and claustrophobic. They are a bitch to drive in urban areas, and they suck gas like a Sherman tank.
>
> I will start in San Francisco and slowly make my way across the country, toward the East Coast, traveling in a north/south zig-zag pattern and probably ending up somewhere in Florida.
>
> I've decided to make tentative plans for all 48 states... This will probably be my "last run" before I 'retire.' Each stop will take 1–2 days. I will keep you updated with an e-mail (and maybe a picture) every few days. I should be in 'your neck of the woods' in late July or early August.

Before he departed, Richard wanted me to do him a favor: get him in touch with an unusual subculture of people I had become somewhat of an expert on—the Real-Life Superheroes (RLSH).

THE BLACK SHEEP OF THE RLSH

BEFORE RICHARD WENT TO PRISON, there weren't a lot of examples of "Real-Life Superheroes." He had read *How to Be a Superhero*, the self-published guide written by the mysterious "Night Rider" in 1980, and there were a few random examples—he was aware of a mysterious costumed and charitable stuntman, the Human Fly, who gained notoriety in the 1970s and had his own Marvel comic book before fading into obscurity. He had read an article about Angle Grinder Man, a British man who had snapped after getting a parking violation "boot" on his car one too many times and ran around England in a costume, sawing the boots off of clamped vehicles in the late 1990s and early 2000s.

Starting in 2005, and expanding rapidly during the next few years, hundreds of people began adopting their costumed personas in what is described as a "movement" or "subculture" of "Real-Life Superheroes."

Some RLSH have attempted crime-fighting, but many more RLSH have a tame humanitarian focus, like handing out food and supplies to homeless people, organizing charity events, or bringing attention to an activist cause. I've sometimes described them as "altruistic performance artists."

Richard wasn't amazed. His opinion was a love/hate cycle that indicated he wanted to be included in the movement but was also harshly critical of the typical RLSH.

"Unfortunately, it's kind of sad to see how some of these guys have dumbed down and homogenized the superhero concept," Richard wrote me. "I accepted the possibility that the Bohemian Grove mission would probably end in my arrest, maybe even my death. I was prepared to make that sacrifice. Would (these RLSH) be willing to do the same? Since when does handing out sandwiches and toilet paper to crackheads, while wearing 'distinctive clothing' make someone a superhero? Doesn't the Salvation Army do that every day without special recognition? If you want to impress me, earn the costume by going after some real criminals."

Despite this, Richard did make attempts to contact a few of the RLSH, particularly ones he saw in a leadership role, like Chaim Lazarus a.k.a. Life, who helped found an organization called Superheroes Anonymous. His attempts, to his disappointment, were unread or ignored.

When Richard's initial attempts to get involved with the RLSH movement were shunned, he dubbed himself "the black sheep of the RLSH movement."

But now the long road ahead must have looked lonely to Richard, because he decided it was time to make a second attempt to try to contact some of his fellow superheroes, hoping to find some boots on the ground that would join him in his protests.

At the time, there was an active RLSH Internet forum at therlsh.net that I was signed up for and checked regularly while working on *Heroes in the Night*. Richard asked me if I would post a message he had handwritten and sent to me, titled "My Open Letter to all RLSHs," on his behalf. I posted the letter along with a couple of paragraphs explaining who Richard was on a private section of the forum.

"Generally speaking, much of what you have read and heard about me, on the Internet, has been intentionally exaggerated by the Government-controlled media, to make me sound like a domestic terrorist," Richard explained to them in his letter. "Other reports took the opposite approach and characterized me as a moron. I assure you that I am neither."

Richard also included several rules for RLSH potentially meeting up with him for a protest, a list of eight demands that instructed the RLSH to make their protest signs, leave weapons at home, do their conspiracy research and that "any occult/reptilian/owl-themed RLSHs should respectfully sit this one out... it's nothing personal. I just don't want to send a mixed message."

Although he would later make some inroads in the RLSH community, initial reaction to Richard and his call for help on the message board was mostly bewildered, contemptuous, and unsupportive. Many RLSH comments said that they thought he was crazy and didn't want to be associated with him. A couple of people, like Razorhawk of the Minneapolis area, expressed an interest in his ideas and a willingness to meet him. He had already talked with other people about the Bohemian Grove in the past.

"I know a lot of people believe this (Bohemian Grove theory), and I think some strange things, so I can't go into it thinking there's something wrong with him," the diplomatic Razorhawk later told me in a phone call. "I think the community rejected meeting him because here was a guy with a criminal record, who had been arrested going after conspiracy theories," Razorhawk says. "Second, here is a guy who *still has* a conspiracy theory. And unless they are into conspiracy theories, or sometimes if they are but not the same ones, they don't want to be involved with people with theories that don't jive with their own."

Razorhawk added that Richard's record didn't deter him. "He had done his time, and I don't think it's proper to be against someone because of that, he paid his debt."

As comments continued to pile on the "My Open Letter to all RLSHs" thread, one RLSH pointed out to fellow hero Knight Owl that his occult owl imagery barred him from showing up at the Thoughtcrime protests.

An EMT and firefighter, Knight Owl responded with a post that joked: "Isn't he an arsonist? Maybe I should show up in a firefighter uniform!" Others viewed Richard as a potentially unstable threat. Zero, one of the founders of the New York Initiative, responded, "If we go, we'll be making it very clear that we're there to keep our eye on him, not to join him."

THE THOUGHTCRIME TOUR

THE LACK OF RLSH interest didn't deter Richard. His next letter to me came in April 2011 and included a neatly handwritten list of all of the cities and states he would stop in, including famous landmarks and spots explicitly chosen because of their relation to conspiracy.

He finished his costume and created several protest signs. "Down With Big Brother," with a circle and slash through an Eye of Providence, read one. "Beware of False Flag Attacks" read another, with an upside-down flag and "CIA" lettered next to it. His pièce de résistance was a sign that had a photo of President Obama with his eyes replaced with slatted lizard eyes, a pentagram on his forehead, and a long serpent tongue drooping out of his mouth. "Reptoid Royalty," the sign read. "No Blue Bloods in the White House!"

Richard packed up his Thoughtcrimemobile and hit the road for his first protest stop, San Francisco, where he marched the streets around the Bohemian Club headquarters on Taylor Street on May 21, 2011. He found a parking garage to change in, then adhered a message to his sign holder that read "The Bohemian Club murders children every July 23!"

"I adapted to the whole parading-around-in-the-open thing better than I expected," Richard wrote. A couple of people shouted things at him like "Alcatraz!" and "Illuminati!" or asked questions, but nothing major, except for one strange encounter.

Richard ended his day of protest by taking a selfie in his costume at the Golden Gate Bridge. Some tourists asked for his photo, too, and then he was approached by a man in his mid- to late 50s, wearing sunglasses. From Richard's letter:

"He approached me and asked, 'are you protesting the Bohemian Club?'

Me: 'Yes, I am.'

'Are you a member?'

'No.'

'I have a friend who was invited to the summer encampment this year. He's an artist. Have you ever been invited?'

'No.'

'Have you ever been there?'

'Yes. I snuck in back in 2002.'

'Did you get caught?'

'Outside the gate.'

'A lot of weird stuff happens there.'

'Yeah... it does.'

'Well, anyway, have a good evening.' (He leaves.)

'You too.'

I definitely got a strange vibe from that guy. He was wearing sunglasses, so he was hard to 'read.' I strongly suspect that he was a Bohemian, himself. This guy had a 'creepy/smooth' tone to his voice similar to the retired Secret Service agent who grilled me in county jail."

ABOVE: Thoughtcrime at the Golden Gate Bridge.

THE LETTER FROM SAN Francisco was the last handwritten message I would receive from Richard for a while. After weighing his options, Richard reluctantly switched to e-mail, giving me updates from public libraries and hotel lobbies every few days while on the road. He always sent along pictures of himself in costume taken with a tripod and automatic timer on his camera. In each photo he is standing stoically in front of a different protest target—Mount Rushmore, the Gateway Arch in St. Louis, the White House, a variety of state capitol buildings, Mason lodges, and other conspiracy-related facilities. Some were obvious, like Ground

Zero in New York City, others more of a deep cut like NASA headquarters in Titusville, Florida (home to a government brainwashing facility, Richard says). It was like a bizarre conspiracy version of *Where in the World is Carmen Sandiego?*

In several states, he also did airport protests rallying against the Transportation Security Administration, holding a sign that read "Down with Big Brother/TSA Fascism," while reading a list of quotes that he read from I was surprised to see weren't from David Icke or other conspiracy figures, but a range of historical philosophers and politicians that ranged from Plato to Mahatma Gandhi to Malcolm X.

"Airports are a 'grey area' in terms of protests. The public gathers there, but it's still considered private property," Richard wrote. "You can be charged with trespassing, but only if you refuse to leave, or disrupt business."

Richard's first airport protest was at San Francisco International as he kicked off his tour.

"Most of the Blue Shirts tried to ignore me. Some of them gave me dirty looks. A lot of the people in line just stared at me, dumbfounded like cattle or sheep (sheeple)," Richard wrote. "They were being 'herded' like livestock. Congress is considering the use of the TSA in railroad stations, harbors, sporting arenas, national parks, and shopping malls in the near future."

Richard was soon confronted by airport security. They asked for his I.D. and searched his backpack, which had a copy of David Icke's book *Children of the Matrix*. One of the officers told Richard he was "creating a lot of attention," to which Richard replied, "That's the point." Citing the private policy clause, they escorted him to the parking lot, using the rail shuttle.

"I had a good conversation with them about fascism slowly creeping into American society. They actually listened... I made it clear to them that *they* (law enforcement) and also the military are the people who will determine whether America degenerates into an Orwellian dictatorship or not," Richard wrote to me. "I told them their children's future depended on it. I shook hands with them before driving away."

I LOOKED FORWARD TO my updates from Richard as he made his way state to state. By June 6 he was in Las Vegas. On June 29 he was in the small town of Riverdale, Iowa, after hearing Obama would be making a stop there at an Alcoa aluminum sheeting plant. A photographer for the *Quad City Times* caught a picture of Richard (the sole protestor at the event) smiling politely and holding his Obama "Reptoid Royalty—No Blue Bloods in the White House" sign while a young girl with long blonde hair, wearing a fringy summer blouse, awkwardly talked to him. The photo got the headline "Alcoa protestor believes Obama is an alien," and a short blurb:

> Richard McCaslin discusses his theory about President Barack Obama's reptile origins with Savannah Holmes, 14, of Provo, Utah, as the two wait for the presidential motorcade Tues June 28, 2011, near the entrance of Alcoa Davenport Works in Riverdale.

Richard had hoped to incite media interest in each state, but this photo caption was the only media hit he'd receive for the duration of the 48-state tour.

BY JULY 18 RICHARD had hit Little Rock and then the "redneck, Republican heaven" of Branson, Missouri.

"There was plenty of honking at me. Whether or not they supported me is anybody's guess. At least I got their attention. Only one guy yelled at me, "Get out of Branson!" I guess anything short of a lynching is a good thing."

RICHARD AND I MET in person for the first time after he arrived in Milwaukee on July 26, 2011. I joined him as he marched up and down Wisconsin Avenue, the main thoroughfare of downtown.

ABOVE: Thoughtcrime with the author in downtown Milwaukee, 2011.

Finally meeting someone in person is always a weird experience. Richard was a little bit shorter than I imagined, physically in athletic shape, and had a bulbous nose. He looked like a Texan, even though he was Ohio-born. His voice had a slight Southern twang. He says Barack O-BAM-a, not O-bAAma. Overall, he was polite and appeared and acted easygoing, though he was prone to awkward silences and had a sort of manic look in his eyes at times.

Richard marched with a sign that read "Down with Big Brother." I decided I had wanted to show solidarity and feel what it's like to be in his shoes, so I made a handwritten sign on tag board that read "No to New World Order!" I held it up and stood next to Richard. My sunglasses hid my gaze as I watched people's reactions to the sight of us. Some people looked confused; others smiled or laughed. A couple of people looked irritated or angry.

We found that Richard had some unknown allies on the streets of downtown. First, a young man with dreadlocks approached us and began shooting video on his iPhone, rapidly speaking about the people needing to stand together against a corrupt government, like Richard was. He shook his hand and parted ways. When we approached a hot dog stand on the corner of Wisconsin and Water streets, the proprietor dropped his hot dog flipping tongs and walked to Richard, giving him a hearty handshake. "I love this," he said, pointing to Richard's Thoughtcrime costume and protest sign.

"You listen to Alex Jones?" he asked Richard.

"Yeah, I have."

"How about David Icke?"

"Oh yeah."

"We need more people out here like you. C'mon, I'll give you a free hot dog. On the house."

After walking a couple more blocks of downtown, Richard and I split ways but made a plan to rendezvous the next day. I was going to take a short road trip with him, to Chicago.

THE NEXT DAY, RICHARD and I stood silently on the moving walkway at O'Hare International Airport, his face in a tight, reflective expression. A jazzy rendition of "Happy Together" by The Turtles blasted out of a saxophone from somewhere, bouncing down the hall. Exiting the walkway, Richard spotted the busker wailing away on the sax and tossed a couple quarters into his case.

"Thanks, man!" the saxophonist said in one sharp exhale, before picking up the riff again. Walking into the airport, Richard appraised the scene. He noted the bathrooms and the exit doors and security, then rode the escalator up to a hall of airline ticket counters. A stream of passengers was entering the TSA checkpoint between the ticket counters to go through the examination process.

"Like cattle," Richard said in disgust, watching them file in. Satisfied with getting a feel for the layout of the airport, we returned to the parking lot where he climbed into the Thoughtcrimemobile to change. When he emerged several minutes later, he was wearing an oddly baggy and bland-looking gray sweatshirt and matching jogging pants. It seemed like a suspicious choice of attire in the hot and humid summer air.

"I'm going to go into the men's room, change out of this, and take my sign out of this," he said, indicating a large portfolio bag. "I'll put the jogging clothes in the bag, walk out of the bathroom, hand the bag off to you, walk as fast as I can to the escalator and then stand in front of the TSA gate for as long as I can. We'll see what happens."

I nodded in agreement, somewhat nervously.

Back inside O'Hare, we passed the busker playing the saxophone again, and then McCaslin shuffled in with the small crowd entering the men's room. He exited a couple minutes later. He was now Thoughtcrime.

McCaslin took a couple steps toward me, handed off the portfolio bag, and then briskly walked toward the escalator holding his "Down with Big Brother" sign. A smaller sign was attached to the bottom that read "TSA FASCISM—I thought Nazis wore brown, not blue shirts!"

As he stepped off the escalator, all eyes that met him were filled with confusion. Some laughed, a little nervously; others looked concerned. Walking to the TSA gates, McCaslin stopped and pulled a piece of loose-leaf paper from his pocket, with a list of quotes he had written down.

"They that can give up essential liberty to obtain a little temporary safety deserve neither liberty nor safety," he said in a loud voice, quoting Benjamin Franklin. He was barely audible over the hum of passengers at the airport. Some people glanced at him curiously as they got in line to be scrutinized by TSA, but most ignored him.

I looked toward the corner of the room and saw a security guard looking at Richard and talking into his walkie-talkie.

He walked down to the next gate and read more quotes from George Orwell and Edmund Burke. By now, there were security guards and airport personnel in every corner watching Richard and talking on their walkie-talkies, but no one approached him.

After he got through his list of quotes, he began walking at a steady pace past me.

"All right, let's go," he said, and we headed for the exits. No one stopped to talk with us.

Richard dropped me off at Union Station to catch a bus back to Milwaukee, and then he was on his way to state number 27 on the Thoughtcrime tour, Indiana.

RICHARD CONTINUED TO SEND me updates and photos. He marched the streets of Detroit, Columbus, Charleston, Harrisburg, then in early August hit New England. His most anticipated stop here was New Haven, Connecticut, home of another notorious secret society, Skull and Bones. He had written a poem about them while in prison, titled "Numbskull and Bones."

Skull and Bones is like a junior version of the Bohemian Grove. It's the oldest fraternity on the Yale University campus, founded in 1832 by William Huntington Russell and Alphonso Taft. (Taft was President Ulysses S. Grant's Secretary of War and father of President William Howard Taft.)

Fifteen members of Yale's Junior class are tapped each year to be members (or "Bonesmen") of the elite club. Like the Bohemian Grove, membership has been of the people (the club was male-only until the 1990s) who will go on to rule the world. Presidents Taft, George H.W. and W. Bush (along with H.W.'s father, Prescott Bush), *Time* magazine magnate Henry Luce, FedEx founder Frederick W. Smith, Supreme Court Justices Morrison Waite and Potter Stewart, Secretary of Defense Robert A. Lovett, and pundit William F. Buckley, Jr. were all members. Many founding CIA members were also Bonesmen. In 2004, there was an interest in the club because, for the first time, two former Skull and Bones members—George W. Bush (Bones 1968) and John Kerry (Bones 1966)—were both running for the presidency.

The club is housed in a large, foreboding building on 64 High Street on campus known as the "Tomb." The sandstone building has few windows, and inside is an Addams Family-style collection of macabre decorations—suits of armor, creepy paintings, and everywhere are skulls. It is a long-standing accusation that Prescott Bush and other Bonesmen stole the skull of Apache leader Geronimo while stationed at Fort Sill in Oklahoma during World War I. The artifact is said to still be in the Tomb's collection, and there have been attempted lawsuits to extract it. Lack of evidence has caused the case to be dismissed as a hoax.

In addition to the Tomb, club members have access to a 40-acre island—Deer Island, located on the St. Lawrence River. Although this used to be a lavish retreat, Alexandra Robbins writes in her book *Secrets of the Tomb: Skull and Bones, the Ivy League, and the Hidden Paths of Power* that as the years have gone by, it has suffered from neglect and has fallen into disrepair.

Like the kooky ooky Cremation of Care ceremony, Skull and Bones has its secret initiation ritual, a mix of fraternity hazing and occult mysticism that is administered to the club's new pledges each year.

Many rumors circulate about this initiation ritual, with most claiming that initiates have to lay in a coffin and confess their most kinky sex secrets to the rest of the club, then go through a macabre set of obstacles designed to frighten them before they are accepted as club members. Each new pledge gets a Skull and Bones nickname. George H.W. Bush was "Magog"; McGeorge Bundy (United States National Security Advisor, 1961–1966) was nicknamed "Odin." The tallest new pledge is given the house nickname "Long Devil."

Yale has other secret societies, like Scroll and Key and Wolf's Head, but Skull and Bones is the oldest and most infamous. Richard stood outside of the Tomb, holding a sign with a half skull and half Reptilian face drawn on it that read "Skull and Bones: Blood-Sucking Reptoids."

AFTER STOPS IN NEW York (where he protested at Ground Zero), Atlantic City, and Philadelphia, Richard headed toward Washington, D.C.

> Baltimore was pretty routine. Washington wasn't. You'll have to wait for the pictures, but here's what happened. I was starting to circle the White House, with my "Reptilian Obama" sign, when a uniformed Secret Service agent drove up and started to question me. Two more on bikes showed up. Once they ran my I.D., the questions really started to fly. Two more plainclothes agents were called in, and they continued the interrogation. To be fair, all the agents were polite and professional. They patted me down respectfully, then asked to search my van, in the parking garage, a few blocks away. I signed their release form, and they went to it. There was nothing illegal in it, so they had to let me go. They were impressed with my outfit. I guess most protestors don't go to this much trouble."

The Secret Service report issued an advisory, circulated to law enforcement, and noted the protest appearance in a couple pages of their files.

"McCaslin approached the White House Complex, dressed as a comic book character," reads part of the report, and in another, "Additionally MCCASLIN [an agent underlines the rest of the sentence] wants the American public to know that POTUS Obama is actually Satan," and that Richard "believes he is an action figure and dresses accordingly" but that the agency ultimately "sent him on his way without incident."

Richard decided to continue his costumed protest.

"Once I got back to the White House, over a dozen people took my picture. I continued up Constitution Avenue to the Capitol, back down Independence Avenue, through the Washington Monument area and back to the parking garage. I then drove up 16th St. and got a pic in front of the Masonic House of the

Temple." At first I didn't pay much attention to this last sentence, as it seemed like just another place on a long list of conspiracy-related stops. But it would be an essential element of Richard's story years later.

"A few minutes after that, the S.S. calls me and asks if they can search my motel room! Yeah, sure, whatever. They met me there and proceeded. The two agents were satisfied with their investigation, wished me luck, then left," Richard concluded on his protest in the nation's capital.

AFTER A STOP BY CNN headquarters in Atlanta and a visit to Orlando, Richard made his final stop of the tour on August 26, 2011, in Miami, Florida.

In an e-mail from Florida, Richard told me his post-tour plan was to move to the Bahamas, loading his car to a ship to sail away from Miami.

I liked this ending for Richard. After years of prison and parole, and after accomplishing a 48-state protest tour, the bitter conspiracy theorist retires to a tropical beach, just out of reach of the country that he feels has done him so much wrong. He would be an expatriate hiding out in the safety of the Bermuda Triangle. I imagined Richard living out his days on a remote beach, perhaps reading conspiracy classics like *Behold a Pale Horse* while sipping out of a hollowed-out coconut. Maybe he would finally find peace.

But that's not what happened at all.

ABOVE: Thoughtcrime protesting outside the White House.

CHAPTER ELEVEN

CRISIS ACTORS

"**H**itler took the guns! Stalin took the guns! Mao took the guns! Fidel Castro took the guns!" Alex Jones, red-faced, his eyeballs bulging, is screaming at Piers Morgan, a British anchor who had a show on CNN called *Piers Morgan Live* at the time. Jones has labeled Morgan a "redcoat." In a rare turn of events, Morgan is dumbfounded and can't get a word in edgewise.

"How many—" he starts, but Jones steamrolls over him.

"Hugo Chavez took the guns! And I'm here to tell you, 1776 will commence again if you try to take our firearms! It doesn't matter how many lemmings you get out there *begging* for them to have their guns taken. We will not relinquish them! Do you understand?!"

It is less than a month after 20-year-old Adam Lanza killed his mother, then walked into Sandy Hook Elementary School in Newton, Connecticut, on December 14, 2012, and shot and killed 20 first-grade children ages six and seven, six adult faculty members, and then killed himself as police arrived on the scene. Morgan had wished for a sensational debate about gun control, but after releasing Alex Jones from the genie lamp, he is having trouble shoving him back inside.

Jones had been so incensed at Morgan's suggestion that guns should be regulated that he had started an online petition titled "Deport British Citizen Piers Morgan for Attacking 2nd Amendment." The post read "we demand that Mr. Morgan be deported immediately for his effort to undermine the Bill of Rights and for exploiting his position as a national network television host to stage attacks against the rights of American citizens." The petition got more than 110,000 signatures before the White House addressed it, saying that they would not be deporting Morgan.

In the decade that had passed since Richard's arrest, Jones' stature as a conspiracy influencer had grown. He was no longer just a fringe commentator in Austin—he had gotten the attention of the mainstream media.

THE RISE OF INFOWARS

BY THE TIME HE appeared on Morgan's show and ten years after Richard's Bohemian Grove raid, *The Alex Jones Show* had reached 120 AM and FM radio stations around the country, drawing in around six million listeners, or maybe more, depending on the source. Jones' radio numbers are always in flux because he'll often get dumped by stations after he receives negative attention for his controversial views.

Where InfoWars programming began to beat out rival talk radio hosts like Rush Limbaugh and Glenn Beck, though, was online. In 2011, InfoWars had a more prominent online following than Limbaugh and Beck combined, and a 2017 report said that InfoWars got around 10 million monthly visits, making it more popular online than mainstream news sources like *Newsweek*.

Jones' following grew from his "in your face" approach, as Richard had described Jones' style. People were attracted to his ambush-style journalism, badgering politicians he ran into in the streets and public buildings of Washington, D.C. or waiting in airports. He immersed himself in protest rallies, screaming at "communists," and provoked confrontations.

Jones also was successful as portraying himself as a truth-slinging David pitted against a six-headed mass media conglomerate Goliath. Jones was not owned by Disney, Comcast, News Corp, AT&T, Viacom, or CBS, as almost 90% of American media is.

InfoWars found revenue for its programming by taking on sponsors and selling an InfoWars line of dietary supplements, which accounts for two-thirds of Jones' revenue, according to a study. The officially endorsed InfoWars line of products (with the logo stamped right on the packaging) includes protein bars, bone broth, Survival Shield X-2, and a male vitality pill called Alpha Power.

"While the rest of the liberal world cries and gets weaker, the Infowarriors and Patriots of the world know that it takes real vitality to push back in the fight against the globalist agenda," the ad copy for Alpha Power reads. Saying it'll boost energy and testosterone levels, "you'll discover what it feels like to be an alpha male all over again!"

BuzzFeed News sent several of the InfoWars products to a lab to be tested, and in the lab's report products were described as "safe, but ineffective," a "waste of money," and as having "no real basis in science." The Survival Shield X-2 turned out to be regular iodine marked up three times the market value.

Other frequent InfoWars advertisers include makers of things like fluoride-free toothpaste, bulletproof vests, and apocalypse survival supplies. Accumulating Patriot Points leads to getting a discount on your InfoWars shopping.

Although Jones was still the leading presence of InfoWars, the media outlet expanded to include other radio shows, correspondents, video producers, and staff.

Paul Joseph Watson is Alex Jones' second-in-command and editor-at-large of InfoWars as well as a writer and sometimes guest host of *The Alex Jones Show*. He also has his own InfoWars-related show on YouTube called *PrisonPlanetLive*, where he has over 1.6 million subscribers. Rob Dew is InfoWars' Nightly News Director, and other shows on the platform include *The David Knight Show* and *The War Room with Owen Shroyer*.

There's also a motley gang of on-the-street reporters who have mimicked Jones' ambush journalism style, sticking mics in people's confused faces to confront, harass, and shout them down in public. They began to hit the streets all over the country, like a demented news agency.

"Why were people in the audience telling people to be calm moments before the bomb went off? Was this another false flag staged attack to take our civil liberties and promote Homeland Security by sticking their hands down our pants in the streets?" queried an InfoWars correspondent named "Bionic" Dan Bidondi, at a 2013 press conference with Massachusetts Governor Deval Patrick about updates to the Boston Marathon bombing, which had killed three people and injured hundreds. Bidondi, a former semi-pro wrestler from Rhode Island, did man-on-the-street reporting for InfoWars when not hosting his own YouTube show *Truth Radio Show Dot Com*.

"No," Governor Patrick responded to Bidondi. "Next question."

"You know what will protect women from getting raped, so they don't have to get an abortion? A gun!" Kaitlin Bennett threw down at the University of Akron students she was confronting in 2019 in an InfoWars video segment titled "Triggered Feminist Gets Destroyed by Kaitlin Bennett." Bennett, a.k.a. "the Kent State Gun Girl," is famous for posing with an AR-10 and a graduation cap that read "come and take it" in her graduation photo. She hosted an open carry rally on campus, and her videos usually consist of her shoving a mic at college students to confront them with disdain on gun rights, censorship, abortion, and other topics.

Although he got out on street level himself sometimes, Jones was mostly found yelling in his Austin studio where he talks for three to four hours a day Monday through Friday and a couple more hours on Sunday.

When Jones needed a break, he'd call in guest hosts like author and film-maker Mike Cernovich, a conspiracy theorist promoter and men's rights activist, known for inflammatory comments on rape, like the tweet he sent commenting on an article that read "A whore will let her friend ruin your life with a false rape case. So why should I care when women get raped?" and blog posts like "When in Doubt, Whip it Out."

During the 2008 election cycle, Jones' passionate hatred for Barack Obama, Hillary Clinton, and Democrats in general, gained him further fame and audience from people with a like mind. Jones is responsible for circulating the popular protest image of Obama wearing makeup similar to Heath Ledger's Joker from *The Dark Knight*.

Jones also produced a popular anti-Obama documentary titled *The Obama Deception* in 2009 which propagated that Obama was conspiring to help orches-trate a one-world government. The film was cited as one of the inspirations for Oscar Ortega-Hernandez, who pulled up to the White House on November 11, 2011, and fired several rounds at the White House with an assault rifle before speeding away from the scene. He was caught at a Pennsylvania hotel five days later and said he thought Obama was the Antichrist. His friend, who had sold him the AK-47 used in the shooting, said the two had watched *The Obama Deception* together. InfoWars, true to form, said the mentally ill Ortega was a "plant" or possibly even a "Mossad agent."

Hillary Clinton was just as bad, if not worse, Jones told his listeners. His rants often included an angle that Obama and Hillary were literally practicing black magick or possessed by demons.

"I mean this woman is dangerous, ladies and gentlemen, I'm telling you. She's a demon! This is biblical. She's going to launch a nuclear war!... Hillary's into like creepy, weird, sick stuff, man. Imagine how bad she smells. I'm told her and Obama just stink, stink stink stink. You can't wash that evil off, man. There's a rotten smell around Hillary. I'm not kidding, people say, they say—folks, I've been told by hired folks, they say 'listen, Obama and Hillary both smell like sulfur' ...I've talked to people that are in protective details, that they've scared them, they say 'listen, she's a frickin' demon, and she stinks, and so does Obama.' And I go 'like what?' 'Sulfur.'"

And, like many conspiracy theorists, Jones often targets Hungarian-born Jewish philanthropist and hedge fund billionaire George Soros as the ultimate liberal boogeyman. He's accused of being a Democratic puppetmaster, as well as secretly bankrolling everything from the Occupy Wall Street movement, to Black Lives Matter, gun control activists, and the Colin Kaepernick kneeling protests. If something is deemed liberal and insidious, the phantom of Soros is sure to be lurking somewhere nearby.

Jones has called Soros "fundamentally evil," with a 2016 InfoWars video titled "George Soros is About to Overthrow the US."

Soros was also a primary target of Glenn Beck, the conspiracy author and former FOX News personality, who now runs his own media site, TheBlaze, a lite version of InfoWars. Beck dedicated two entire 2010 episodes of his FOX News show to Soros conspiracies, which he laid out with the help of three chalkboards and literal marionette puppets to explain the intricate conspiracy web to viewers. Beck continues to accuse Soros of funding everything from communist organizations to migrant caravans.

When he wasn't talking about his list of Democrat enemies, Jones would scream for attention any way he could get it. One of Jones' most famous over-the-top moments occurred when he flew off the handle while talking about a potential "gay bomb" of chemicals being added to the water supply, perhaps referencing a study by UC Berkeley that showed atrazine from pesticides in water supplies caused frogs to gender-switch.

"I don't like them putting chemicals in the water that turn the frickin' frogs gay!" he yelled, red-faced, then pounded his desk with a stack of papers. "Do you understand that?! I'm sick of this crap! I'm sick of social engineering! It's not funny!"

But what was going to get Jones more mainstream news attention than anything was his promotion of the "crisis actors" theory.

Up until this point, I had viewed conspiracy as amusing, like the moon landing hoax, or sometimes interesting, like the JFK assassination theories. I enjoyed learning about these ideas, even if there was usually no way I would believe it. The spreading of the sickening "crisis actors" theory changed all that for me.

LIKE MANY CONSPIRACIES, THERE'S some grain of truth to be found in the crisis actors theory insomuch as "crisis actors" do exist. They're hired by companies like CrisisCast who set up scenarios for law enforcement to work through as a training program. These actors might set up a scene of a terrorist hostage situation in a closed-off section of an airport so law enforcement can get firsthand experience learning how to deal with a panicked group of people, mass casualties, and active shooters. Somehow this spun into a wild theory that crisis actors are used to stage horrifying hoaxes of mass shootings.

As these shootings became an all too regular occurrence, the theory began to circulate that the government staged the shooting events to cause a catalyst that will lead to the repeal of the 2nd Amendment. The victims are fabrications, and the grieving loved ones seen in media are just actors playing a role. The supposed evidence is that in several cases the same "actor" appears to play different grieving people in various tragedies because they have a similar appearance.

Susan Orfanos, for example, lost her son, U.S. Navy vet Telemachus Orfanos in a mass shooting in a bar in Thousand Oaks, California, one of 12 people killed at the Borderline Bar & Grill on November 7, 2018. He had escaped the Las Vegas shooting at the Harvest Music Fest a little over a year earlier, on October 1, 2017.

"I don't want thoughts. I don't want prayers. I want gun control," Orfanos told reporters about losing her son. But soon a meme was circulating among conspiracy theorists that showed a picture from the interview paired up with two other photos. "Just so you know, not only was she a mom of the California and Orlando shootings, she was a victim of the Las Vegas shooting, too!!" the meme post shared, adding three laughing emoticons with tears in their eyes.

The other two photos were not of Orfanos, but of Christine Leinonen, who lost her son in the 2016 Pulse Club shooting in Orlando, and Jan Lambourne, who survived the Las Vegas shooting with a gunshot to the abdomen. All three women resemble each other insomuch as they are all Caucasian women with glasses and somewhat in the same age range, and theorists said it was the same person wearing different wigs and glasses. Soon the juxtaposed photos were rapidly being shared via Twitter, Instagram, and YouTube.

Similar examples were picked up from the vast database of people responding to different shootings. A somewhat similar grieving brunette younger woman was found in footage from the Sandy Hook and Aurora shootings as well as the Boston bombings.

In other variations of the mass shooting hoax theories, conspiracists say that the shootings did happen but were a type of "false flag" event set up by the Deep State, who got a shooter to do their bidding through a "Manchurian Candidate" style of brainwashing program.

That's what Richard McCaslin believes happened at the Aurora, Colorado shooting on July 20, 2012, when James Eagan Holmes, heavily armed and wearing ballistic gear, walked into a movie theater and killed 12 people. For a period of a few years, I knew I could count on a message from Richard whenever a large-scale shooting or event happened. He usually didn't take time to say hi but jumped straight into the conspiracy. Sure enough, later the same day Aurora happened, I got a message from Richard with his thoughts.

> Tea, This shooting has CIA / MK Ultra / Project Monarch written all over it! I haven't heard all the details, but this guy was waayy too equipped and prepared just to be some psychotic fanboy. I don't buy the "lone wolf" scenario either. Somebody in that theater had to open the emergency exit for him because you can't open them from the outside. HLN reported that a few people saw someone (Holmes' handler?) answer a cellphone call during the movie, get up and leave through the emergency exit. Keep in mind that Columbine isn't that far away and that region of the country is a major center for the military-industrial complex. Bottom line... this psy-op was another attempt by the Establishment to scare the American people into giving up their 2nd Amendment rights!

Richard ended up driving to Colorado to protest the "false flag" outside the theater where the shooting had happened. From Aurora and the other 15 mass shootings of 2012 to the 2017 Texas Sutherland Spring First Baptist Church shooting where 26 people died, most mass shootings have a conspiracy attached to them. But the favorite targets for the crisis actor theory have been Sandy Hook and the Stoneman Douglas High School shooting in Parkland, Florida, another school shooting where 17 people died. The teenage Parkland survivors went on to make appearances at rallies and in the media, pleading for gun control legislation. One of the most frequent Parkland spokespersons, David Hogg, became a favorite target for the theory as he was the son of a retired FBI agent. Hogg was soon as reviled a liberal name as Clinton, Obama, and Soros (and later Alexandria Ocasio-Cortez and "the Squad"). His family began to receive death threats from conspiracy theorists.

After his appearance on Piers Morgan's show, Jones propagated the crisis actors theory several times on his show, specifically related to Sandy Hook and Parkland.

"Sandy Hook is synthetic, completely fake with actors, in my view, manu-factured," Jones told a caller on his show in January 2015. "I couldn't believe it at first. I knew they had actors there, clearly, but I thought they killed some real kids. And it just shows how bold they are, that they clearly used actors."

SANDY HOOKERS

IN OCTOBER 2016 ROBBIE PARKER was walking in Seattle to a hotel to meet members of his family. Parker and his wife had lost their six-year-old daughter, Emilie, at Sandy Hook. A middle-aged man in khakis and a sport coat approached him and asked if his child had died in the shooting. When Parker answered that he had lost his daughter, the man unleashed a string of obscenities at him, then followed him for blocks "jabbering in my ear," Parker said in an interview.

Parker had been a favorite target because, still grieving the death of his daughter, he let out a nervous laugh before he broke down in a news interview shortly after the shooting. A lot of crisis actor theories are built about perceived behavior from grieving people. The loved ones of the victims are not sad enough or too sad or seem like they're reading a script, conspiracy theorists say.

"He's laughing, and then he basically goes over and starts breaking down and crying," Alex Jones said on his show, imitating fake crying. "This needs to be investigated. They're clearly using this to go after our guns!"

Parker was not the only parent to receive harassment. Sandy Hookers[6] are among the most unhinged and frightening conspiracy theorists out there, and they've stalked and harassed the Sandy Hook parents through phone calls, e-mails, and in-person confrontations.

Shortly after the shooting, Sandy Hookers began creating media on the event, including self-published books and YouTube video "documentaries," and discussed their theories on sites like 4chan.

InfoWars gave the arguments a consistent microphone. InfoWars correspondent Dan Bidondi traveled to confront lawyers of the family and family members in Newtown, in front of a courthouse.

"Yer a buncha frauds, a buncha criminals! Scumbags! Sandy Hook was an inside job!" Bidondi screamed at them.

Other popular Hooker media produced included a book edited by Jim Fetzer and Mike Palecek titled *Nobody Died at Sandy Hook*, published by Moon Rock Books. The company went on to publish a series of similarly titled books like *And Nobody Died in Boston, either*, as well as *The Parkland Puzzle: How the pieces fit together*, and *Political Theater in Charlottesville*. Fetzer was an InfoWars guest.

---

6   They prefer to call themselves "Sandy Hook Investigators" or "Sandy Hook Truthers," but this is the term I'm using.

Another InfoWars guest, Peter Klein, produced documentaries that worked on the theory that Sandy Hook was staged, *We Need to Talk About Sandy Hook* in 2014 and a 2015 follow-up titled *The Life of Adam*, which studied Sandy Hook shooter Adam Lanza.

But the most dogged Sandy Hooker was Wolfgang Halbig, who made his pursuit of Sandy Hook conspiracies a full-time hobby.

"What's your bottom line, what do you think really happened at Sandy Hook?" Jones asked Halbig in an InfoWars video.

"I can tell you children did not die, teachers did not die on December 14, 2012. It just could not have happened," Halbig responded with a smirk.

Halbig, who was briefly a Florida State Trooper, a part-time employee at U.S. Customs, and a retired school security director (he also tried to sell his school system on a phony bomb detection device called the Quatro Tracker), harassed families and lobbied the Connecticut government with repeated information requests. In one video confrontation, he approaches the Newtown Volunteer Fire Department and antagonizes them about their response to Sandy Hook until a firefighter pushes him, at which point Halbig calls 911 to report an assault.

Halbig, via InfoWars, promoted many of the Sandy Hook conspiracies—that the school had allegedly been abandoned for years and was used as a movie set; that Porta-Potties, sent for because of the mass of grieving people and media who had assembled at the closed-off school, had arrived too quickly, proving it had been premeditated. A theory that Jones helped spread, swirling his hand around in a circle, suggested that the Sandy Hook crisis actors were being led around in circles through the building with their hands up, over and over. What the video really shows is adults being evacuated at a different structure and being led outside from the back door to the front of the building.

One of the strangest conspiracies alleged that CNN host Anderson Cooper was not broadcasting live from one of the Sandy Hook funerals, but was recording in front of a green screen because at one point the tip of his nose seems to disappear, evidence that theorists said was part of a green-screen glitch. Why Anderson needed to fake the news report in a studio produces more questions than answers.

Fundraising efforts by Halbig to file more Freedom of Information Act costs and trips to Newtown to investigate were publicized on InfoWars shows.

In a 2015 e-mail, Halbig asked InfoWars Nightly News Director Rob Dew to thank InfoWars host David Knight for an interview, saying the publicity "has raised $1,545.00 since last night."

All of this Sandy Hooker media inspired InfoWars fans to engage with the Sandy Hook families themselves.

In November 2015, a Sandy Hooker named Matthew Mills was arrested for harassing the family of Victoria Soto, a 27-year-old Sandy Hook teacher that had died trying to protect the children in her classroom. Mills entered the Vicki Soto 5K run in Stratford, Connecticut, a charity event organized by Soto's family. After the run, he confronted Soto's younger sister Jillian about a photo that had circulated online of the Soto sisters he believed was "photoshopped." Mills said he considered himself a "journalist." Soto asked Mills to leave her alone, but he kept pushing the photo toward her, telling her that her sister didn't exist until the police arrived.

In the photo, Mills explained after his arrest, "people say the rocks don't match up, the shadows don't match up." The prior year Mills had been arrested for grabbing the microphone away from Seattle Seahawks linebacker Malcolm Smith during a Super Bowl press conference and saying "Investigate 9/11. 9/11 was perpetuated by people in our own government."

Mills pled guilty via Alford plea procedure and was sentenced to a one-year sentence followed by a two-year probation, and ordered not to have further contact with the Soto family.

In December 2016, a 57-year-old Tampa, Florida woman named Lucy Richards threatened Lenny Pozner, whose six-year-old son, Noah, had died at Sandy Hook. Richards harassed Pozner with multiple voicemail messages and e-mails, including a text that read "you gonna die, death is coming to you real soon" and "LOOK BEHIND YOU IT IS DEATH."

Richards, a devoted follower of InfoWars, had gotten Pozner's e-mail from Alex Jones after he shared it on his show, also showing a map where Pozner's post office box was located.

Pozner had attracted more attention than most Sandy Hook families because he was vocally challenging those who were spreading the lies about the tragedy. Pozner has said that he had been interested in conspiracy theory himself, and had even listened to *The Alex Jones Show* after dropping his kids off at school, but for him entertaining the ideas were the same as "watching a good science-fiction movie," as *New York* magazine reports.

Perhaps because of this, "he decided the best way to quell the controversy and shut down the conspiracy theorists was to make himself personally available on social media, to answer people's questions, and provide proof of Noah's existence," a statement reads on the website for HONR, a nonprofit Pozner founded to "end the continued harassment and intentional torment of the victims' families" of Sandy Hook and other mass-casualty events.

Pozner posted copies of Noah's birth announcement, report cards, autopsy reports, and death certificate, but if anything, this added fuel to the fire. Hookers created social media groups dedicated to stalking the Pozners, posting Social Security and credit information, and creepy videos of their house and Noah's grave. Eventually conspiracy rhetoric and threats grew so great that Pozner ended up moving over and over—seven times in five years—as Sandy Hookers found out where he and his family lived and continued to harass them.

Richards went to trial in June 2017 and pled guilty. As part of a plea deal, some of the charges against Richards were dropped, and she was sentenced to five months in prison, followed by five months of house arrest, followed by three years of supervised release. During this period she was told that she would need to record her computer activity, and part of her sentence was that she was to "cease consuming InfoWars programming."

Another of the Sandy Hook parents, Jeremy Richman, who had lost his daughter Avielle at Sandy Hook, found himself harassed after Wolfgang Halbig had promoted a particularly disgusting conspiracy that Avielle was still alive and wasn't even Richman's daughter.

Like Pozner and other Sandy Hook parents, Richman, a neuroscientist, had created an organization. He had hoped that the Avielle Foundation could do some good in the world, honor the memory of his daughter, and help him cope with her loss. The Avielle Foundation's mission is "to prevent violence and build compassion through neuroscience research, community engagement, and education."

Halbig's website, SandyHookJustice.com, accused Richman and Avielle's mother, Jennifer Hensel, of trying to "deceive and defraud the American public and collect donations for The Avielle Foundation, claiming she is dead, when in reality, she is alive and was never their daughter." Halbig's evidence was photos that allegedly showed Avielle (or someone that looked like her) alive and well.

But despite his efforts with the foundation, Jeremy's heart was broken, and the grief was too much. In March 2019, he committed suicide.

For the time being, the remaining Sandy Hook parents were stuck in Hell—they had not only lost their young children in a massacre, but they were also being bombarded by conspiracy theorists accusing them of faking the tragedy as the conspiracy continued to spread on the Internet.

Some small retribution for the families would be arriving soon.

CHAPTER TWELVE

RETURN OF THE PHANTOM PATRIOT

R ichard only spent three days in the Bahamas. A September 4, 2011, e-mail to me read:

Once I checked with Immigration, it became apparent that I wouldn't be staying. In order to file for residency, you have to already own property in the U.S. To get a work permit, a potential employer must write a letter of recommendation and then Immigration will mull it over for several months. In other words, I was screwed.

Richard bought a return ticket to the States and headed to Las Vegas. I heard from Richard sporadically over the next few months. He found an apartment in downtown Vegas and protested a couple times as Thoughtcrime. On 9/11, less than a week in town, he found a local group of Las Vegas Truthers led by a local character with a big, bushy beard known as "9/11 Bob." He joined them protesting on the strip.

"We greeted each other like old friends!" Richard e-mailed.

THE RETURN

A FEW MONTHS LATER, in an early January 2012 e-mail, Richard outlined a new superhero action.

"I plan to make an appearance as the Phantom Patriot in San Francisco on January 20, the tenth anniversary of my arrest," Richard wrote, saying he would dress in a replica of his original Phantom Patriot costume, march with a protest sign, and try to drum up interest from the local media.

"The main feature of the protest will be for me to stand in front of the Bohemian Club Mansion, unmask, then read a prepared statement... The Bohos will probably call the cops, but I'm not on parole anymore, so the area restrictions are invalid now."

Wow, this is getting pretty intense, I thought.

He asked me if I could put him in touch with Motor-Mouth, a fast-talking, rambling Real-Life Superhero that led a small team of San Franciscan RLSH named the Pacific Protectorate. I had met him at an RLSH team-up in Vancouver while working on *Heroes in the Night*.

"I'm well aware I'm the 'black sheep' of the RLSH community, but it would be nice if some of the Pacific Protectorate guys showed up to stand with me," Richard explained. And then, something I wasn't expecting—Richard wanted me there, too.

"I can't guarantee media coverage, but your presence would help," he wrote. "I'll make you an offer. If you have the time, but not the money, then I would be willing to pay for a round-trip ticket." He added, "This mission is a *go* whether I do it myself (as usual) or these guys man up and show up."

I thought about whether or not I should go. If Richard bought my ticket, I didn't want to be beholden to him to write Phantom Patriot propaganda. Finally, I decided to go, but first I spoke to Richard, letting him know that his purchase of the plane ticket could not be seen as a sign that I was not planning to do anything but try to write about the experience and him objectively. He said he understood. But there was a bit of a curveball when I explained to him that "Tea Krulos" was not my real name and he would have to use my legal name to purchase a ticket. He seemed a bit weirded out, so I explained it was just a pen name, and that hundreds of artists, writers, musicians, actors, and more used them, including "everyone from Mark Twain to Ice Cube," I wrote to him.

He seemed to relax when I explained it, but he had one last word on it:

"I know what a pen name is. By the way—Mark Twain was a Bohemian Club member, and Ice Cube is a Freemason. You might want to rethink your examples."

OK, I thought. *Let's go to San Francisco.*

AFTER STRIPPING OFF MY jacket, sweatshirt, shoes, and belt, I stuffed them into a gray tote bin. I unzipped my backpack and set my laptop into another gray bin and emptied my pockets on top of it. Noticing a toe sticking out of a hole in my sock, I held the waistline of my pants, so they didn't droop down and reveal my buttcrack. Then I stepped into a sci-fi-like full-body scanner, held my hands up and my feet apart while a gyroscope scanner swooshed around me, and TSA watched me with a cautious eye. Cleared, I retrieved my possessions and sat on a bench to put myself back together.

Did Richard have a point about TSA? I wondered as I sat waiting for my flight, drinking coffee.

I HAD BEEN ABLE to contact Motor-Mouth, who turned out to be somewhat of a budding young conspiracy theorist himself. He agreed to meet Richard for his protest and recruited his teammate Mutinous Angel, who was oblivious to what he had volunteered himself for, to join in.

During my first day in San Francisco, I met up with Richard so the two of us could scope out the area he'd be protesting in the next day. As soon as I crossed the street and shook his hand, the conspiracy started rolling.

"Did you see all of these Occupy protesters walking this way?" was the first thing Richard said.

I had, I told him. As I had walked up Market Street, I had seen small groups of protesters here and there carrying handwritten signs, all heading the opposite direction I was walking.

Although Occupy camps had started to fizzle out by 2012, the protest was still active in the rainy streets of San Francisco. I initially thought this movement, although on a different wavelength, would be something Richard might embrace and try to be a part of, or appreciate on some level. After all, the members of the Bohemian Grove were the very definition of the "one percent." But like his quick disappointment with the RLSH, Richard's opinion of the Occupy movement soured when he placed them within the dark depths of the conspiracy. Richard told me he believed protestors were being manipulated as a strategy to discredit and eventually shut down protest movements, in a campaign of sabotage.

"9/11 Bob and I have concluded that the Occupy Las Vegas 'inner circle' are obviously 'Obamanoids.' There are reports that New World Order billionaire George Soros is bankrolling several of the Occupy groups across the country. Maybe that's why Soros started this movement... to ruin the concept of protest in the eyes of the general public and to 'outlaw' any diehards (like me)," Richard wrote to me.

Now Richard had a theory that this particular Occupy demonstration had been arranged by a Bohemian Club puppetmaster to distract attention from his protest. Somehow, the Bohemian Club had gleaned information on his protest, probably getting the info by spying on his e-mail. That idea might sound paranoid, but then again, conspiracy theory turned reality in 2013, when Edward Snowden revealed that the National Security Agency had a far-reaching surveillance program called PRISM. The NSA collected phone data on millions of Americans and tapped directly into the servers of Internet companies, including Facebook, Google, Microsoft, and Yahoo. Snowden leaked documents to *The Washington Post* and *The Guardian* after working for the NSA as a contractor. Reports revealed that the NSA surveillance was far-reaching and could hack into live communication and stored data.

Richard and I walked down the rainy streets until we found the Occupy event, about a hundred people trying to stay dry with raincoats and quickly assembled tent canopies, handing out leaflets and signing people up for networking lists. Richard attempted to question volunteers on when and who had organized the event, to try to give credence to his theory it had been hammered together last-minute to distract from him, but the volunteers on hand didn't have specifics.

AFTER WE LEFT OCCUPY, Richard asked me to join him as he cruised around town, hand-delivering some "press packs" he had made up to local media. Each included a zine-style version of the comic he had drawn about his Bohemian Grove raid, and a press release of sorts that talked about his planned protest the next day.

"It is a sad day in America when someone has to resort to gaudy street theater to get the truth out to the masses, but you have left me no other choice," the last line of the press release read.

Richard was hoping I might be able to "talk the talk" and get people interested in covering his story. We made about five stops to San Francisco TV stations and newspaper offices, Richard navigating around with his GPS. He looked up driving directions to a local TV news station, and we showed up and approached a glass door with an intercom system on the door. I pushed the intercom button.

"*Fffft fffchhh zzzzp...*" a staticky, chopped-up voice replied. Richard and I looked at each other, quizzically.

"Ah, hello. We want to drop off a press release here," I said, pulling on the door. It was locked.

"*Ffffsss sssffff chhh....*" I tried pulling on the door again, but it was still locked.

"Hello?" I said, pressing the button, then tried the door again.

Richard slid the press pack in between the door and doorframe. "Let's go," he said, dismayed.

Our luck didn't improve from there. We ran into a succession of locked, unattended doors, and disinterested secretaries, who at best would throw the press pack onto a big stack of paperwork.

Richard and I parted ways, establishing a time and meet-up spot at a park—Union Square—just a couple blocks from the Bohemian Club for the next day.

THAT NIGHT I HUNG OUT with some members of the California Initiative, a group of people who had ties to the Real-Life Superhero community, led by a couple named Rock n Roll and Night Bug. The California Initiative and the Pacific Protectorate had different philosophies on the whole superhero thing, leading to a rare case of two RLSH teams in the same city. Rock n Roll and Night Bug had a charming, sunny California family and a young family friend, Angelita, who was willing to shoot video of the protest the next day. The California Initiative was concerned about a possible situation—perhaps Richard might flip out, or alternately, maybe a passerby might flip out on us. Rock had decided that it might be prudent to have her, Night Bug, and team member Eon on hand nearby.

The next morning, Rock, Night Bug, and Eon dropped Angelita and me off at Union Square to meet up with Richard and the Pacific Protectorate. The California Initiative parked and got seats to keep an eye on us discreetly outside the Honey Honey Café & Crepery across the street from the Bohemian Club.

After a couple of quick phone calls and a walk around the perimeter of the square the park was in, we found Motor-Mouth and Mutinous Angel, then turned the corner and discovered Richard standing quietly, as still as a statue, with his sign ("The Bohemian Grove Murders Children Every July 23!") while passersby gaped at him. His skull mask stared blankly ahead, grinning maniacally. The Phantom Patriot was a striking appearance, and I saw more than one person walking by give a look of fear, including a frightened mother quietly herding her child away from his direction.

After Motor-Mouth, Mutinous Angel, and Angelita made their introductions, we headed up to the Bohemian Club's front doors. Richard handed his sign to

Mutinous Angel and his copy of a book he'd be reading from, *Trance-Formation of America* by Mark Phillips and Cathy O'Brien, to Motor-Mouth. Angelita started rolling video. At the last minute, Richard asked me to step in frame and introduce him. I wasn't sure what to say, so I improvised:

"My name is Tea Krulos. I'm a journalist, and I'm here in front of the Bohemian Club with Richard McCaslin who has returned once again as the Phantom Patriot and is going to say a few words here today."

Richard removed his skull mask and looked intently at the camera. Motor-Mouth handed him a single sheet of loose-leaf paper covered with Richard's careful handwriting.

THE BOHEMIAN CLUB SPEECH

"MY NAME IS RICHARD McCaslin. Ten years ago, I was arrested outside the Bohemian Grove. My goal was to expose the Bohemian's crimes of pedophilia, torture, murder, and treason against the American people. In 2002, I failed to convince a jury that these atrocities were occurring because I had no proof. Today, however, I have all the proof America needs to condemn these sociopaths. This book, *Trance Formation of America*, was written by Cathy O'Brien and her husband, Mark Phillips. Cathy O'Brien is the only vocal and recovered survivor of the CIA's MKUltra Project Monarch mind-control operation. On August 3, 1977, the 95th U.S. Congress opened hearings into the reported abuses concerning MKUltra. On February 8, 1988, Cathy O'Brien was covertly rescued from her mind-controlled enslavement and scheduled execution in Bohemian Grove by intelligence insider Mark Phillips. Their pursuit of justice has been denied for reasons of national security. In other words, many of Cathy and her daughter Kelly's abusers were high-ranking politicians, like Gerald Ford, Ronald Reagan, George Bush Sr., Dick Cheney, Senator Robert Byrd, and both Clintons.

"I will now read pages 170 and 171 of *Trance*. Cathy O'Brien writes," Richard began, opening the book.

I looked at the doors to the Bohemian Club behind him. The windows on the doors were slightly tinted, but I could see two men in black suits, one speaking into a walkie-talkie on the other side of the door. Richard began to read.

THE SECOND MOST DISTURBING MOMENT I had while researching this book was reading *Trance Formation of America: The True Story of a CIA Mind Control Slave*. The first was realizing that I hadn't taken adequate notes on my initial read-through of the book and would need to go back and reread long sections. The text reads like an intense, rambling non-consensual torture erotica, the worst political porn ever created.

The first sentence of chapter one of Cathy O'Brien's section (her husband wrote the first 80 pages) describes how O'Brien's father began molesting her as a baby, and continues through a graphic depiction of abuse she claims she received from the world's most powerful political leaders and famous entertainers. O'Brien claims that she was entered into a MKUltra-style CIA brainwashing program called "Project Monarch" at a young age and then was used brutally as a sex slave, drug mule, and encoded-message delivery person to the world's most powerful men. Her "handlers," who tortured her with brainwashing techniques and pimped her out, she says, included her father, who sold her as a slave to U.S. Senator Robert Byrd, and later her first husband, Wayne Cox, a country musician.

The brainwashing program continued with her second husband, a Nashville ventriloquist named Alex Houston, who toured the South with his dummy, Elmer. The duo started performing in the '50s and often played clubs and festivals opening for famous country music acts. They also found some success appearing on TV programs like *The Porter Wagoner Show* and *Hee Haw*. The duo produced at least one comedy album and a couple of singles, like the holiday spoof "Here Comes Peter Cotton Claus," and a ventriloquist dummy's take on women's lib, "Burn Your Bra, Baby." Houston died in 2017.

Whenever these songs or TV show clips appear on blogs and YouTube, you'll find a steady stream of commenters who have read *Trance Formation of America* and leave comments like: "Do you realize who this is? This is the criminal who mind-controlled Cathy O'Brien in the MK-Ultra program for her owner Senator Byrd!!!! Really!" and "Houston, I wish you to burn in hell forever!"

O'Brien claims in her book that Houston used mind control to condition her to become a sex slave that serviced Canadian Prime Minister Pierre Trudeau (who enjoyed a bestiality film of O'Brien having sex with a French poodle named Pepe), musician and "CIA operative" Jimmy Buffett, and dozens of other senators, military commanders, and various other world leaders like Nicaraguan President Daniel Ortega, Haitian dictator Jean-Claude "Baby Doc" Duvalier, and Fahd bin Abdulaziz Al Saud, King of Saudi Arabia. All of these men, O'Brien claimed, shared the same taste in a sex slave they found desirable.

Houston and O'Brien were married in 1980, he being almost 30 years older than her. One of O'Brien's most disturbing allegations about the ventriloquist is that he "flesh carved a hideous witch's face for Senator Byrd's perversion" into her "upper vaginal wall."

"Not only did this surgery give Byrd a vagina suited to his minute, under-developed penis, it also provided an equitable 'curiosity' to be displayed over and over again in both commercial and non-commercial pornography and prostitution," O'Brien explains.

O'Brien also claims that as a "Presidential Model" sex slave she was abused by a long lineage of U.S. Presidents and Vice Presidents, starting with her teenage years and President Gerald Ford in 1974.

"That night, I wore my Catholic uniform as instructed and went into a dis-sociative trance as my father drove me to the local National Guard Armory, where I was prostituted to Ford. Ford took me into an empty room, pushed me down on the wooden floor as he unzipped his pants, and said, 'pray on this.' Then he brutally, sexually assaulted me. Afterward, my memory was compartmentalized through the use of high voltage. I was then carried out to the car where I lay in the back seat, muscles contracted, stunned, in pain, and unable to move."

O'Brien claims in her book that her worst tormentor from this pack was former Vice President Dick Cheney, who had an "oversized penis" and an angry streak that would lead him to beat her often. O'Brien says that Cheney would make his sex slaves strip their clothing, then run naked through the woods of an unknown property of Wyoming so that Cheney could pursue them and hunt them down in his version of "The Most Dangerous Game." When Cheney would find his prey, O'Brien explicitly describes being beaten and sexually abused.

Ronald Reagan, whom O'Brien says she also serviced, made his mind control slaves drink his urine, produced porn and, like all the politicians talked about in her account, loved to snort massive amounts of cocaine. O'Brien also says she was used for sex by Hillary and as a cocaine smuggler for Bill Clinton, and her daughter Kelly, also brainwashed in the program, became a favorite sex slave for President George H.W. Bush.

O'Brien says all of these experiences "regressed" and only came forward after she met Mark Phillips, who helped "de-program" her and she was able to recall the traumatic experiences under hypnosis. Although it seems likely that O'Brien has had traumatizing experiences of some sort (though not with the people she names), the book is entirely based on her word. Conspiracy die-hards, like any group of fanatic believers, are quick to be skeptical of any "mainstream" media reporting but will completely believe a self-published, poorly sourced book like *Trance Formation of America* as gospel truth, simply because it is presented as nonfiction. If it wasn't accurate, *Trance* defenders often say, why weren't Phillips and O'Brien sued for libel by the book's subjects? One possibility would be that the subjects either haven't been made aware of the underground tome or don't want to give it the satisfaction of the spotlight with a libel suit.

RICHARD'S READING FROM *Trance Formation of America* is two pages in which Cathy O'Brien describes what she purports to be her time as a sex slave in a strange, perverse sexual playground somewhere in the Bohemian Grove. She claims slaves of advancing age or faulty programming were ritually sacrificed in the Grove. Instructed to perform sexually "as though her life depended on it," O'Brien claims she was led through myriad horrific perversions for the world's elite men. She says there was a necrophilia-themed room where she was "heavily drugged and programmed" to simulate that she was dead. She was forced to perform sexually in a pornography-themed room with former President Gerald Ford and was "brutally assaulted" by former Vice President Dick Cheney in the "Leather Room," a dark, leather-lined room. "Cheney jokingly claimed I 'blew his cover' when I recognized his all-too-familiar voice and abnormally large penis size," O'Brien writes.

She says she was locked in a triangular-shaped display case "with various trained animals, including snakes. Members walking by watched illicit sex acts of bestiality, women with women, mothers with daughters, kids with kids, or any other unlimited perverse visual display."

"THERE WAS A ROOM of shackles and tortures, black lights and strobes, an opium den, ritualistic sex altars, a chapel, group orgy rooms including poster beds, water beds, and kitten houses." Richard read loudly outside the Bohemian Club. "I was used as a rag doll in the toy store, and *as a urinal,*" Richard's voice cracked with anger, "in the golden arches room. From the owl's roost to the necrophilia room, no memory of sexual abuse is as horrifying as the conversations overheard in the [underground meeting room in the Grove] pertaining to the New World Order. I learned that perpetrators believed that controlling the masses through propaganda mind manipulation did not guarantee there would be a world left to dominate due to environmental and overpopulation problems. The solution being debated was not pollution/population control, but mass genocide of selected undesirables."

Richard took a deep breath and handed the book over to Motor-Mouth. He looked intensely into Angelita's camera.

"This book was published in 1995. Its sequel, *Access Denied,* came out in 2004, but the mainstream media has never mentioned them. If you think Cathy and her daughter Kelly's case doesn't affect you, consider this. Many of her abusers were the real masterminds behind 9/11, and they are still planning more false flag attacks in the near future. For instance, Dick Cheney has cooked up a scenario in which the CIA and Israeli Mossad would launch a false flag attack on an American warship in the Persian Gulf, then blame it on the Iranians. If the U.S. retaliated against Iran, Russia and China have already vowed to defend their ally. That means World War III, and that is exactly what the New World Order wants," Richard looked down at his paper momentarily. His face flushed with anger. He stared at his notes for a second, then pointed at the building behind him.

"Don't let these cold-blooded *reptiles* destroy the world!" He shouted. "In 2002, I was alone when I faced these bastards!" His voice cracked with emotion, and he was teary-eyed. "Today, I stand here with the Pacific Protectorate, and I ask America—all Americans—to do the same thing. Thank you."

Motor-Mouth put a hand on his shoulder. Richard wiped the tears from his eyes and turned away from the Bohemian Club. "C'mon, let's get out of here," he said, walking away, but then stopped and turned to us again. He still had tears in his eyes. "It feels good. I've waited ten years for this. *Ten years!*"

It hit home to me that this is all Richard wanted for the last ten years—allies, people to stand shoulder to shoulder with him. People to listen to him. He tried to deliver his message, and now via in person and through a video soon to be uploaded to YouTube, he would share that message. It seemed like a weight had been lifted off of him, and I thought that perhaps Richard had finally found some closure.

But I was wrong about this, too.

CHAPTER THIRTEEN

PIZZAGATE AND OTHER NEW RICHARDS

O n December 4, 2016, a 28-year-old man named Edgar Maddison Welch (he usually goes by his middle instead of first name) began a five-and-a-half-hour drive north from his home in Salisbury, North Carolina to Washington, D.C. Welch was on a mission uncanny in its similarity to Richard McCaslin's raid.

Welch and Richard had a common interest in creating independent film (in a WriteAPrisoner.com profile, Edgar says his nickname is "Hollywood"), which Welch pursued while going to school in Salisbury (or as he calls it, "Smallsbury"—the population is around 8,500 more than Richard's hometown, Zanesville), at Cape Fear Community College. IMDB lists him as a production assistant to two low-budget films, one acting credit as "Raver/Victim" in the critically panned vampire thriller *The Bleeding* (2009), and the writer of a nine-minute short film called *Mute* (2011). *Mute* depicts a college student who struggles to be understood but finds a friend (or perhaps a romance) by the end of the film. Welch, looking very much like Kurt Cobain, appears as an extra.

Welch had been enraged and driven to action by Internet reports of a secret pedophile ring operating out of a pizza parlor named Comet Ping Pong by high-profile Democrats including Hillary Clinton, her advisor and Chief of Staff John Podesta, and others in their campaign. The conspiracy theory started on Reddit and spread like wildfire on the Internet and was branded as "Pizzagate."

Welch was well-armed for his raid—he had a handgun and an AR-15 semi-automatic rifle, and he had a loaded 12-gauge shotgun for backup in his car. Like Richard's note to Chely Wright, one of Welch's last acts was to text a Bible verse to his girlfriend. He also has Isaiah 40:30–31 (which says that faith in the Lord will give the weary strength) tattooed on his back.

One difference between Welch and Richard is that while Richard had no one to leave behind, Welch has family. He's the father of two young girls from his ex-wife and has a girlfriend and other family—unlike Richard, both of his parents were still alive.

Richard and Welch both did not plan a mass shooting bloodbath but were convinced they were doing heroic acts and would be freeing imprisoned child slaves. But like Richard, Welch would find nothing.

UNLIKE THE BOHEMIAN GROVE story, which took a slow ride for decades and decades to reach conspiracy lore, the Pizzagate theory spread to millions of people in a few quick weeks online.

After Clinton campaign staff e-mails were posted on WikiLeaks, the Pizzagate theory was strung together from e-mails by Podesta. Theorists noted that he seemed to be sending an awful lot of e-mails about his love for food, especially pizza, including e-mails where he set up fundraising events at Comet Ping Pong.

But was Podesta referring to pizza pizza or *pizza*, a code word for something much more depraved?

A "pizza pedo code" of unknown origin circulated online that supposedly listed words that were "early Internet and Deep Web" code words for child pornography. *Cheese* meant "child" while *cheese pizza*, the list stated, was "child porn." *Sauce* equaled "orgy," and *Domino's* was a substitute for BDSM. Other foods like *hot dog* and *pasta* were code for "boy" and *ice cream* meant "male prostitute."

That means an e-mail, like this exchange about a free ice cream event in Podesta's e-mails, had a secret meaning:

"I consider ice cream, its purchase, and its consumption a rather serious business. We can't just toss it out willy-nilly in casual references especially with the word 'free' involved."

According to the code theory, that would mean Podesta was speaking about a free male prostitute. But the code doesn't make sense in an e-mail where Podesta's friend Herb talks about a gift he received in the mail:

"I immediately realized something was different by the shape of the box, and I contemplated who would be sending me something in the square-shaped box. Lo and behold, instead of pasta and wonderful sauces, it was a lovely assortment of cheeses, Yummy. I am awaiting the return of my children and grandchildren from their holiday travels so we can demolish them."

According to the supposed code, this person is saying he received an assortment of *children* instead of a *little boy* and a wonderful *orgy* and that the *children* would be demolished by him, his children, and grandchildren. Were conspiracists suggesting that Podesta's associate was so depraved he was planning an inter-generational pedophile gangbang orgy with his family?

After the premise was established—that Podesta was helping run a child sex trafficking ring, an Internet army of conspiracists began scrutinizing everything they could about Comet Ping Pong and the businesses surrounding it, Podesta's life, and his colleagues. They found alarming symbolism everywhere.

Comet Ping Pong had a secret basement room, the conspiracy says, where the child sex slaves were imprisoned, inspired by a photo of what looks like an empty walk-in cooler. The theory was soon being sounded off in YouTube videos, conspiracy radio shows, and on Reddit and other forums. InfoWars picked up the story and began talking about it, giving the theory an even bigger platform, and others help spread the word, like Mike Cernovich and Jack Posobiec (the "Far Right's Twin Trolls," as the *Daily Beast* called them). Cernovich wrote an article on his blog titled "Reveal Clinton's Inner Circle as Sex Cult with Connections to Human Trafficking," and Posobiec tweeted the theory and stopped in Comet Ping Pong to shoot videos for Periscope, including filming a child's birthday party in a back room.

The conspiracy grew legs. Lieutenant General Michael Flynn (briefly Trump's National Security Advisor) tweeted that Hillary's e-mails included "sex crimes with children," and his son, Michael Flynn Jr., was ousted from Trump's transition team after he retweeted the conspiracy, writing "Until #Pizzagate proven to be false, it'll remain a story."

WEIRDO PIZZA PLACE

ONE OF THE REASONS Comet Ping Pong, owned by restaurateur and art gallery proprietor James Alefantis, was ripe for conspiracy is because it is, as Slate.com calls it, "D.C.'s Weirdo Pizza Place," adding that "Comet is a platform for art from the margins." It's a family-friendly establishment by day, but at night the ping pong tables get moved for punk shows, art openings, and LGBT events.

A photo circulated by conspiracy theorists showed one of the restaurant's employees dressed for his drag act for a Halloween show—covered in fake blood, writhing on the floor. For conspiracy theorists, it was a shocking proof of a scandal. They had no idea how an individual might be a pizza cook during the day and a drag performer at night unless there was a satanic pedophile agenda behind it. Comet Ping Pong has been described as a "dive," but that's not accurate; it's something freakier and harder to understand to those who aren't in an urban culture—it's hip.

Comet Ping Pong serves Duck Rabbit Milk Stout and Snake Dog IPA and says on its menu that many ingredients are "farmed and harvested in a sustainable manner." You can get a wood-roasted spaghetti squash for an appetizer, and for a pizza entrée maybe try the Ca-Lamb-ity Jane.

And then there's the art.

Internet researchers found that Comet Ping Pong had once had a display of paintings by Kim Noble, an artist with dissociative identity disorder. Noble does a variety of different painting styles from her different personalities. Some of her art includes haunting portraits of children, including one that depicts the outline of what might look like a child chained to a wall.

Pizzagaters also zeroed in on John's brother Tony Podesta's art collection, which conspiracists found in a magazine spread. Tony Podesta's collection features a sculpture by Louise Bourgeois, an odd piece that depicts a backward bent body with no head titled *The Arc of Hysteria* (1993). Pizzagaters say the piece is inspired by a Polaroid found in the apartment of serial killer Jeffrey Dahmer, who bent one of his dead, headless victims in the same pose. However, a sketch similar to the sculpture by Bourgeois can be found from 1989, before Dahmer was caught.

Tony Podesta also owns paintings by Biljana Djurdjevic, a Serbian artist known for eerie paintings, sometimes featuring children that look dead or unconscious.

Being alarmed by creepy art is also the primary impetus of the Denver International Airport conspiracy, which has plagued the airport since it opened in 1995. Conspiracy theorists say that a series of secret hidden tunnels lead to bunkers where the rich and powerful will head to when the end times are upon us, and they've hidden the story in plain sight within the airport's art.

Murals by artist Leo Tanguma titled *In Peace and Harmony with Nature* and *Children of the World Dream of Peace* in the baggage claim area of the airport feature scenes of what looks like a dystopian future. In one, an oppressive soldier wearing a gas mask and waving a sword stands near the wreckage of a building, while a woman with a dead baby weeps nearby. The second mural features a group of people in ethnic clothing from around the world carrying bundles of swords gathered by a toppled statue of the same soldier from the first mural. The murals, Denver Airport Conspiracists say, represent an apocalyptic vision of a war followed by a globalist New World Order.

Another frightening piece of Denver International art is a sculpture of a 32-foot-tall blue horse with blazing red eyes named *Blue Mustang* (but nicknamed "Blucifer") that stands kicking its hooves in the air outside the airport and is said to represent a horseman of the apocalypse. The sculptor, Luis Jiménez, was killed by the sculpture when the blue horse's head fell on him in his studio and severed an artery in his leg in 2006. The statue was installed at Denver International in 2008.

The runways are also supposedly laid out in the shape of a swastika, and a dedication marker inside has Freemason symbols on it, among other conspiracy clues.

To help talk about all this rumor, Denver International made the strange decision to install a helpful voice: an animatronic talking gargoyle that interacts with passengers and answers questions, including ones about alleged conspiracies.

WELCH'S RAID

PIZZAGATE SOON SPREAD NOT only to include Comet Ping Pong but pretty much everything it touched. Nearby businesses were included in the widening web. Besta Pizza, just around the corner, was said to have a symbol similar to one supposedly representing pedophilia, as was nearby restaurant

Terrasol. The Beyond Borders offices, Little Red Fox market, and the Politics and Prose bookstore were soon all also connected, with theorists speculating there might even be underground tunnels running between the businesses to help smuggle child sex slaves.

"And they're all about a four-minute drive from John Podesta's home, kinda coincidental huh?" a YouTube video exploring the theory questioned. The businesses all reported getting threatening phone calls, e-mails, and social media messages from Pizzagaters.

Like Richard, Welch's downward spiral into conspiracy started with a bout of depression after a harsh turn in life. Just a couple months before his Pizzagate raid, Edgar had accidentally hit a 13-year-old boy who was walking with friends on the side of a road. The boy suffered head, torso, and leg injuries and had to be airlifted to a hospital. Welch's parents, Harry and Terri Welch, told the press that the aftermath of the accident left the ordinarily energetic and outgoing Welch "melancholy and quiet" and "traumatized."

Welch began a deep binge on Pizzagate conspiracy media for three days, leading to his voyage to Comet Ping Pong. Welch, like other conspiracy "citizen journalists," said his inspiration was to "self-investigate." He perhaps felt that if he could save child slaves, he might make good with the universe for his injuring the boy in his accident.

Welch was interested in Alex Jones and InfoWars, saying he found Jones "eccentric" and adding that "he touches on some subjects that are viable but goes off the deep end on some things." The significant influences for his raid, though, were InfoWars-produced videos titled "Pizzagate is Real" and "Pizzagate: The Bigger Picture." Unlike Richard, he tried to recruit two of his friends in his mission by sending them links to the videos, but they didn't take him seriously.

Welch entered the pizzeria with his guns, and after drawing on an employee carrying frozen dough, panicked customers and employees quickly cleared out of the building. Alone and with a growing police presence outside, Welch searched for the hidden basement room, where enslaved children were shackled awaiting a terrible fate.

But as Welch stormed through Comet Ping Pong (he was inside the restaurant for 45 minutes), his assault rifle clutched tight, he must have felt a growing sense of disappointment. Thinking he had found a secret room, he fired at a locked door several times, only to reveal a dusty closet space that held computer servers.

There was no secret basement room filled with enslaved children, and, in fact, no basement at all. The weird art on the wall turned out to be just weird art. The cheese pizza was just cheese pizza.

Welch's raid ended up like Richard's on the road outside of Bohemian Grove. He walked out with his hands up, gave up his weapon, got down belly-first on Connecticut Avenue and was arrested by Washington, D.C. Metro Police.

The most significant difference between Welch's and Richard's stories is that Welch's "investigation" changed his mind. He admitted his erroneous thinking and apologized.

"Truly sorry for endangering the safety of any and all bystanders who were present that day. Unfortunately, I cannot change what I did, but I think I owe it to the families and community to apologize for my mistakes," Welch said in a statement. "I regret how I handled the situation."

Richard, on the other hand, only intensified his feelings about the Bohemian Grove. When I interviewed him while driving through the desert terrain of Nevada, I asked if he could go back and do the Bohemian Grove over, would he change anything? I was trying to see if he had any regrets. Richard stared in silence at the bright yellow stripes passing on the highway for a minute, then answered.

"I would do it differently. I think I'd probably rent a bulldozer or a large truck and push the owl idol over," Richard said on his alternate plan. "I wanted to burn it because I thought it was wood. If I could have destroyed it some other way, that would have been a better symbolic gesture. It would have been more feasible to push it over into that little pond that's in front of it."

Conspiracy theorists, of course, immediately assigned the whole Welch raid as part of the Pizzagate conspiracy. Welch was labeled as a form of crisis actor, a plant from the Deep State, his brief experience in indie film production cited as a smoking gun.

WELCH WAS ORDERED TO pay restitution to the restaurant for damages and sentenced to four years in federal prison.

An interesting twist was that this was one of the few times Alex Jones issued a retraction. At first, he offered a rambling, half-assed apology a few months after the event in February, but erased it. In March 2017 Jones read a six-minute prepared statement in which he said he was sorry for spreading the Pizzagate conspiracy and that he did not believe that the restaurant and its owner, James Alefantis, were part of a child trafficking ring. Of course, Alefantis' attorneys leaning on Jones hard for a retraction probably helped in his decision.

Welch's story is one that resonates strongly with Richard's, but he's not the only one. Lots of similar stories have popped up since Richard's arrest in 2002. They're a blip in our crazy news cycle for a minute before they're largely forgotten.

MORE CONSPIRACY RAIDS

ALEX JONES POPS UP like a bad penny in stories of unhinged people. In addition to the Sandy Hookers mentioned, his words have influenced people to act violently and break the law.

While working on my book *Apocalypse Any Day Now*, in which I talked to doomsday preppers, a woman (who wanted to remain anonymous and was called "Tara" in the book) that was a former prepper spoke to me about the downward spiral of her husband. Her husband told her that they, along with their son, needed to prepare for an invasion by the Deep State that was going to round people up and take them to Federal Emergency Management Agency (FEMA) camps, which, the conspiracy goes, are sites set up not as emergency shelters, but as concentration camps that enemies of the New World Order will be herded into.

To sharpen their survival skills, Tara's husband made them camp outside in their tents in Wisconsin in winter. He began using their sparse finances to stockpile weapons and supplies. He refused to let their son, who had autism, go to the doctors as he believed they were part of the conspiracy. And often in the background was the scratchy, twanging baritone of Alex Jones on the radio.

"I can pick that man's voice out from across a house, and it's like nails on a chalkboard for me. He spews ignorance and fearmongering, and my husband soaked it up like a sponge, absorbing every word and vomiting it back out whenever he saw an opening in a conversation," Tara told me about listening to InfoWars. After her husband held a knife to her throat and threatened to kill her, Tara took their son, slipped away from her husband while he was asleep, and went to police.

In 2010 45-year-old Byron Williams, inspired by listening to Alex Jones and Glenn Beck, planned an attack at places in San Francisco that have a piece of yarn attached to George Soros. Williams planned to raid Tides Foundation, which works to further progressive policy and the San Francisco offices of the ACLU, both of which have received funding from Soros, who was up to "all kinds of nefarious activities," according to Williams. He was pulled over in Oakland after police spotted him speeding and weaving in traffic on Interstate 580. Williams engaged in a shootout with the California Highway Patrol for 12 minutes on the side of the highway. Two officers were slightly injured. Williams' ballistic vest saved him from gunshots, and he surrendered. Williams was sentenced to 401 years in prison.

In 2016, two Georgia men, Michael Mancil, 30, and James Dryden Jr., 22, were discovered to be putting together a plan to travel over 3,400 miles to Alaska to raid the High-frequency Active Auroral Research Program (HAARP) facility in Gakona, Alaska. They had stockpiled AR-15s, four Glock handguns, a rifle, and two thousand rounds of ammo as well as communication radios for their mission.

HAARP was developed and built by the U.S. Air Force in the 1990s to study the ionosphere. The facility spreads across 40 acres and features a fenced-in array of 180 antennas. Just the sight of the rows of odd-looking antennas spread as far as the eye can see probably inspired conspiracy imagination.

Conspiracists say that the facility is a government-controlled weather manipulation facility capable of causing hurricanes and other extreme weather, earthquakes (Hugo Chavez blamed the Haitian earthquakes of 2010 on a HAARP-like program), or a mass mind-control center.

In 2015, the Air Force turned HAARP over to the University of Alaska, which continues to use the facility to study atmospheric and satellite communications research, but the transfer hasn't deterred the theories.

Mancil and Dryden not only believed the weather manipulating machine theory, but somehow concluded that HAARP was "storing souls" in its facility. Things unraveled when the two men were busted for producing methamphetamines, and authorities discovered the plot.

In many cases, Jones tried to deny his violent followers as being a "false flag" or downplaying his influence on them, though the one thing they have in common is that they were InfoWars fans.

With more and more people referencing Jones as at least part of the inspiration for their violent actions, how would Jones escape blame? Starting in 2017, that was an issue he would have to deal with repeatedly.

CHAPTER FOURTEEN

THE INFOWARS PRESIDENT

T here's a pivotal moment in Trump becoming president, a night when the seed for his 2016 run was planted: the White House Press Correspondents' Dinner, April 30, 2011. Leading up to that event, Trump had been the most vocal proponent of a conspiracy called Birtherism, the theory that says President Barack Obama was not a United States-born citizen, that he was born in Kenya and that his Hawaiian birth certificate was a fake.

"Why doesn't he show his birth certificate? There's something on his birth certificate he doesn't like," Trump told the hosts on *The View*, March 23, 2011.

A week later, Trump was on *The Laura Ingraham Show*, where he said:

"He doesn't have a birth certificate, or if he does, there's something on that certificate that is very bad for him. Now, somebody told me—and I have no idea if this is bad for him or not, but perhaps it would be—that where it says 'religion,' it might have 'Muslim.' And if you're a Muslim, you don't change your religion, by the way."

Over the next week, he'd talk about Birtherism on the *Today* show on NBC and on *Morning Joe* on MSNBC and any media outlet that would listen.

But now Obama had the mic. Dressed sharply in a tux, he mentioned he had released his long-form birth certificate earlier in the week and then said he was about to show video of his birth, playing a clip from *The Lion King* of Simba being held up and presented to the animal kingdom. Then Obama zeroed in on Trump.

"I know he's taken some flak lately, but no one is happier, no one is prouder to put this birth certificate matter to rest than The Donald. And that's because he can finally get back to focusing on the issues that matter, like—did we fake the moon landing?" The audience, about three thousand members of the media, erupted into laughter. A camera panned to Trump, who offered a sickly, stiff half-smile.

"What really happened in Roswell?" Obama continued when the laughter died down a little. "And where *are* Biggie and Tupac?" More big laughs and enthusiastic applause. Trump tried to smile again but was staring angrily. Nobody loves media attention more than Trump, but here he was the butt of the joke.

"All kidding aside, we obviously know about your credentials and breadth of experience," Obama continued. "No seriously, in a recent episode of *Celebrity Apprentice*... at the steak house, the men's cooking team, uh, did not impress the judges from Omaha Steaks, and there was a lot of blame to go around. But you, Mr. Trump, recognized that the real problem was a lack of leadership, so ultimately you didn't blame Lil Jon or Meat Loaf—you fired Gary Busey. And these are the type of decisions that would keep me up at night!" Loud laughter. "Well handled, sir!" Obama called out. Trump smiled slightly and nodded. "Well handled! Say what you will about Mr. Trump, he certainly would bring some change to the White House," Obama said, turning to a screen behind him, which displayed a photoshopped image of the White House redone with a giant "TRUMP: The White House" sign in neon, gold pillars, crystal chandeliers, bikini babes hanging out in a fountain and golfers milling about the lawn.

The whole room was filled with people laughing their ass off—Trump the conspiracy nut! Trump the tacky! Trump the reality show clown! Here was Trump, often accused of being racist, getting the mic dropped on him by a younger, suave, black President.

Up next was host Seth Meyer, at the time head writer and "Weekend Update" anchor for *Saturday Night Live*. He continued a more brutal roast of Trump.

"Donald Trump has been saying he'll run for president as a Republican— which is surprising since I just assumed he was running as a joke."

"Donald Trump often appears on FOX, which is ironic because a fox often appears on Donald Trump's head."

By this time, Trump had stopped attempting to smile.

"Donald Trump said recently that he has a great relationship with the blacks," Meyer wound up, delivering, "but unless The Blacks are a family of white people, I bet he's mistaken." Obama, sitting next to him on the dais, began to crack up, his shoulders shaking with laughter. Meyer kept slinging jokes for several long minutes.

After the dinner, Trump and Melania and their security detail beelined out the door. The room had become enemies—Obama, the dishonest media, *Saturday Night Live*. When he became president, he would decline going to the White House Correspondents' Dinner every year.

It's the moment Trump's conspiracy theorist confidant Roger Stone thinks the Trump candidacy began.

"I think that is the night he resolves to run for president," Stone said in a PBS interview. "I think that he's kind of motivated by it. 'Maybe I'll run. Maybe I'll show them all.'"

THE CONSPIRACY CAMPAIGN

ROGER STONE HAD FIRST urged Trump to consider making a run for the presidency after he met him in the '80s. Stone, political advisor and former lobbyist (his firm in the '80s included his friend Paul Manafort), had worked in some capacity on campaigns for Richard Nixon (he has a tattoo of Nixon's face on his back), Ronald Reagan, Jack Kemp, and Bob Dole. Stone continued to encourage Trump to run almost every election cycle, and Trump came close to making a serious bid in 2000 and again in 2012.

When Trump's campaign got rolling in 2015, with Stone as an advisor, it quickly showed it was playing by Stone's playbook. One of Stone's rules for politics was "Attack, attack, attack, never defend," embodied by Trump stomping his Republican opponents in the primaries. He blasted "Low Energy Jeb" Bush and "Little Marco" Rubio until only "Lyin' Ted" Cruz was left. Trump's campaign had been seen as a joke when he started, but he had punched his way through and trashed Cruz, even speculating at one point that Cruz's father had somehow been involved in the JFK assassination. Now he was facing off against "Crooked Hillary."

Trump had been underestimated. Many people were sick of the Bush and Clinton dynasties in control of the nation's most powerful office. George H.W. Bush had spent eight years as vice president, then four as president, followed by eight years of Bill Clinton, then eight years of George W. Bush. Obama was the first fresh name in 28 years, but even then, Hillary Clinton spent four years of his administration in a top position as Secretary of State.

There was a lot of fear, anger, and disenfranchisement out there. If Trump could tap into it, he could beat Hillary.

Stone soon found an ally to help him find dirt on Hillary and orchestrate an attack: James Corsi, another conspiracy theorist who would, for a time, have his own InfoWars show. As reported by Jeffrey Toobin for the *New Yorker* in an article titled "Roger Stone's and Jerome Corsi's Time in the Barrel," Stone and Corsi first connected after they both penned books to coincide with the 50th anniversary of the assassination of JFK in 2013. Stone's book, *The Man Who Killed Kennedy: The Case Against LBJ*, as the title suggests, pins Vice President Johnson as the force who orchestrated the fateful day in Dallas. Corsi's book *Who Really Killed Kennedy?* blames a Deep State conspiracy of the CIA and organized crime as the force behind the assassination. Corsi had a prior bestseller on John Kerry that came out in the 2004 election cycle, *Unfit for Command* (co-authored with John O'Neill, who served with John Kerry), the central piece of the political hit job "Swift Boat" attacks.

What connected Corsi with Trump was his 2011 Birtherism bestseller *Where's the Birth Certificate?: The Case that Barack Obama is Not Eligible to be President*. Trump and Corsi discussed the book and Birtherism several times.

Stone fell out of the Trump campaign in an official capacity in 2015 but was still a strong advocate of his bid for the presidency.

And so Stone and Corsi, after hearing the Russians had hacked Hillary campaign e-mails, hatched a plan to needle WikiLeaks and see what they could find. Julian Assange, founder of WikiLeaks, had dumped some of the e-mails and promised more would be on the way. Stone and Corsi worked their contacts to try to get info from Assange about what was in the pipeline. Stone cryptically tweeted, "Trust me, it will soon the Podesta's [sic] time in the barrel. #CrookedHillary," about six weeks before WikiLeaks dumped a massive amount of Podesta's e-mails. Focus on the e-mails stole the spotlight for the last month of the campaign and damaged the Clinton campaign.

Stone also recognized the value of Alex Jones. Trump appeared on Alex Jones' show in December 2015, shortly after announcing his candidacy, hoping to tap into Jones' audience of millions.

"Your reputation is amazing," Trump told Jones on air. "I will not let you down."

Jones and Stone worked together to campaign for Trump. At the Republican National Convention, the duo crashed liberal show *The Young Turks* on media row. Jones walked on the set and pointed a mic in host Cenk Uygur's face, then tried to hand him a T-shirt with an image of Bill Clinton on it that read "RAPE." When Stone jumped into the fray, it turned into a chaotic shouting match, and a fistfight almost broke out.

"Alex, this ain't your fucking show, and Roger, this surely ain't your fucking show!" Uygur shouted.

Jones and Stone also took time together to peddle Stone's book (co-written with Robert Morrow) *The Clintons' War on Women*, which presents all of Bill Clinton's sexual abuse allegations, outside the convention.

In 2017, Stone was offered a spot on InfoWars, co-hosting a show called *War Room*, and he worked for a while as an InfoWars talking head, and continued to be a frequent guest.

On election night Alex Jones and Roger Stone covered the returns together live for InfoWars. Like many Americans, they were surprised by what they saw unfolding, sure that a conspiracy of massive election fraud—a theory Trump would promote, even after he won, would place Hillary as Commander-in-Chief. To their delight, Trump was victorious.

"Is this Valhalla? Is this the best moment of your political life?" Jones asked Stone, as InfoWars staff handed them glasses of champagne.

"It's amazing," Stone sighed happily as they clinked their champagne glasses together.

Days later, according to Jones, President-elect Trump called Jones to thank him and his InfoWars listeners for their support.

"He said, listen, Alex. I just talked to kings and queens of the world, world leaders, you name it, but he said it doesn't matter, I wanted to talk to you, to thank your audience," Jones reported.

Later Jones would claim that InfoWars had been offered White House press credentials, a claim that was rebuked by White House spokespersons Hope Hicks and Sarah Huckabee Sanders. Still, James Corsi, who said he was setting up an InfoWars Washington bureau, was able to get a day pass to gain access to the White House press room.

Using his platform as president, Trump began to promote conspiracies day one when he argued that the media was lying about the size of his inauguration crowd and that he had won despite massive cases of voter fraud—three to five million fraud votes—in California, a claim with no substantiation.

Dozens of conspiracies would follow consistently. Trump claimed that Obama had tapped the phones in Trump Tower during the campaign, that climate change was a "Chinese hoax," that Democrats had inflated the death toll in Puerto Rico after Hurricane Maria to make him look bad, and as the Midwest elections approached he floated stories of a sinister caravan of migrants marching toward the southern border from Central America. The caravan, Trump tweeted and told reporters, contained MS-13 gang members and Middle Eastern terrorists.

When 79-year-old Supreme Court Justice Antonin Scalia died, Trump seemed to entertain the conspiracy that he had been murdered (he died of natural causes).

"It's a horrible topic. But they say they found a pillow on his face, which is a pretty unusual place to find a pillow," Trump responded when asked about the theory by conservative radio host Michael Savage.

He even tried to spin away the famous *Access Hollywood* tape where he brags that when you're famous, you can "grab 'em by the pussy" as a conspiracy against him.

"We don't think that was my voice," he reportedly explained to a senator and later an adviser.

All of this "cements his status as the InfoWars president," as CNN's Brian Stelter noted in an opinion piece. A conspiracy theorist now held the most powerful office in the world.

FAKE NEWS. SAD!

THE MOST PROMINENT CONSPIRACY, according to Trump, was the media bias against him. "Low Ratings CNN," "The Failing New York Times," and other news agencies critical of him were "Fake News," an "enemy of the people," and even guilty of "treason," while FOX News (especially his favorites, *Fox & Friends* and *Hannity*) received his praise and conspiracy sites like InfoWars were often retweeted by him.

While Trump was calling out mainstream media as "fake," the proliferation of actual fake news was in overdrive, being pumped out by Russian troll farms, data companies, and political extremists.

The most disturbing development to the fake news industry is the quickly improving technology of deepfakes.

At first, like many emerging technologies, deepfakes were used in porn, where celebrity faces were juxtaposed on porn star bodies. Funny videos appeared, like Steve Buscemi's face grafted to Jennifer Lawrence's body accepting an award, but the technology quickly evolved into something that could be weaponized for politics, as U.S. Director of National Intelligence Dan Coats warned Congress in January 2019.

In June 2019, artists working on an exhibition called *Spectre* posted a video on Instagram that appeared to be a clip of Facebook CEO Mark Zuckerberg being interviewed on CBS.

"Imagine this for a second: One man, with total control of billions of people's stolen data, all their secrets, their lives, their futures," the Zuckerberg deepfake says. The video followed a month after Facebook's refusal to remove an altered video of House Speaker Nancy Pelosi that was slowed down to make it appear that she was drunkenly slurring her words, uploaded to a Facebook group called "Politics WatchDog," that quickly went viral with millions of views.

The spreading of deepfake videos might be done by those who see them as confirmation bias by those who don't care if it's true or not, entering us into an era where fake videos dropped on voters could undermine elections or cause panic with a false emergency alert.

TRUMP EMBOLDENS WHITE SUPREMACISTS AND OTHER EXTREMISTS

IN ADDITION TO THE CONSPIRACIES he was promoting, Trump's rise to power had emboldened violent people, people much more dangerous than Richard McCaslin. White supremacy, sometimes trying to cloak itself as an "alt-right" movement, was on the rise.

The alt-right label began to catch on with Richard Spencer, a white nationalist, who called his webzine *The Alternative Right*, launched in 2010. He tried to give the white nationalist movement a more accessible, low-key look as opposed to the traditional white power groups that featured hillbillies in goofy Klan robes or skinheads covered in tattoos. The alt-right grew to include white identity groups and men's rights movement groups, like the Proud Boys.

In Charlottesville, North Carolina in August 2017, a rally to "Unite the Right" was held, inspired to protest the removal of a statue of Confederate General Robert E. Lee. The event produced shocking images of men marching with tiki torches chanting "Jews will not replace us!" A protester, Heather Heyer, died and several were injured after a man rammed his car into anti-racist protestors.

Trump responded in a contentious press conference by saying the protest had "very fine people on both sides" and tried to throw half the blame on the "Alt-Left."

Although not all conspiracists are white supremacists, the two do overlap on a Venn diagram.

At the heart of many white supremacist theories is that there is a Jewish plot to take over the world, to replace white people with themselves and other ethnic groups, leading to a "white genocide." White power literature claims we are already controlled by ZOG, the Zionist Occupational Government, Zion and Zionist referring to the Land of Israel.

Belief in these theories goes back to a document called *The Protocols of the Elders of Zion*, a hoax document that first circulated in Russia in the early 1900s, purporting to show an uncovered secret plan that outlined how Jews were plotting global domination. Even after it was revealed to be fraudulent, it kept rolling off the press. When Nazis came to power, it was added to the curriculum of some German schools.

Another white supremacist conspiracy says that the Holocaust didn't happen or was greatly exaggerated. Holocaust deniers rely on junk science and say evidence was a hoax perpetrated by the Jewish people to advance their causes by falsely portraying themselves as victims.

Even if he didn't endorse them directly, President Trump was a president who white power groups believed was an advocate for them. Trump proclaimed that a mighty border wall would be built to keep Mexican "rapists and murderers" out, and that Mexico would pay for it. His travel ban caused chaos at airports as travelers from Muslim countries were denied entry to the U.S. In 2019 he told congresswomen of color that criticized him that they should "go back" to "the crime-infested places from which they came" and in another tweet called them "savages."

Hate crimes increased in America during Trump's campaign and presidency, and in 2018 a record number of hate groups—1,020—was documented by the Southern Poverty Law Center.

On August 3, 2019, a 21-year-old gunman, Patrick Crusius, drove from Dallas to the border town of El Paso, where he shot and killed 22 people and injured 24 more at a Wal-Mart store. He had published an anti-immigration white power manifesto on 8chan before the shooting, and several parts of it parroted Trump's rhetoric. The shooter described the Hispanic "invasion" as his inspiration to kill, a word Trump frequently uses to describe immigration, as well as Trump's favorite term to describe media: "fake news."

Other extremists were also motivated to act in Trump's name.

In October 2018, a 57-year-old man named Cesar Sayoc mailed 16 pipe bombs to top Democrats including Barack Obama, Joe Biden, Bill Clinton, Sen. Kamala Harris, as well as CNN and top Democratic supporters like George Soros and Robert De Niro.

Sayoc was found living in a van (his parents had kicked him out of their house) plastered with pro-Trump stickers and memes attacking liberals in Adventura, Florida. He pled guilty to 65 felony counts in April 2019 and told a judge that going to Trump rallies was "like a newfound drug."

In a similar case, 50-year-old Lt. Christopher Hasson of the Coast Guard, a white nationalist, was arrested in February 2019 after it was discovered he was stockpiling weapons and researching home addresses of prominent Democrats like Nancy Pelosi and Chuck Schumer, media figures, and Supreme Court justices.

In both cases, Sayoc's and Hasson's hit lists read as enemies of Trump.

And that will be Trump's legacy more than anything else—the rabid frenzy of paranoia, anger, conspiracy, xenophobia, hatred, and violence he has inspired.

CHAPTER FIFTEEN

WHERE THE HECK IS PAHRUMP?

T he woman next to me on the plane spent most of her trip playing poker on her phone, gearing up for a vacation to Las Vegas. Walking through the Las Vegas airport, tired from a day of flying from Milwaukee to Dallas, then barely making my connecting flight to Nevada, I walked through the terminal, my senses overloaded by row after row of slot machines projecting noise and flashing lights.

As I approached the baggage area, I heard a voice say, "Hey, Milwaukee!" I turned to see Richard, leaning against the airport wall. He was no longer living in Las Vegas, though. The T-shirt he was wearing teased his new home, with block letters inside an outline of the state of Nevada that read, "Where the Heck is Pahrump?"

IN 2012 RICHARD'S FRIEND LON suggested that, instead of blowing through money on rent for his small Las Vegas apartment, he invest some of his remaining inheritance on buying property. After searching, Richard found a home out in the desert community of Pahrump, about 63 miles northwest of Las Vegas, close to the California border ("walking distance," Richard says) and 30–40 miles to Death Valley. One selling point was the low price—a high unemployment rate, foreclosure rate, and general slow economy has led to housing prices as cheap as the gravel that decorates most Pahrump yards. The landscape is dotted with abandoned trailer homes, and Richard found a ranch house with two bedrooms, two baths, a living room, kitchen, and den for $53,000. The other big selling point was the large Quonset hut on the property that looked like a mini corrugated metal airplane hangar.

"I would like this place to be the 'Superfriends Hall of Justice' (or at least the blue-collar/redneck version of it) of the West Coast RLSH," Richard wrote me in August 2012, as he was in escrow. "I feel bad for Motor-Mouth, when the reporters [from *Stan Lee's Superhero Academy*] were at his house (a dumpy duplex in Oakland), and they asked him if he had a 'lair.' Maybe this will make us more legitimate in the eyes of the media."

Richard was envisioning what is probably the largest-ever RLSH headquarters by square foot, a meeting place for his team, the Pacific Protectorate. After his Bohemian Club protest, Motor-Mouth had made Phantom Patriot a member of the team. In general, Richard had made some connections to the RLSH community. He joined them a couple years in 2012 and 2014 at the big HOPE meetup event in San Diego, where RLSH gather to spend time together doing a handout of supplies to San Diego's homeless population. His reception there had been wary, but accepting by those who knew his history.

"He's a nice guy," an RLSH named Geist reported. "He kept his conspiracy theories to himself and stayed on task." I was glad Richard had made a social connection with the group.

Richard described his new home in an e-mail to me:

"Yeah, it's kind of a hump out to Pahrump and I'm not sure if any (prospective) members of a 'Las Vegas Protectorate' will want to drive clear out there for meetings and training sessions, but I haven't found anything in Vegas (like this) that I can afford. Actually, if things get any worse in this country (and they probably will) I don't want to be living in ANY major metropolitan area. Pahrump is kind of famous for its 'anti-government weirdoes.' I should fit right in... HA!"

Indeed, Pahrump, an unincorporated town of 36,441 people, is a strange little desert community.

Local newspaper *Pahrump Valley Times*, whom I followed on Facebook, once reported about vandalism to the "Welcome to Pahrump" sign. Someone had added a banner beneath it that read "Well come [sic] to Dark Side Hee Haw."

An odd but apt local motto, as it seemed Pahrump was a desert town full of quirky celebrities, odd stories, and desert recluses.

The town was home to radio talk show legend Art Bell, original host of the definitive voice of weirdness, *Coast to Coast AM*. Bell broadcasted from his home studio in Pahrump, built in a cave. He founded the Pahrump radio station KNYE 95.1FM, and after leaving *Coast to Coast AM* hosted a show called *Midnight in the Desert*, starting in July 2015. Later that same year he signed off from the program, saying that unknown persons he believed wanted him silenced had intruded and fired gunshots on his property. Bell died in 2018.

Toward the end of his life, Michael Jackson bought a home in Pahrump in 2008, where he homeschooled his children, recorded in a home studio, and tried to hide out from the media.

There's also the story of Ron Wayne, one of the original three partners (along with Steve Jobs and Steve Wozniak) of Apple. He designed the company's first logo and wrote the manual for the Apple I computer. Uncertain about the future of the company, he cashed in his 10 percent share of the company for $800. That share would be worth about $22 billion today. Wayne lives in a modest home in Pahrump, supplementing his monthly government check by selling rare stamps, coins, and gold.

Dennis Hof, who lived in nearby Crystal, Nevada, was owner of seven brothels, including the Moonlite Bunny Ranch (featured in HBO's *Cathouse* series) and authored his autobiography *The Art of the Pimp*. A Libertarian, Hof became a Trump Republican in 2016 and ran for Nevada Assembly. He was dubbed the "Trump of Pahrump" by his friend, none other than Roger Stone. Hof died in 2018 at his Love Ranch South brothel after his 72nd birthday party, his body being discovered by friend and porn legend Ron Jeremy. Despite being dead, he won election to his Nevada Assembly seat posthumously.

Hof was at one point briefly engaged to another Pahrumpian, Heidi Fleiss, the famous "Hollywood Madame" who used to make "10,000 dollars on a slow night" providing prostitutes to Hollywood's rich and famous. She's had a tamer life in Pahrump, where she owns an ultralight flight park and tends to her 25 pet parrots.

"I saw her at Wal-Mart one time. She looks like ten miles of bad road," Richard would later tell me, as we drove through Pahrump toward his house. We passed by a lot of red dirt and gravel, tumbleweeds, fireworks stores, and fast-food joints. We stopped at the Pahrump Nugget Hotel & Gambling Hall on the main drag to eat at their 24-hour greasy spoon diner, then headed toward Richard's home. I asked him what his neighbors were like as we turned onto the dusty road to his house.

"A father and son live there, both widowers," Richard said, pointing one direction. "And over there, you know The Misfits?"

"Like the punk band?" I asked, curious to where this was going.

"Yeah. He used to be their chiropractor," Richard said, nodding to the house next to his.

I had more questions about these neighbors and was also coming up with the theory that perhaps all 36,441 residents of Pahrump each had a strange life story, but Richard was already out of his truck and leading me to his superhero headquarters, which he had named "The Outpost," for a tour.

TRYING TO WRAP UP this book, I had told Richard that I wanted to get some final interview material, but that while I was visiting in Pahrump, I'd be glad to participate in whatever he wanted me to, in addition to interview sessions. What it turned out he wanted was for me to co-star in a new Phantom Patriot video with him, as he was trying to switch from producing comics to making YouTube videos. Comics, he felt, weren't working out.

Richard had tried to get his story out there while he was on parole. He sent copies of his *Prison Penned Comics* to Marvel and DC (both of whom don't accept unsolicited submissions) and later would claim that each publisher stole elements of his life story in some way. He cited Marvel's 2010 *Ultimate Avengers: Crime and Punishment*, written by Mark Millar, who also penned the Real-Life Superhero-inspired *Kick-Ass,* as one example. Part of the storyline has the skull-faced Ghost Rider tracking down a gang that engaged in a satanic ritual to gain wealth and power. I think Richard's conclusion that he inspired the story is a stretch.

The Court of Owls storyline introduced in *Batman* the following year did give me pause for a moment. Written by Scott Snyder, the Court of Owls became popular new villains in the Batman universe as a secret society that controls Gotham City and beyond. They disguise their identities with owl masks, and their headquarters has a *giant statue of an owl* as its centerpiece. If the story idea hadn't come from former Batman portrayer Richard directly, it seems the Bohemian Grove might have inspired it.

When I went to visit, Richard had already produced three Phantom Patriot videos. He had hired a company, Las Vegas Motion Pictures, to shoot and edit. He found them the old-fashioned way—flipping through the Las Vegas Yellow Pages.

His first video, *Phantom Patriot: An Inside Look*, showed off The Outpost and he hoped it would help recruit more members of the Pacific Protectorate to join him. Inside his fort, as I soon got to see firsthand, was a museum dedicated to himself—a row of blank-faced mannequins wearing replicas of various costumed personas he had invented, including the Lynx, Thoughtcrime, and Phantom Patriot (he later changed them to variations of Phantom Patriot costumes), and one wearing a Marines uniform. The mannequins all stood with a slight bend in their knee, one hand slightly raised, and eerily looked as though they might all come to life and take a step forward to try to shake hands with you.

A glass display case in a corner of The Outpost had copies of the comic publications Richard had created, as well as a copy of my book *Heroes in the Night* (which featured a couple of paragraphs on him), a DVD of the *Dark Secrets: Inside Bohemian Grove* doc, and a plastic owl (the kind put on roofs to scare away crows) labeled "Moloch." The walls were covered with protest signs he had made, like REJECT REPTOID RELIGION and BEWARE OF FALSE FLAG ATTACKS, along with photos from protests and RLSH meetups.

He had a weight bench and punching bag, and a body-shaped target with a rubber Reptilian mask for crossbow training. And in the middle of the room was a round table where he hoped Real-Life Superheroes could assemble for meetings.

The next year he produced a video titled *Phantom Patriot Report 2013*, which showed clips of the Phantom Patriot doing a patrol in Las Vegas with Motor-Mouth, a visit to The Outpost from a new RLSH named Def Con, and protests on his new Phantom-Cycle, a four-wheeled bicycle to which he attached protest signs and a bullhorn to the handlebars, so he could cover more ground in his weekly protests out on the Vegas Strip.

All of this was fun, but there was a disturbing segment in *Phantom Patriot Report 2013* that showed that Richard was still obsessed with Chely Wright and his thought process on her had become completely delusional.

LIKE ME

AS IT TURNED OUT, Wright was having her own American dream-turned-nightmare. Back when Richard had met her in 2001, something substantial was weighing on Wright—she was in the closet about being gay. She knew that the heavily Christian country music industry would not be welcoming of her lifestyle, and she was terrified about coming out. The fear and pressure had tormented her so much that at one point she was close to ending her own life, as she describes in her 2010 autobiography *Like Me: Confessions of a Heartland Country Singer.*

"I went upstairs to my bedroom, got on a stepladder, and reached up high into my closet. I easily located the loaded 9mm handgun," Wright says in her book. She stuck the gun in her mouth, but after a few tense moments, she burst into tears, put down the weapon and collapsed into bed.

Richard had told me he had tried to go "cold turkey" on his obsession with Wright, but after reading *Trance-formation of America* by Cathy O'Brien, he believed he had discovered a conspiracy on why Wright had not fallen in love with him: government mind control. The disinterest in him after their auction date, her tired appearance that night, her lesbianism, and many other aspects of her life were all were signs of Project Monarch, just as Cathy O'Brien had explained. O'Brien's book has numerous passages that cite the country music industry as part of the conspiracy.

O'Brien claims she was used as a mind-controlled sex slave by Kris Kristofferson and that country singers like Loretta Lynn and Barbara Mandrell were fellow slaves.

Richard had now gone off the deep end about Wright. His video, which would make almost no sense to the casual or even a deeply entrenched conspiracist, dissects alleged hidden symbolism in Wright's album cover for *Never Loved You Enough*. His analysis is on the following page.

How long had he stared at this album cover to see the secrets floating in it?

Before I left Pahrump, Richard asked me if I had read *Like Me* yet, as he had suggested. I had, I told him. He handed me a stack of photocopies of handwritten notes he had taken on the autobiography. There were eight pages of notes, mostly page numbers and sentence fragments.

"Page 13–15, 3rd-grade crush on Miss Smilie," notes one line. "Page 102–104, dated Vince Gill," reads another and "page 139, 1994 lesbian sex on tour bus rumor."

I wasn't sure what conclusions Richard was trying to reach, but it was clear he had gone through Wright's autobiography with a fine-toothed comb, noting any reference to dating, travel, and other random quotes. Toward the conclusion of his "My Memories of Chely Wright" document, he wrote:

"For years, I had been telling myself that my feelings for Chely were just a celebrity crush that got way out of hand. However, crushes don't last for over 12 years. For months, I've had this irresistible urge to go public with my connection to Chely and expose Project Monarch to the public. I have to help her, no matter what the cost. That's what you do when you love someone!"

Richard McCaslin's analysis of Chely Wright's
Never Love You Enough album cover.

The album's original release date was September 11, 2001, but as the events of 9/11 unfolded, September 25 was chosen as the new release date.

According to Richard, the stroke of the 'h' and the 'l' form the twin World Trade Center buildings.

The 'c' and the 'e' stand for "controlled explosives" which is what secretly took down the Twin Towers, Richard says.

Wright is wearing a gold bracelet and Richard notes, "Could the explosions heard below the World Trade Center have been the bank vaults before the planes hit the towers and the means to cover the robbery of the gold from the buildings?"

Richard says Wright's arm forms a pyramid with her eye at the top like the Eye of Providence "Illuminati symbol"

After e-mailing Wright's management company requesting to talk to Wright for this book, I got a short but understandable response: "Chely is not interested in speaking about Richard McCaslin or anyone associated with him."

THERE WERE MANY TIMES where I had hoped Richard was on the right path to finding... something. In 2011 I had hoped he might find a happy life retiring in the Bahamas. In 2012, I thought his protest in front of the Bohemian Club in San Francisco had brought him closure. When he built a small network of 9/11 Truthers on the Las Vegas Strip and befriended Motor-Mouth and his Pacific Protectorate team, I had hoped he was making a support network. After the Bohemian Club protest, Richard had drawn a comic zine titled *RLSH Team-Up* that starred Phantom Patriot, Motor-Mouth, and Mutinous Angel in a fictional story where they raided the Bohemian Club and beat up a group of robe-clad Reptilians who were preparing to sacrifice a young boy. Richard drove to the Bay Area a couple of times to join the Pacific Protectorate on patrol and had even spent a Thanksgiving dinner with Motor-Mouth's family.

ABOVE: Richard as Phantom Patriot with members of the Pacific Protectorate on a charity mission, 2013.

But except for Lon, Richard had a hard time maintaining friendships. He quickly soured on Motor-Mouth and his crew, especially when he invited them to a team-up as a celebration of the completion of The Outpost, but everyone he asked flaked out, one by one. He sent me photos of the recently finished headquarters the day of the planned meetup, with this message:

"Here's the finished product... pretty cool? Unfortunately, you may notice that nobody is at the table. NOBODY HAS SHOWN UP!" Richard wrote, fuming and running through the excuses the RLSH he had invited had given. "I'm still running the charity handout and patrol tonight by myself."

Months later, frustrated by the flakiness of his team, he quit the Pacific Protectorate.

There were times, too, he lost his temper with me. After his San Francisco protest, he had been angry that I hadn't reported it on my *Heroes in the Night* blog and chastised me in an angry e-mail.

"TOTAL BULLSHIT!! ...I expect the mainstream media to ignore me, but I thought you were better than that! Do you want my mission to fail, because (so far) it looks like it!" Richard wrote. "I'm not some newbie begging for attention. I 'paid my dues' before half these guys were even born!" He concluded, "Do the RIGHT THING, do the SMART THING and FIX THIS!"

His sudden burst of anger toward me caught me off-guard and made me nervous.

I placated him by writing a short article on my blog, and our correspondence returned to normal. I knew our next falling-out might be a final one, so I wanted a chance to interview him at least one more time.

PHANTOM PATRIOT RETRO CINEMA

RICHARD'S LATEST ENDEAVOR was a series he called *Phantom Patriot Retro Cinema*. His first idea for the format, which he did in episode one, was to act as a horror host, like Elvira or Svengoolie, or something similar to *Mystery Science Theater 3000*. Richard would introduce an old film with bumper segments, throwing in some jokes and a pinch of conspiracy theory.

He created a sidekick for the show named G'nik, a rubber alien mask with an Elvis wig on it mounted in a plexiglass box. G'nik (read it backward) was "an Elvis enthusiast from the planet Memphis-3," that the Phantom Patriot had saved from a UFO crash in the Nevada desert.

I couldn't help but think that G'nik was also sort of a companion like in the movie *Cast Away*, where Tom Hanks, stranded on an island, paints a face on a volleyball and names it Wilson, talking to it to keep from going insane. I imagined Richard ranting to G'nik in the abandoned Outpost, while his blank rubber face stared back at him.

The first episode rolled out. Richard's acting is a little stiff, but he showed creativity in show design and writing, particularly in working with their environment.

"Greetings Earthlings, take me to your casino, ha ha ha," G'nik says, introducing himself. Richard tells G'nik he's about to show him an episode of the old 1950s British series *The Adventures of William Tell*.

"Is this program based on the medieval Earthling that shot <censor beep> with a crossbow?" G'nik asks Richard.

"*Apples*. He shot an *apple* off his son's head with a crossbow," a flustered Richard responds in the comedy bit.

After the first episode, Richard changed his mind about the nature of the show and wanted to film his fictional adventures instead of showing old films.

He told me he wanted me to join him as a superhero for a second episode of *Phantom Patriot Retro Cinema*, in which I would reprise a persona I developed for my book *Heroes in the Night*. Spoilers: for the epilogue of that book I created my own Real-Life Superhero persona, Argyle Gargoyle, which I soon changed

ABOVE: Behind the scenes: Phantom
Patriot punches Illuminus.

to Argo, and joined Real-Life Superheroes on patrol in Milwaukee. I told him I would be glad to participate but pointed out that I didn't have acting experience.

Soon after making travel plans to Pahrump, Richard sent me photocopies of a handwritten script for an episode called "Assault on Area 51." The story was that Argo (whom Richard changed in the text to Argoyle) and Phantom Patriot would team up to defeat his enemy Illuminus in a showdown in conspiracy hotspot Area 51. It was a dense script, and I wondered how we could film all the scenes in three days.

AFTER A TOUR OF The Outpost, we hung out at Richard's house, where he had set up a guest bedroom for me to stay in for my visit.

I was curious as to what his house might be like. I thought it might be something like the doomsday preppers I had studied for my book *Apocalypse Any Day Now*, packed with food, water, medical and survival supplies. But what I found was a house that was surprisingly sparse and empty-feeling. There was furniture, but no art on the walls. Richard didn't drink coffee but generously had gotten me some instant coffee for my stay. While looking for a coffee mug, I noticed his cupboards were almost bare—a few cans of food, a couple of plates and bowls. His fridge had orange juice and eggs, and little else. One small room of the house had nothing but shelves containing his comic book collection and a vacuum cleaner. We sat on his couch and watched the news, and then I went to bed—Richard wanted us up early as we were to start filming in The Outpost at 9 a.m.

I couldn't sleep and stared at the bedroom ceiling. *What was I doing here? Why was I writing this book?* The silent night in Pahrump was broken by a coyote howling off in the desert, then another and another. I laid for a long time listening to coyotes and wondering what was going to happen next in the story of Richard McCaslin.

IN THE MORNING, we shot some scenes in The Outpost, with Las Vegas Motion Pictures director of photography Greg Benoit. Then we all headed out to Area 51, which, along with Roswell, New Mexico is one of the most famous pieces of UFO conspiracy lore. Area 51 is part of an Air Force base where it is said the government is supposedly storing one or more UFOs, reverse engineering alien technology, and maybe even has preserved dead alien bodies or captives in an intergalactic jail cell. Many of the stories of the secret base come from Bob Lazar, who in 1989 made media appearances claiming he had been hired to work at Area 51, where he studied alien crafts (and their fuel, element 151) and learned about extraterrestrial life from the Zeta Reticuli system and their interactions with humans throughout history. Since then, Lazar has been labeled as either a brave whistleblower or a pathological liar. His story received renewed interest when a 2018 Netflix documentary titled *Bob Lazar: Area 51 and Flying Saucers* was released.

In 2019, Area 51 received a lot of attention when a Facebook event page called "Storm Area 51, They Can't Stop Us All," was created. It became viral and millions of people said they were "going" or "interested."

"Let's see them aliens," the page's event description suggested. The page was intended as a joke and led to the creation of hundreds of funny memes and videos. As the interest rose, there were concerns that in the mass of people responding to the event, some might be taking the idea of the raid seriously, so the Air Force and other officials issued warnings to potential trespassers.

The plot of Richard's "Assault on Area 51" story was that the Phantom Patriot, Argoyle, and G'nik were supposed to enter the secret base stealthily (I was glad to find out we would be using a stand-in site instead of actually attempting to do this, as trespassers are quickly arrested) to confront Phantom Patriot's eyeball-headed nemesis Illuminus.

The plan in driving out there was to shoot scenes on the nearby Extraterrestrial Highway, marked by a sign with UFOs on it, a wink at the area's notoriety and the skywatchers who gather around Rachel, a one-horse town on the highway of about 50 people. Rachel's big destination is the Little A'Le'Inn, a diner, gift shop and bar, serving UFO hunters since 1989. The Little A'Le'Inn was featured in an episode of *The X-Files* and the alien comedy *Paul*. Conspiracy legend Milton William Cooper once gave a presentation there. As we left The Outpost, I discovered Richard's plan was pure guerrilla filmmaking. He was willing to drive all the way out to Rachel, to shoot a scene where the heroes rendezvous after their big battle with Illuminus at the inn, but hadn't thought or cared to call ahead and see if it might be OK for a cameraman, a couple of colorfully clad people, and a rubber alien head in a plexiglass box to shoot scenes outside the establishment.

It wasn't, as it turned out.

"No hon, you can't film here without permission from the owners," a waitress with a beehive hairdo told us, leaning out the front door. The owners weren't around, she added; we'd have to e-mail them. Richard apparently wasn't expecting this response, because after the waitress ducked back inside, he swore and stomped around angrily outside the Little A'Le'Inn. I sheepishly entered the establishment to check it out and buy souvenirs and to give Richard a moment to cool off. The scene was later recreated at Las Vegas Motion Pictures using a green screen and a photo of the exterior of the building.

After the rejection at the Little A'Le'Inn, we did a couple more shots, mostly vehicles driving along desert roads and entering a gate on an abandoned lot to simulate driving into Area 51. Then we headed back to Pahrump and drove down a dirt road off the highway to spend the rest of the long day in a big dirt pit owned by Nevada's Bureau of Land Management. It looked like the spot was mainly used for dumping trash and shooting empty beer bottles. Richard had painstakingly cleaned up the garbage ("I had to haul an entire mattress out of here," he told us) for his set.

This was where the climactic scene of the episode would take place—the heroes confronting Illuminus, played by an actor named Matt hired via Las Vegas Motion Pictures. We would spend the entire next day there. There were a lot of action fight scenes that were supposed to be shot, including my chance to shine as Argoyle pulled out a slingshot and said "Hey, Illuminus! Face front, true believer!" and then shot him in the crotch with a bouncy ball.

The grueling shoot got worse for me as Richard asked me to pull off a stunt in his ATV.

This is an example of Richard's strange relationship with money. Three years in the Marines and six years in prison had not left him with extravagant tastes. He had an organized budget and schedule—he exercised every morning, had a lean, inexpensive diet, and no vices other than his weekly trip to the comic book store on Wednesdays. He rarely ate out and only occasionally treated himself to seeing a superhero movie in the theater. He had tried to find work in Pahrump, anything—he applied at McDonald's, Home Depot, and everywhere else in town, but didn't get any callbacks and was trying to budget his remaining inheritance carefully.

But then again, he would go out and spend thousands of dollars on an ATV because he thought it would look cool in his video. He saw it as an investment—he hoped his *Phantom Patriot Retro Cinema* show would somehow make him money, either by rental or purchase sales online and on DVD or by selling the show to a network.

As the Phantom Patriot and G'nik confronted Illuminus, I was supposed to drive Richard's ATV down a dirt hill to surprise and distract Illuminus. The problem was, I told Richard, I had never driven an ATV before, and looking down the steep hill, didn't feel prepared to do the stunt. He shook his head, irritated. I'd be just fine, he told me. I did a couple of practice runs, taking it slow. It was jarring and bumpy, but I made it.

The cameras starting rolling. I drove down the hill and slid the ATV next to Illuminus, dust flying in the air.

"Cut!" Richard yelled. "No, you got to do it faster. Way faster!"

Now I was getting irritated. We had been filming all day with no breaks in the desert, and the whole experience was wearing me down. I was tired, hungry, and dazed from the sun. I circled back up out of the pit and prepared to do the stunt run again. I cruised down the hill faster, bouncing and flying through the air in the ATV.

"Cut!" Richard yelled. "Faster!"

I sped angrily back up the hill, circled, and hit the gas. This time I hit a mound of dirt the wrong way. The ATV jumped sideways and crashed into the side of the hill. My body flew through the front of the ATV (I wasn't wearing the ATV's seatbelt as it didn't fit me) and smashed into the reddish-brown dirt. I saw stars flash in my eyes, then blacked out for a second.

When I came to, I was lying on my back in the dirt. I felt like my mask was choking me, so I peeled it off, blinded by the bright sun. The wheels of the ATV were still spinning next to me. I felt an intense pain in my leg, and for a second, I thought it had been severed in the crash. I propped myself onto my elbows and saw Richard, Greg, and Matt rushing toward me. Richard turned the ATV off, and they helped me to my feet. I gave myself a dusty pat-down to make sure everything was still there and in one piece. My leg was shooting with pain, and it was hard to walk or even stand. I stumbled over to Richard's van and drank a bottle of water. They shot a couple scenes without me before I eased back in, limping back into the action.

Hours later, as the hot Nevada sun began to set, Richard was losing his temper, snapping at cast and crew. There were still several scenes that hadn't been shot, and he blamed it on Greg and Matt being late (Greg had picked up Matt, and they had gotten lost trying to find the pit) and on Greg doing too many takes. He was particularly getting upset with a stunt that wasn't working where a lit smoke bomb was supposed to time correctly with the ATV's hood flying open. The timing to get it right was ridiculously improbable, and it just wasn't working out.

"Damn it!" Richard yelled, kicking up a cloud of dust and dirt.

Finally, as the sun sank, Greg called it a day on filming and gave Richard a talk, telling him most of the shots had been accomplished, and the couple that remained could be done with a Tea Krulos stunt double wearing my Argoyle costume. Richard, still obviously frustrated and angry, reluctantly agreed. We returned to his home in silence. Richard made us La Choy and instant rice for dinner. I took some ibuprofen and went to sleep.

IN THE MORNING, RICHARD had calmed down quite a bit. I walked into his kitchen to find him making eggs and bacon. He was staring out the window, smiling, and turned to me.

"Look, rabbits!" he said cheerfully and pointed outside. I walked over and saw several baby jackrabbits chasing each other around his desert yard.

We drove to Las Vegas so I could catch my flight home. I used the car ride to ask him some interview questions. As the miles went by, we talked and laughed about several different topics—stories from his time in prison, Real-Life Superheroes, and life in Las Vegas.

AFTER MY ADVENTURES FILMING with Richard in Pahrump, he created one last Phantom Patriot video, which was posted to time with the presidential election in November 2016. This one was designed to be more "art therapy" aimed at the election cycle, which featured two people much despised by Richard—Hillary Clinton and Donald Trump.

Unlike other conspiracy theorists, Richard had not warmed up to Trump. In the *Prison Penned Comics* he created in 2005, he had an illustration showing influential members of the Bohemian Club. Trump was among them (although in reality, it appears, surprisingly, that he isn't a member). His dislike of Hillary can be found all the way back in an early Phantom Patriot booklet he handed out in 2001 before his arrest, which included a poem he wrote titled "Queen Hillary," with the opening lines "Bitch from hell/liar through and through/Hillary plans to trash/ the red, white, and blue."

In this video, Trump is joined by ex-presidents Carter, both Bush presidents, Bill Clinton, and Obama as well as Pope Francis in old enemy Illuminus' headquarters in a cave. They are all depicted as Reptilians until they drink blood and transform into their presidential forms, created in the video by actors wearing cartoonish rubber masks from a Halloween store. Hillary Clinton and Sarah Palin soon show up, too, and there are cameos from actors as Bernie Sanders, who is portrayed as a buffoonish Bolshevik, and Richard's old inspiration, Alex Jones.

Richard packs a ton of conspiracy deep cuts into this episode. The Reptilians read from *The Emerald Tablets of Thoth the Atlantean*, purported to be an ancient text from Atlantis translated by Dr. Maurice Doreal in 1939, but more likely a pulp-era hoax made from plagiarizing the works of H.P. Lovecraft and other writers. Richard's script also references the homophobic conspiracy that Michelle Obama is secretly transgender and the one that says Hillary Clinton has already died and been replaced with Teresa Barnwell, a woman who has carved out a career as a Hillary impersonator due to her uncanny resemblance to the politician.

Perhaps the harshest "art therapy" in the video is saved for the Alex Jones scenes, where an actor portraying Jones is depicted as a creepy jester jack-in-the-box. He's announced as entertainment for the assembled Reptilian world leaders, as he bounces up from the box, his shirt reading "Disinfo Wars."

"You globalist scum make me sick! Donald Trump is the real deal! I am the resistance!" Jones croaks, as the assembled Reptilians applaud. Jones' phone rings and his clown gloved hands grab his phone.

"Yes, Mr. Turner, I'll pass that on to Sheen, Rogan, and Ventura! You can count on us, Mr. Turner!" the jester Jones says obediently, referring to three of Jones' high-profile conspiracy-oriented friends—Charlie Sheen, Governor Jesse Ventura, and Joe Rogan, host of *The Joe Rogan Experience*, apparently implying they are all on the payroll of media mogul and CNN founder Ted Turner. Later in the broadcast, Phantom Patriot gets the satisfaction of knocking the Jones clown out, hitting him with his shield.

Phantom Patriot appears halfway through the video, bursting through a brick wall with G'nik and an armed militia of citizens—a farmer, a nun, a soldier, and a police officer—who place the former presidents and other leaders under arrest.

"This is an illegal coup, and I order you to drop your weapons," Obama protests as the Deep State members are rounded up.

"In order for this to be an illegal coup, your group would have to be the legitimate government, which you have never been," Richard sneers.

"Preach on it, PP!" G'nik chimes in.

"None of you were fairly elected by the people. All of you were secretly chosen from Illuminati bloodline families. You have never represented us. You're the tools of the globalists and Zionists, the Rothschilds, the Rockefellers, and the Vatican!" Richard tells the prisoners.

"Amen, brother," G'nik agrees.

Then they get what they deserve, in Richard's opinion—the miserable line-up is corralled into Guantanamo Bay to share a cell, all wearing orange prison jumpsuits. Their overpowering Reptilian thirst growing, Trump and George H.W. Bush end up fighting over who gets to eat a rubber prop rat.

THE STARDUST AND FANTOMAH SHOW

IN 2017, RICHARD MADE one more attempt at creating a show, which he was hoping would act as a pilot he could sell to Comedy Central or Adult Swim on Cartoon Network. If that failed, he would try to sell DVDs online and in comic book stores. He was hoping to create a cult hit, he told me. His idea was to create something similar to *Space Ghost Coast to Coast*, which had taken an old animated Hanna-Barbera superhero and made him the cartoon host of a talk show. Richard found two public-domain Golden Age comic book heroes, Stardust the Super Wizard (one of the stars of *Fantastic Comics*, 1939–1941) and Fantomah "Mystery Woman of the Jungle" (featured in *Jungle Comics* 1940–1944), and made them a married couple and talk show hosts, broadcasting from a spaceship.

I didn't think it was a bad idea, considering we live in an era where it seems like every superhero property ever created is being optioned for movies and TV shows. I didn't have faith that Richard was going to find success as a viral hit, though, as he had no social media presence and "cult hits" can be hard to manufacture.

Richard mailed me a DVD when it was completed, and as the show rolled, I was pleasantly surprised. It was awkward and hokey but entertaining. The production values were good. What impressed me the most was that there was no mention of conspiracy at all, just clean, Golden Age comic book fun, and I thought he might find an audience of comic fans. The fake black and white newsreels were a nice touch, and the actors were having a gleeful time with their roles. *Perhaps Richard was moving in a new, healthier creative direction,* I thought.

The show features the superhero couple scooping fellow Golden Age heroes Deuce the Daredevil and Black Terror out of World War II and beaming them aboard their ship. Richard played Deuce the Daredevil as well as the video's villains, The Claw, and The Voice. As always, Richard wrote the script and made all the costumes and props. Las Vegas Motion Pictures hired the actors that played the other characters and handled production.

But as it turns out, Richard could only make it 17-and-a-half minutes into the narrative before conspiracy reared its ugly head.

A flashback shows comic book action as Deuce the Daredevil and Black Terror battle The Claw to retrieve an A-bomb he's stolen. Back in the studio with their hosts, the talk turns to a discussion of the Manhattan Project.

"Truman's excuse about the bombings at Hiroshima and Nagasaki being preferable to a full-scale invasion never seemed genuine to me," Black Terror shrugs.

"To be perfectly honest your president and his Masonic advisers had ulterior motives unleashing such devastation..." Stardust begins to say as Fantomah shoots him a dirty look and elbows him.

"Husband, what did I say about temporal anomalies?" she scolds him in a whisper. "If we reveal to them the extent of the Illuminati's influence on this reality, it will be more than their mortal minds can handle!"

I sighed and shook my head. It was apparent that Richard couldn't escape the conspiracy, even for a short time.

AFTER OUR DRIVE BACK to Las Vegas that weekend following the long video shoot in Pahrump, Richard pulled up to McCarran International. I was exhausted from travel and two days of shooting all day with few breaks, my leg was throbbing with pain, and after the strange weekend, I was glad to be heading home to Milwaukee. I limped out of Richard's van and turned to say goodbye to him through the passenger window. We shook hands, and he told me he'd let me know when the video was done and posted on YouTube.

That was the last time I was to see Richard McCaslin.

CHAPTER SIXTEEN

THE WAR AGAINST SCIENCE

PART I: THE EARTH IS FLAT

JERAN CAMPANELLA STOOD ON the stage of a ballroom in a hotel in Frisco, a suburb of Dallas. Flanking him on either side are two projection screens, where words are swirling and flipping around, a list Campanella calls "The Lies," which are "everywhere and they encompass everything."

"Sugar and tobacco science, public water fluoridation, global warming and climate change science, GMOs and Monsanto, big pharma and medicine, flu shots and vaccines," Campanella reads off as the words circle around the screen. The words "Fear Porn" appear.

"Health insurance industry and medical malpractice, biotech, the pesticides, the EPA, oil industry and free energy, education system, false history, of course, big bang and evolution is a farce, common core math is a joke," Campanella lists.

The words continue to flash: "federal reserve banking, stock market and financial scams, censored on YouTube, Hollywood, alien agenda, Satanic message, music industry, kidnapping and human trafficking, child sex exploitation, sexualization of minors, government, mainstream media, fake news, IRS, NSA,

NSF, FTC, DEA, DOD, EPA, etc., CIA, false flags and covert government opera-
tions, political scene, election fraud and dishonest polls, left vs. right, Military
Industrial Complex, War on Drugs, weapons and arms dealing, and Official 9/11
Story," all swirl around in an exhausting list.

"What makes you think, with all of those lies, that they're telling you the
truth about space?" Campanella rhetorically asks the audience of about five
hundred people. These people, called Flat Earthers, are the fringe of the fringe.
Campanella (of Monterey, California) is speaking at the 4th annual Flat Earth
International Conference, the largest meet-up for Flat Earthers.

"I do not feel like I am spinning, living on a ball or flying through space at
66,000 mph around a 93-million-mile distant sun," Campanella's speaker bio
reads. "So to me, those are facts, and to change those facts, I need sufficient
evidence to make me give up my senses. Well, it has been a year, and you have
called me stupid, and you have yelled and screamed, but I have been given no
evidence to abandon the truth."

Campanella, wearing a backward baseball cap, a black polo shirt, a thin beard
framing his face, paces the stage as he talks. Hanging to Campanella's left is a
large disc, a map of the world as Flat Earthers believe it looks like. It's round
like a record, with what we call the North Pole dead center. The continents
swirl around it, and Antarctica, instead of being a solid mass, surrounds the
perimeter like a crust on a pizza. The icy wall of Antarctica is what prevents
ships from sailing off the edge and keeps our water supply in. Above, the sun
and moon rotate around a circle, like watch hands, and are much smaller than
science tells us (Flat Earthers say the sun is about 30 miles wide), with the
moon generating its own light. The constellations are not stars eons away, but
tiny twinkling lights that slowly rotate in a zoetrope above us. An invisible dome
made of an unknown material keeps the heavens intact above us. Beyond that
dome is nothing. Like people did in the Dark Ages, Flat Earthers believe that
we are the center of the universe, and they dismiss photos of other planets as
complete fabrications, along with pictures of the earth.

The main Flat Earther villain is the National Aeronautics and Space Administration. The name of Campanella's talk was titled "NASA: Going Nowhere
Since 1958." He gets big laughs from the audience when he says "Let's start
with my opinion of NASA," and shows a roll of toilet paper with the agency's
logo on it. Around the conference, I saw several people wearing shirts or hats
with a parody of the NASA logo that read "LIES" on it. Another speaker, who
calls himself Paul On a Plane (pseudonyms or people referring to themselves
as their YouTube page name like this are common amongst Flat Earthers), says
NASA is "just a CGI factory." Another speaker, Darryl Marble, showed a clip of

a NASA scientist on a TV show who says that for the agency, "the only limit is our own imagination," which doesn't provoke inspiration for this audience, but a sneering ripple of laughter.

To accept flat earth means believing in a conspiracy of massive proportions. Not only would NASA (which has 17,219 employees) be involved in the cover-up, but so would every government and private space agency on earth (there have been 327 crewed space flights from 1961–2019). Also complicit would have to be astronomy programs, explorers of Antarctica, creators of global navigation systems, the entire industry that creates and launches TV and other satellites into orbit (almost five thousand satellites currently orbit the planet, but Flat Earthers say they are just hanging in the sky, suspended by weather balloons), and probably large parts of the airline and shipping industries, as well as the military, among others. That's a secret being kept by tens of thousands of people, with no whistleblowers coming forward.

As to why NASA (and other agencies) would go to these great lengths to fabricate space exploration, Flat Earthers say it's simple: money. They point to NASA's $21.5 billion annual budget as the motivation for keeping the lie alive. In Darryl Marble's talk, "Flat Earth According to D. Marble," he showed a slide of a NASA lunar rover from 1969 that Marble says had a price tag of $9.5 million. Marble struggles to catch his breath after laughing when he shows the photo of the rover, which looks like a clunky golf cart. Marble has short dreadlocks, is wearing a flat earth medallion around his neck, and his T-shirt features a cartoon version of Morpheus from *The Matrix* holding a disc-shaped earth in his hands. Marble points to features on the lunar vehicle that look like an upside-down umbrella and lawn chairs. He tells the audience he tried to figure out why the rover had such a substantial cost.

"Then I looked closer, and I'm like ope! I got it! Check this out, I did some digging on the Internet, man, check out what I found," Marble says as he shows a doctored web page showing lawn chairs from a True Value hardware store with a $3.5 million price each. The audience bursts into laughter.

Marble, like Campanella, believes that his senses tell the truth, and like other Flat Earthers, he likes to conduct experiments to prove that the earth has no curvature. He demonstrated one in which he brought a carpenter's level onto an airplane, balanced it on a drink tray, and affirmed his belief when he saw it remained straight. In another experiment, he had a friend shine a light across a lake. There appeared to be no curvature. And in another investigation by Marble, he tracked the moon moving across the sky above a parking lot with a video camera in a time-lapse recording. Marble says the video proves the moon is moving, but not the earth.

These were the people Dr. Daniel White had told me in my interview with him that had a curious (and I would add, creative) mind, but not the right tools to make sense of their ideas. The theory has a long, colorful history with several ups and downs before the Internet age.

HISTORY OF THE FLAT EARTH

ANCIENT GREECE WOULD APPEAR to be where humanity first figured out that the earth was a sphere. Pythagoras and his group of followers used math and astronomy to reach the deduction, and the idea spread. Over the following centuries, scientists and explorers—Copernicus, Galileo, Newton, Magellan, to name a few—would add evidence that the world was round.

For every step of scientific progress, though, there was a reaction of fear and anger from some quarters that the Devil was behind these new ways of thinking.

The first wave of Flat Earthers launched from the teachings of Samuel Briley Rowbotham (1816–1884), who wrote and lectured under the pseudonym "Parallax" and was a "traveling lecturer and quack doctor" in England, according to Christine Garwood's *Flat Earth: The History of an Infamous Idea*. Calling his ideas "zetetic astronomy," Parallax didn't have blogs or YouTube videos at his disposal, but spread his message by self-published booklets with titles like *Zetetic Astronomy: Earth Not a Globe!* (published in 1885) and by giving talks at lecture halls, where he was often heckled, but occasionally found new followers.

One of Parallax's followers was a fiery Biblical literalist named John Hampden, who put out a wager of five hundred pounds that he could prove the earth had no curvature in 1870. Alfred Russel Wallace, a colleague of Charles Darwin, took him up on the challenge. Hampden wanted to repeat the Bedford Level Experiment, which had first been performed by Parallax in 1838 on the Old Bedford River in Norfolk, England. Parallax had claimed that a telescope lined up with a flag on a boat six miles away, which was proof that the world was not curved.

The referee for Hampden's wager was a neutral party named John Henry Walsh, editor of a sports magazine called *The Field*. The trio traveled to Norfolk and set up the experiment. Looking through the telescope, Walsh determined that the test proved curvature and awarded the five hundred pounds to Wallace.

Hampden did not take losing the bet with good sportsmanship. He ended up stalking and harassing Wallace and his family for years, sending letters that contained death threats. Here's part of one addressed to Wallace's wife:

Madame—if your infernal thief of a husband is brought home some day in a hurdle, with every bone in his head smashed to pulp, you will know the reason. Do you tell him from me he is a lying infernal thief, and as sure as his name is Wallace, he never dies in his sleep.

You must be a miserable wretch to be obliged to live with a convicted felon. Do not think or let him think I am done with him.

Lengthy court battles followed. The bet was deemed invalid, and Wallace had to return the wager to Hampden. However, in the libel suits that followed, Hampden had to pay massive fines repeatedly and eventually spent time in prison for his actions.

From there, the flat earth torch passed to Lady Elizabeth Anne Blount, who founded the Universal Zetetic Society in 1893 and published a magazine called *The Earth Not a Globe Review*. I was soon to hear some modern flat earth music, but Lady Blount is the originator of hymns and poetry that joyfully share the message of the theory.

The International Flat Earth Research Society was a descendent of Lady Blount's group, founded in 1956 in Dover, England, by Samuel Shenton. He was the first Flat Earther to be caught in the awkward position of having to try to explain away photos of the planet taken during the Space Race.

Other groups formed, some serious and others not so much—the Flat Earth Society of Canada with the motto "we're on the level" was a satire or subversive philosophy group formed by poets and other writers at Saint Thomas University in New Brunswick in 1970. Meanwhile, the International Flat Earth Research Society of America, founded in 1972, was completely serious and gained thousands of followers, who received a quarterly newsletter called *Flat Earth News*. Charles Kenneth Johnson ran the organization from his home, located on five acres of land in the Mojave Desert, about 20 miles east of Lancaster, California. Johnson died in 2001, but the Flat Earth theory would be back.

FLAT EARTH 2.0

THE POPULATION GROWTH OF "Flat Earth 2.0" picked up steam in 2015 and can largely be attributed to YouTube. Mark Sargent was not the first, but an early proponent of flat earth and got a lot of people to fall down a rabbit hole with his series of "Flat Earth Clues" videos.

Other early members of Flat Earth 2.0 included Matt Boylan (who also goes by Math Powerland), who would go on incoherent video rants, and Eric Dubay, an anti-Semitic Flat Earther who made documentaries like "Adolph Hitler vs. the Jew World Order," portraying Hitler as a misunderstood hero, causing Dubay to be shunned by many Flat Earthers. Unlike Boylan and Dubay, Sargent doesn't come off as a lunatic and is charismatic, well-spoken, and funny. The "Flat Earth Clues" videos began to rack up thousands and then millions of views. Many viewers laughed his ideas off, but for a small percent, they stuck. He was a personality to identity-fuse to. Sargent, a former professional computer game player and software trainer, reveled in his newfound status as a celebrity in a fringe movement. Other flat earth YouTube celebrities were formed. Campanella's YouTube channel, "Jeranism," has over 147,000 followers.

Researchers from Texas Tech University went to two Flat Earth International Conferences and through their interviewing discovered that almost

ABOVE: Flatearthmodels.com at the Flat Earth International Conference 2019.

100% of Flat Earthers had been introduced to the concept through YouTube videos, and that most of them had been steered that direction after searching for videos on other conspiracies like 9/11, Sandy Hook, and the moon landing. In January of 2019, YouTube announced they would be tweaking their algorithms to stop recommending content that "comes close" to violating their site policies, explicitly listing "9/11 trutherism, miracle cures, and flat earth" as examples, but it was too little, too late. Flat earth had been spreading on YouTube for over four years by then, and a passionate new subculture had been born.

2019 was year four for the Flat Earth International Conference, which in the past took place in Denver, Raleigh, and Alberta, before showing up in Dallas. The conference is produced by a production company called Kryptoz Media and featured 28 guest speakers over two days. There was a main ballroom, a smaller workshop room, and a handful of vendors set up in the hotel hallway, selling books, flat earth shirts, stickers, and posters. One of the most popular booths was the one set up for Chris Pontius, of Flatearthmodels.com. Pontius creates well-crafted, intricate domed models and clocks shaped like the flat earth model, which run from several hundred to a few thousand dollars.

Flat Earthers are aggressively ridiculed by almost everyone outside of their group, which forges stronger bonds within their community. It's an idea that fellow conspiracy theorists can't hang with for the most part. One conspiracy researcher (who spoke to me off the record) told me he believed Flat Earthers were part of a government "psy-op program" to discredit people like him. Even Ken Ham, the notorious Creationist who built the Ark Encounter and Creation Museum in Kentucky (he claims the earth is only 6,000 years old and that humans co-existed with dinosaurs), dismisses flat earth theory as over-the-top.

"It simply isn't taught in Scripture, and the science doesn't support it," Ham wrote in a blog post on his *Answers in Genesis* site.

To fight back, Flat Earthers refer to people who believe the world is a sphere as "globers," or "globeheads," a derogatory nickname for over 99.99% of the population.

There are two schools of thought in the Flat Earther movement. The first is a pseudoscience approach, in which Flat Earthers claim experimentation that proves the world is not a sphere, like Daryl Marble's experiments bringing a level onto an airplane or time-lapsing the moon moving in the sky above him. The second is an intense Biblical literalism that claims that scripture confirms the belief. Most, but not all, Flat Earthers believe in Biblical proof of a flat earth.

"We live in a world that hates truth," Matt Long told the audience for his talk "Flat Earth and the Great Perception." Long, of Fort Worth, Texas, uses the screen name "Flat Worth," co-hosts a podcast with his wife titled *Woketown*, and studies "Biblical cosmology," according to his speaker bio. Long says that the Bible refers to the earth "as a circle, not a ball," in the Book of Isaiah. Other verses refer to the world as having "four corners," a feature Long says is not available on a sphere but could apply to a disc. He invites the audience to visualize a pizza cut party-style, with the little triangle pieces as corners.

"Just like John mentions in Revelation that he can see the angels standing on the four corners of the earth, it makes sense that he can see them all in the same place because they were all standing in one place at the center of the Biblical flat earth, otherwise known as the North Pole, the place that all compasses point," Long said, "which potentially sits beneath the emerald rainbow of the very throne of God—the northern lights, which John saw in Revelation 4:3."

Long talked at length about the importance of having a "good vs. evil mindset," and proof of NASA "evil," he says, can be found right in their logo. He says the two red slashes in it don't form a rocket shape, but the forked tongue of a snake, the famous Bible villain, and that the word NASA is derived from the Hebrew word *nasha*, "to deceive."

After Long spoke, there was a brief break, and then the hall filled back up for a live recording of one of the most popular Flat Earth podcasts, *Globebusters*. Like the ghost hunting group they took their name from, the Globebusters are a quartet. Jeran Campanella, who had given the NASA talk, was joined by Bob Knodel, Iru Landucci, and a man calling himself "Taboo Conspiracy." The audience is treated to the *Globebusters* theme song sung live by the musicians who recorded it. The song is not exactly a parody of the *Ghostbusters* theme song, but a riff on it.

"There simply is no curve in sight! And you know we don't spin all day and night!" the theme's singer soulfully belts out. The podcast airs every Sunday and is three to four hours long.

The Netflix documentary *Behind the Curve* followed the Globebusters in their unsuccessful experiments to prove the world was flat. In one, a Flat Earther purchased a $20,000 ring laser gyroscope for the team to use. If the machine showed them that the gyroscope drifted 15 degrees every hour, it would confirm the world is turning on an axis... and that is precisely what the expensive experiment showed. But rather than admit defeat, cognitive dissonance pushed the Globebusters further into flat earth experimentation. At the end of *Behind the Curve*, they set up a light to shine through three boards with holes in them spread 3.88 miles apart. If the light would shine straight through the holes, the Globebusters reasoned, it would prove there is no curvature to the earth. If the world is curved, they will have to move the light up to make up for the difference. It's an experiment similar to the one that Hampden failed to win and lost his five hundred pounds to, way back in 1870. And like Hampden, the test did not go in their favor, with the Globebusters disproving their own theory. The failed experiments and the sounds of laughter of Netflix viewers across the country did not deter the team as they sat on the conference stage.

The Globebusters ended their show with a live Q-and-A session, but most people who got the mic didn't have a question but wanted to expound on their own philosophy or ideas. One audience member, who introduced himself as being from Alabama, started talking about the dome above us.

"My question is—how high do we suppose that is?" he asked.

Knodel responded that "there is a lot of evidence, in my opinion anyway, for something being up there at around 100, 120 kilometers," adding that lighting seems to flatten out around that height, suggesting a dome was blocking it.

THE CONFERENCE TOOK A lunch break, and I walked across the street to a 7-Eleven to get a slice of pizza. There was a bench nearby, so I sat down to eat there before heading back in. An awkward-looking guy in a trenchcoat with a conference lanyard on walked by.

"Hello, fellow Flat Earther," he told me quietly, wiggling his fingers in greeting.

"Hey, man, how's it going?" I replied. He looked like he was going to say something else, but overcome with shyness, he slinked away. I saw him a few times at the conference, sitting alone, watching the speakers with rapt attention. He seemed awkward, shy, lonely, and perhaps looking for social acceptance here.

IN THE AFTERNOON, I checked out a talk by a speaker named Shelley Lewis titled "Coming Out of the Flat Earth Closet: A Call to Activism." Lewis' bio says she is a former Army paratrooper, a holistic health practitioner, a certified lymphologist, vegan chef, photographer, and received a Bachelors in Science from West Point, where "she entertained hopes of becoming an AstroNOT." After 9/11, she began descending into the rabbit hole and had recently become a Flat Earther, and was co-director and co-producer of an upcoming documentary called *The Plane Truth*.

At the conference, she's created a talk based on breaking down a quote attributed to Mahatma Gandhi: "First they ignore you, then they laugh at you, then they fight you, then you win."

For the "laugh at you" part, Long had strung together a long montage of Flat Earthers being ridiculed on late-night talk shows and other comedy programs. James Corden and Jimmy Kimmel and stand-up comedians laughed it up at the flat earth idea. In a clip detested by Flat Earthers, Neil deGrasse Tyson ("He-Who-Shall-Not-Be-Named," as Mark Sargent calls him) calls them out on Comedy Central's *The Nightly Show with Larry Wilmore*. DeGrasse Tyson tells flat earth believers he's going to show them how gravity works before dropping a mic on the floor. The clips were filled with the laughter of studio audiences, which echoed around the dark conference ballroom, while the Flat Earthers sit in silent scorn as the clips drag out over excruciating long minutes.

One of the goals of Lewis' talk was to motivate people to get out and do some "flat smacking," a term that means to smack a globehead with the harsh flat earth reality, dropping a "truth bomb" on them by handing out pamphlets, trolling a "Research Flat Earth" sign in public, or confronting people on the street. Like Jehovah's Witnesses, Flat Earthers brave the disinterested public in hopes of a conversion.

Lewis offered Bizarro World takes on terms often applied to Flat Earthers in an attempt to flip the script back on critics. She talked about cognitive dissonance referring to people who blindly believe what scientists tell them, and said these scientists and those who trusted them were suffering from the Dunning-Kruger effect, the irony being that Flat Earthers are examples of Dunning-Kruger on steroids. The term refers to people thinking they have much more knowledge on a subject than they have and an inability to recognize their lack of expertise. Dunning-Kruger might lead someone to believe that watching YouTube videos and reading a couple of poorly sourced blog posts puts them on an equal playing field to people who have completed college-level studies and have had field experience.

THE FLATTYS

ARTISTICALLY, FLAT EARTHERS ARE more creative than other conspiracy subculture counterparts. A couple of listings made me excited about the conference's evening entertainment, but I was quickly disappointed. First, the program listed a "Flat Earth Game Show," which I assumed was going to be a wrong-answer-only extravaganza of flat earth knowledge with contestants hitting buzzers to answer questions about life under the dome. It turned out to be a staged game show that was going to be part of a comedy movie about a guy who encounters Flat Earthers. Mark Sargent played the game show host, and other guest speakers portrayed the game show contestants.

I focused on pondering the next thing listed in the program—a flat-earth-themed comedy show. I was hoping for amateur stand-up from Flat Earthers, perhaps giving a vicious roast of globeheads or maybe some Seinfeld-style observations of day-to-day life under the dome. But what we got instead was a vile alt-right comedian named Owen Benjamin. Benjamin had been pursuing a Hollywood comedy career, appearing on MTV's *Punk'd* and in films like *The House Bunny* and the Adam Sandler film *Jack and Jill*,[7] and was a cast member on the TBS sitcom *Sullivan & Son*.

Then he spiraled into conspiracy. Show business doors began to close and platforms de-monetized Benjamin as he began to endorse and talk about anti-Semitic conspiracies about the Jews ruling the world. The last thread in his Hollywood career was severed by a comedy song he created called "That Nigga Stole my Bike."

"I did that song because I wanted to do a joke with a word in it that's so taboo. OK, the N-word is absurd—if you ever say the N-word, you've cucked yourself. Because I will argue right now that necrophilia is infinitely more offensive than nigger," Benjamin explained to the Flat Earther audience. Between that and jokes bashing gay and transpeople, his career was pretty much over.

"I used to have my fancy pants and lollipops... everyone has a satanic Achilles, right? Mine was never money, it was I liked the status I had at the Hollywood Improv. They painted me in the mural, I was hanging on the wall like a conquering gladiator, and I could walk in there any night of the week, and famous people would be like 'hey man, I can't wait to see your new jokes and stuff,'" Benjamin said, pacing the stage. "They took down my picture, they persona non gratis'd me because of my stance against trans-child abuse, you know the child abuse which is trans-children—and they called me all these names of stuff. Now that did hurt, but once I realized that's all a nonsense loop, it never ends, then you're free. They're literally kicking you out of Hell."

Liberal Hollywood had booed and shunned him, but here in the ballroom full of Flat Earthers, he was a rockstar. Flat earth has gotten a couple of celebrity endorsements. Rapper B.o.B.'s support of the theory is what had led to Neil deGrasse Tyson calling out Flat Earthers and dropping a mic to demonstrate gravity on the Comedy Central appearance, and B.o.B. retaliated by recording a Tyson diss track titled "Flatliner." Basketball star Kyrie Irving said he believed in flat earth before an all-star game, which got a lot of media attention, and Shaquille O'Neal also said he believed in the argument before back-pedaling and saying he had been joking.

Benjamin told the audience his conversion to the belief came after he was challenged to debate the topic by a Flat Earther.

"I was like fuck this guy, so I got all my guys together, and I was like 'give me all the globe proofs you got!'" Benjamin told the conference. "I'm about to turn

---

7   A film that Sandler won both the worst male and female performance Razzies for because of his dual role as the title characters.

this asshole into dust! And then the more they gave me globe proof, the more I was like 'more, more though!'" he said, cycling his hand, gesturing his need for more info, as the audience laughed.

"I don't want to do this. I want to win, I want to stay on the side of the normal people, and then eventually I had to face reality, and that's it," Benjamin said on his new status. "When I realized the globe argument was total nonsense, I had to face the reality that we're not on a spinning ball, and it's great, people shouldn't be afraid of that."

Benjamin's set was more free-flowing rant than routine. His set was about 40 minutes of offensive jokes and him tooling around on a keyboard, improvising like a drunk at a house party, before rambling through audience questions for an hour. At one point a man got on stage and proposed to his girlfriend. The targets during his set included mocking "cultural appropriation," noting how he and a friend had been scolded at a Halloween party for wearing sombreros and calling themselves "Hose A" and "Hose B" (a joke on the name "Jose") and the latest liberal villain, teenage climate activist Greta Thunberg ("I'm not going to be browbeaten by a 15-year-old foreigner who looks like she has fetal alcohol syndrome," he told the crowd).

His most rabid dialogue came when an audience member asked him "How does homosexuality help us win the culture war?"

"It doesn't," Benjamin replied. "I'm not blaming the homosexual in a sense; I'm blaming the evangelical homosexual that's like 'everyone should be like me.' I can't stand those people; it's one thing if someone's brain is wired a little wacky and they're like 'Hey man, ya know, I'm just into this shit,' and I'm like 'all right buddy, we can still be buddies, just don't ever bring it up around anyone I care about.' Uh," Benjamin exhaled loudly and laughed. "But it's the ones that are like 'oh, vaginas are disgusting, like, you're gross, like, vaginas are gross.' I'm like... 'You really wanna do this?' Like, I don't want to get graphic 'cause I think there might be some kids in the room, but vaginas are not gross, and assholes are insanely disgusting," Benjamin said as the audience cheered and laughed. "Fertile sex makes life, which is great, and sodomy makes fake AIDS and death."

There were quite a few kids at the conference, and in the room for Benjamin's set. Another audience member asked how to talk to their children about flat earth.

"How to break the earth is flat with your kids? Never tell them it's round. That's why we're homeschooling," Benjamin responded. "Like we're going to get to a point, guys, the homeschool movement is growing, there's going to be a point where someone's going to have a spinning ball, and kids are like 'what?!' Like, dude, we're never going to introduce that concept to them," Benjamin told the conference. The ballroom filled with cheering.

I DID FINALLY GET to see some Flat Earther entertainment the second night of the conference when things concluded with the Flat Earth Video Awards or the "Flattys," a ceremony to acknowledge Flat Earthers who had made influential videos over the last year. Mark Sargent co-hosted the awards with a woman named Karen B, the secretary of a "nonprofit scientific research group called FECORE."

Among the categories were Best Flat Earth Awakening Video (awarded to Owen Benjamin), Best Flat Earth Proof Experiment (which went to a group called Flat Earth Los Angeles), and Best Flat Smacking.

The awards show had a few live music performances. Flat earth has a vibrant music scene. As Sargent mentions in his book *Flat Earth Clues: End of the World*,[8] flat earth songs can be "in just about every genre you can think of: rock, rap, folk, country, techno, they all spoke of an awakening, a disappointment, and a journey," and adds that a playlist on his YouTube channel has over three hundred entries.

The most well-known musician in the community is Flat Earth Man, a country singer who has crafted a self-titled album of songs related to flat earth conspiracies, with songs like "No Photographs of Earth," and "Do You Still Believe We Went To The Moon." Although he appears and sounds like he stepped out of a Texas honky-tonk, Flat Earth Man is British.

But the genre that has the most output is flat earth hip hop or, as I've dubbed it, "flat hop." B.o.B. was the highest-profile rapper to do a flat earth song, but real flat hoppers are exclusively devoted to singing about conspiracy. The awards show featured a hybrid live and pre-recorded performance of a song called "Flat Smackin: The All-Star Remix" by WesBlazeMuzik, with eight flat hoppers dropping verses and repeating the refrain "Eat. Sleep. Debunk the globe, repeat."

Another crew calling themselves The B-Boys did a live performance of a song called "Lean Flat."

The awards kicked off with a premiere of what is the flat hop magnum opus, a video titled "Epic Rap Battles of History: Globe vs. Flat Earth," a parody of the famous "Epic Rap Battles of History" YouTube show (which pits figures from history or fictional characters against each other, i.e., Blackbeard vs. Al Capone or Sherlock Holmes vs. Batman). Unlike the short rap-offs the video is based on, this song stretched for nearly 13 minutes and featured a cast of people Mark Sargent lists in his *Flat Earth Clues: End of the World* book as "Enemies of the State." Joining the rap are actors portraying Neil deGrasse Tyson, Bill Nye,

---

8   All 2019 conference attendees got a free copy of this book, signed by Sargent with the inscription "Keep it flat!"

physicist Brian Cox, and at one point, the corpse of Charles Darwin is revived to combat the flat earth theory.

Most revealing is the depiction of "Science" in the video. A young boy is trying to teach a girl (at one point depicted as a literal globehead) about flat earth, when the girl summons Science. Here the field is represented by an anthropomorphic S character that is feminine and dorky, while also being a supernatural monster. Science has big, goofy teeth wrapped in braces, and tape holding together the bridge of her glasses. The girl looks in a mirror and says "Science" three times as the character giggles evilly, lightning flashing to reveal a gory S made of bones and gore as it appears like Bloody Mary or Candyman.

As the video awards and flat hop performances continued to drag on, I suddenly felt an overwhelming feeling that I needed to leave. I had spent two days embedded in a group of people that believe we are trapped in God's terrarium and that "space is fake." As I walked down the aisle, flashes of light and loud sound from the video awards blared behind me as I looked back and forth at the Flat Earthers one last time in the ballroom, trying to figure out who they were. I walked rapidly through the hotel reception area and out the exit doors.

THE FLAT EARTHER PRESENTATIONS I saw often featured slides that showed famous quotes from Nikola Tesla, Plato, Benjamin Franklin, and other historical figures. Nothing adds a little boost to your theory like making it look as if a famous dead guy agrees with you. In her presentation, Shelly Lewis presented a quote by Victor Hugo: "No force can stop an idea whose time has come."

The Flat Earther time has come. Or in this case, come, gone, and come back again—kind of like the measles.

PART II: VACCINES CAUSE AUTISM

IT WAS A DARK, dreary day as I walked past farmer's market vendors lining the perimeter of Wisconsin's State Capitol Building, a white dome towering into the gray cloud-filled sky. The smell of rain was in the air. I followed the sound of an enthusiastic, amplified voice until I saw a crowd of about 150 gathered on the stairs of the Capitol, the traditional spot for all manner of protests and rallies in the state of Wisconsin. A few of them held signs that say things like "Believe Parents NOT Pharmaceutical Companies," "My Child My Choice" and "People Who Do the Research Don't Vaccinate."

This rally was called "Wisconsin United for Freedom," which I found on the page of a group called Informed Choice Wisconsin. These people were what media and others would commonly call "Anti-vaxxers."

The crowd included many families with children. Shortly after I arrived, the event organizers, concerned about the incoming rain, asked all the children to line up on the Capitol steps to lead the crowd in singing "The Star-Spangled Banner."

"C'mon up here, don't be shy, don't be shy," a woman with a mic said as rows of kids—a couple dozen—lined up on the stairs with their hands over their hearts, rain clouds rolling in above the dome of the Capitol Building behind them, and they began to sing. One of them, a girl no more than eight years old, was wearing a shirt that reads "My body, my choice, no mandatory vaccines!"

Absorbing this sight, I couldn't help but think of the many tasteless jokes and memes I've seen on social media about kids dying before they complete elementary school.

When I would post about Flat Earthers, people would crack jokes about how foolish they were. Sandy Hookers drew a response of disgust, but Anti-vaxxers prompted a special kind of vitriol. They were viewed as dangerous and contagious.

"Making fun of anti-vaxxers is a lot like unvaccinated children—it never gets old," a friend had joked on my Facebook after I posted that I was attending the rally.

"America the dumbest," another friend commented. "A thousand people without the benefit of modern medicine ... that's how an outbreak happens," said another. I also had several comments from friends saying that they hoped I had worn a face mask

ABOVE: At the Madison Anti-vaxx rally, 2019.

so I wouldn't get polio or other diseases. "You're gonna get the plague. Dibs on your stuff," one friend posted.

Fear and anger about Anti-vaxxers in Wisconsin had led to a letter circulating in a neighborhood in Sussex (about 20 miles outside of Milwaukee), signed "Concerned Moms of Wisconsin," that outed a family as Anti-vaxxers.

"Protect yourself, your family, and your community by using caution when interacting with these people," the anonymous letter read.

AT THE MADISON RALLY, the rain began to fall as the kids finished singing "The Star-Spangled Banner." The crowd had come with ponchos and umbrellas, keeping them dry as the marker on their protest signs began to drip and smear.

The rally had a motley line-up of speakers—holistic health practitioners, activists, an Internet radio show host, a couple of state representatives, and the founder of the Nurses for Vaccine Safety Alliance, among others.

Like a lot of social groups, Anti-vaxxers don't like the term they've been stuck with. "I am not Anti-vaxx. I'm vaccine informed," explained one protest sign. "Informed" sounds more inviting and enlightened than "Anti."

"Please don't label us, please don't call us anti-vaxxers," Representative Chuck Wichgers, of the Wisconsin State Assembly, told the crowd, on his message to the powers that be in the Capitol behind him.

"Many doctors say 'I don't give [vaccines] anymore because the first 20 years of my practice I didn't see a lot of autism, Alzheimer's, all these things, seizure disorders, celiac disease, autoimmune diseases,' they didn't deal with any of that," Wichgers claimed to the crowd. "And then all of a sudden, it started picking up. And then it started picking up more and more. And they (the doctors) said 'I don't want to do them anymore'. So you know who's doing them? The pharmacies!"

THE RISE OF ANTI-VAXXING

THERE ARE SOME STEREOTYPICAL ideas of what a conspiracy theorist might look like, but they come in all shapes and sizes. One of the people who helped distribute the Anti-vaxxer message more than anyone else is actress, model, and TV host Jenny McCarthy.

In 2007 McCarthy announced that her son had been diagnosed with autism two years earlier, writing about it in her book *Louder Than Words: A Mother's Journey in Healing Autism*. For the next few years, she made the Anti-vaxxer argument on *The Oprah Winfrey Show*, *Frontline*, *Larry King Live*, and other media as well as at Anti-vaxxer rallies.

McCarthy's inspiration, along with leagues of other Anti-vaxxers, was British gastroenterologist Andrew Wakefield, who co-authored a 1998 paper that linked the measles, mumps, rubella (MMR) vaccine with autism and bowel illnesses.

The British General Medical Council had a tribunal on Wakefield in 2010, concluded he had acted "dishonestly and irresponsibly," and leveled charges of abuse of developmentally disabled children. *The Lancet*, the journal that had initially published Wakefield's 1998 paper, retracted their decision to publish, stating that Wakefield's conclusion had "been proven to be false." As a result of the tribunal, Wakefield was removed from the UK Medical Register for unethical behavior.

Despite this, Wakefield continues to have a strong following of Anti-vaxxers, and promotes his views, writing books and directing a 2016 documentary titled *Vaxxed: From Cover-Up to Catastrophe*.

FRAUDULENT OR NOT, WAKEFIELD had tapped into a distrust of the medical field and the nightmare of America's health care system. Looking around at the protest, I noticed many signs that read "Stop Big Pharma" or something similar. I think the anger and frustration there is understandable. "Big Pharma" is an aggressively greedy industry, full of stories like the "Pharma Bro" Martin Shkreli, former CEO of Turing Pharmaceuticals. Shkreli purchased the manufacturing license to the drug Daraprim and then raised the price from $13.50 to $750 per pill before he went to prison for securities fraud.

Besides a broken health care system and a greedy drug industry, conspiracists can draw from a history of government malfeasance. One example is the Tuskegee Syphilis Study. Between 1932 and 1972, the U.S. Public Health service told about six hundred African-American men from Alabama that they were being given free health care. Some already had syphilis; others were infected and weren't told they were carrying the illness (they were told they were being looked at for what was colloquially known as "bad blood") and they were at no point given treatment, so the effects of the untreated disease could be studied. Their funeral costs were covered in the plan, so researchers could ensure they would get autopsies.

The Tuskegee Syphilis Study was not the only experiment carried out on American citizens, often the least protected in society—patients at mental institutions, prisoners, and poor African Americans. In various studies, these victims were exposed to hepatitis, malaria, injected with live cancer cells, had Asian flu sprayed in their nose, and gonorrhea injected into their urinary tract.

LIKE FLAT EARTHERS HAVE FOUND their enemy organization in NASA, Anti-vaxxers have made it their mission to confront the Center for Disease Control (CDC). One of the Madison rally speakers, Lynette Brown, host of a show called *Forsaken Generation* on the online Freedomizer Radio, has been one of the leaders of the effort, coordinating an "Inundate the CDC ACIP Meetings" Facebook page. The CDC's Advisory Committee on Immunization Practices has three annual meetings in Atlanta, which are now packed with what one report called "rowdy" Anti-vaxx activist "warriors" (as they call themselves) to confront the board of experts. The growing presence of the passionate Anti-vaxxers attending has led to new rules on disruptive behavior as well as adding heightened security measures.

CDC INUNDATIONS ARE FILLED with anger, but one of the most significant rallying points of the Anti-vaxxer movement is genuine grief. When I had arrived at the Madison Anti-vaxx event, the first person to speak was a distraught 14-year-old girl named Ashlyn. She was talking about her mom and crying.

"She's the one that makes sure I'm always OK at school and at home," Ashlyn said, choking back tears, her voice cracking. "You guys are awesome, thank you. And here's my mom," she said, handing the mic to her mom, Heidi.

A GoFundMe page set up for Ashlyn told the story: in 2018, 13-year-old Ashlyn received the human papillomavirus (HPV) vaccination, and two months later she began to pass out randomly and then experienced seizures. Doctors at first suspected dehydration or stress, but the seizures continued—at stores, while playing softball, out with friends, at home—everywhere.

Heidi claims she was introduced to an ER doctor; "she confirmed that yes, this is a side effect from the vaccination and yes, that is what is causing Ashlynn's seizures." After going through neurofeedback and biofeedback training, "she continues to have seizures but has them controlled to about 1–2 a week."

"I chose this for Ashley," Heidi said into a mic at the rally as the rain fell. "But I chose not to give vaccinations to my other daughters!" The crowd cheered. "I do not want the government to tell me what to do for my children. It's my choice! Better yet, do not let the pharmaceutical company tell our government what I should be giving to my child!" The crowd cheered again, louder.

Another speaker, Destiny, also had a tragic story—the death of her teenage son, who was just about to start high school. In the summer of 2018, he got the HPV vaccine. About a month later, he collapsed at football practice, and he was diagnosed with acute disseminated encephalomyelitis (ADEM) disease. He died less than a month later.

"I watched his brain malfunction because it was so swollen, and I watched him have seizures and lose all control of his bodily functions," Destiny told the rally crowd, crying. "I seen his life slip away right before my eyes. All because a doctor thought this vaccine would save his future partners. I listened. I wanted my son's future partners to be safe. I was so naïve, and I should have done my own research years ago. Trying to explain to my children to live without their brother is something I never thought I would have to do."

Destiny's and Heidi's grief and anger at the rally is palpable.

"Making sense of all this is impossible. I'm pissed!" Destiny says into the mic before bursting into tears. "The pharmaceutical companies killed one of my children and destroyed the other four's lives. I will forever fight for your children, and I will forever fight for mine. I will tell everyone about vaccine injury. We will move mountains in honor of my son!" she says as she hands off the mic, the crowd clapping and voicing their support.

OUTBREAK

THE RALLY I ATTENDED was happening amid a time when Anti-vaxxers were under scrutiny and pressed in the media. In the month before the May 2019 rally, the news cycle was full of stories about a growing outbreak of measles, a disease declared eliminated almost 20 years prior. By the end of April 2019, there were over seven hundred reported cases of measles for the year, with outbreaks in five states and reports of the disease in 17 more, the highest number of measles cases since 1992.

Wisconsin has a significant role in the Anti-vaxx battle as it's one of 18 states that allows students to go to school without vaccinations due to personal convictions.

When the measles outbreak began to spread in April 2019, a reporter asked President Trump what he thought of the situation outside the White House before Trump boarded a helicopter.

"They have to get the shots!" Trump shouted to reporters over the noise of the helicopter blades on April 26. "The vaccinations are so important. This is really going around now. They have to get their shots."

In true Trump fashion, this is a reversal of what he previously had to say about vaccinations.

"Healthy young child goes to doctor, gets pumped with massive shot of many vaccines, doesn't feel good and changes- AUTISM. Many such cases!" read a Trump tweet from 2014. Once he was in the White House, Trump-appointed administration were identified as Anti-vaxxers.

Thayer Verschoor, who worked at the Department of Veteran's Affairs, shared a list of reasons to vote for Trump, which included comments on Birtherism, and said Trump was "warning America" of poisonous vaccines and their dangers, he wrote. Darla Shine, wife of White House Communications Chief Bill Shine (and CEO of the Happy Housewives Club), has long supported Anti-vaxxers. As the measles outbreak began, she tweeted out:

"I had Measles Mumps ChickenPox as a child and so did every kid I knew- Sadly my kids had MMR so they will never have the life long immunity I have. Come breath on me!"

Unlike Flat Earth theories, the Anti-vaxx platform is widely accepted by other conspiracy theorists, the loudest of these, not surprisingly, being Alex Jones. Jones has hosted Andrew Wakefield on his show, calling him a "hero" and a "pioneer."

The claims Jones has made range from the HPV vaccine causing paralysis and seizures in children around the world, an impending "forced vaccination," and that Bill Gates, a "modern-day Stalin," is not doing philanthropic work in Africa trying to eradicate polio, but is using his charity as a front for a eugenics program using vaccinations to "sterilize and destroy" third-world countries. Richard McCaslin told me he believed this theory and that other vaccine programs were possibly used to inject citizens with a microchip device to monitor their behavior.

Anti-vaxxer response to the measles outbreak was to scoff at it as being overblown by the media or, as one of the Madison rally speakers, Kevin Barry, suggested, "a hoax to scare people so legislators can take away religious freedom."

Barry is the author of a book titled *Vaccine Whistleblower: Exposing Autism Research Fraud at the CDC*. "This is not an epidemic. The story should have been 155 kids have an itchy week, and now they're immune to measles," Barry told the cheering crowd.

ONE OF THE LAST SPEAKERS on the Capitol stairs was, as he was introduced, "a chiropractor, a family man, and a downright truther, he speaks his mind, he gets down to the nitty-gritty of the matter, and we love him for it, here to tell us what's really going on, the Wild Doc, Dale Brown!" Dr. Brown, who runs a natural health clinic in Tennessee, addressed the crowd as rain bounced off his cowboy hat.

A couple minutes into his speech, Dr. Brown told the crowd to Google a CDC whistleblower. "Just search it—congressional video—C-SPAN, Senator Posey or Representative Posey," Dr. Brown says.

I did as Dr. Brown suggested and found a 2015 C-SPAN video with Representative Bill Posey, Republican, representing the 8th district of Florida, where he brought up documents given to him by Dr. Bill Thompson, formerly of the CDC, who says that in a 2004 report he and his co-authors omitted information about vaccines and possible connections to autism.

"He got scientists confessing to committing fraud in 2015, and since then our government has done *nothing*," Dr. Brown told the crowd, who booed loudly.

"Shame on them!" someone from the crowd shouted.

"When you look at research, studies show that eczema and asthma increase anywhere between 10–15 times in the vaccinated population. If you take those two conditions alone... shoot, eczema, allergies, increase the risk of suicide. Suicide is the number one killer of our children right now, in the thousands. Thousands of people die each year from asthma. Vaccines are adding to that and causing those conditions..."

That's when the sole protestor showed up to the rally. Dressed in jean shorts, a T-shirt, and an '80s-style headband, it seemed like he randomly wandered into the rally. He shouted something about "polio and measles."

A chorus of booing was hurled at him.

"Quiet down!" someone shouted angrily.

"Excuse me, we're more than willing to have a conversation with you, but if you just want to step over to the side..." the event organizer said, taking the mic from Dr. Brown.

"Hey, did you just hear me say that a senior scientist from the CDC confessed to committing fraud?" Dr. Brown asked the protestor, taking the mic back. The protestor yelled something again about polio, and this time an event volunteer in a Wisconsin Rally for Freedom T-shirt stormed toward him.

"Let me talk to him, wait wait wait," Dr. Brown said.

"Have a nice day!" someone called out sarcastically.

"Please, no, let him stay. Don't chase him off!" Dr. Brown pleaded.

"Have a nice day, sir," the event organizer said, grabbing the mic again. "Research vaccines!"

The volunteer frog-marched the protestor out of the rally as he continued to yell things about diseases preventable by vaccines.

"Bye, Felicia!" a teenage Anti-vaxxer hurled snidely as he walked by.

The entire scene at the rally, the Anti-vaxxers versus the vaccinated, reminded me that at the heart of this and other conspiracies is the culture war in America. It feels like the country has never been as divided, and conspiracists see it as a battle on their beliefs and rights and that they need to fight back against.

CHAPTER SEVENTEEN

Q

On March 13, 2019, Gambino crime family boss Francesco "Franky Boy" Cali was found dead in the street in front of his house, where he had been shot ten times. It was the highest-profile mob killing in decades, and for days there was speculation: was the murder sparked by romantic jealousy, or more frightening, was a new war erupting between New York's five mafia families?

As it turned out, it wasn't an underworld hitman that had taken out the mob boss, but a 24-year-old drifter turned vigilante from Staten Island named Anthony Comello who was obsessed with a far-right conspiracy theory called "QAnon."

ON OCTOBER 5, 2017, Trump gathered with a group of people attending a military dinner for a photo op.

"Maybe it's the calm before the storm," Trump told the media. "Could be. The calm before the storm." When media pressed him as to what he meant, he replied, "You'll see." To those uninitiated, it was just a typical unclear Trumpism. But some saw it as a more profound message.

Later that month, the first message from a person or persons named "Q" first appeared on 4chan (then moved to Reddit and 8chan) on October 28. The code letter referred to Q-level security clearance, a.k.a. Top Secret.

Q's messages began to paint a story of an upcoming moment in history called "The Storm," an Alt-Right, Make America Great Again pure fantasy, cult-like in the group's devotion to cognitive dissonance. Trump and Special Counsel Robert Mueller were secretly working together, Q reported, the public animosity between them all a talented act. The carefully orchestrated Storm being plotted by them would sweep down and round up all of the Democrat villains: Crooked Hillary (finally the shouts of "Lock her up!" would be heard), John Podesta and his pedophile Pizzagate ring, Obama, George Soros, the Hollywood elites, the Dishonest Media, David Hogg and all the other Crisis Actors, would be part of a mass arrest. Some speculated that they would all be sent to rot in cells in Guantanamo Bay, much like the ending of Richard's last *Phantom Patriot's Retro Cinema* episode.

As for who this Q might be, it didn't matter to QAnon, the quickly growing group of Q followers, who interpret the "crumbs" or clues of information Q leaves in his "drops." It was clear to QAnon that Q was a government insider, while some thought it was Trump himself, or someone working closely with him in his administration. Another suggestion was that Q was John F. Kennedy Jr., who faked his 1999 death in an airplane crash to lurk in the shadows, watching and waiting to emerge at the right time.

"It came down to two choices for America. Launch a military coup to seize the government from whichever cabal puppet was in the White House or win legitimately, take control of the NSA, expose the criminals for what they are and arrest them all," writes one of the authors of *QAnon: An Invitation to the Great Awakening*, a collections of essays by members of QAnon. The book has become an Amazon bestseller. An app called QDrops, which sent alerts about the conspiracy, was a top seller in Apple and Google app stores until Apple dropped the app after NBC News investigated.

Celebrity QAnon believers like Roseanne Barr, former Major League Baseball pitcher (and Breitbart podcast host) Curt Schilling, and singer Joy Villa (famous for her pro-Trump dresses worn to the Grammy Awards, including one with a brick and barbed-wire motif, representing the border wall), helped spread the word of Q.

QAnon began showing up at Trump rallies wearing MAGA hats and holding giant cardboard Qs.

"Where we go one, we go all," became the motto of the group, a phrase to identify their unity as part of the approaching Storm.

"THESE, THE CRUMBS, in time, will equate to the biggest drops ever disclosed in our history," Q promised in a message posted November 4, 2017.

Q's messages range from pep talks to cryptic riddles. Some of them remind me of the quatrains of soothsayer Nostradamus, whose cryptic predictions were later interpreted to predict all sorts of historical tragedies, from the Great London Fire of 1666 to key moments of World War II to 9/11. Part of the criticism of the quatrains was that the wording was so vague that it could have applied to a great many different things. Here's typical Q vagueness (BO probably stands for Barack Obama):

Q47: NOV. 2, 2017, 12:08:46 (EST)

You can paint the picture solely on the questions asked.

Be vigilant today and expect a major false flag.

Does anyone find it to be a coincidence there is always a terrorist attack when bad news breaks for the Ds?

What is that called?

Military relevant how?

BO could not and would not allow the military to destroy ISIS- why?

How was ISIS formed?

When?

How has POTUS made so much progress in the short time he's been President?

Alice & Wonderland.

Some of Q's predictions have been a total failure.

On November 1, 2017, Q predicted that in the next couple of days Clinton staff members John Podesta, the Pizzagate mastermind, and Hillary's chief aide Huma Abedin would be arrested. Abedin is another favorite target for right-wingers, and subject of a conspiracy that states she is secretly working with Islamic extremists like the Muslim Brotherhood. Monica Crowley, a FOX News analyst who became Trump's senior director of strategic communications for the National Security Council, had pushed the conspiracy relentlessly.

Following Podesta's and Abedin's arrests, and realizing more were on the way, mass riots would break out, followed by a period of military control to restore order, Q reported. QAnon waited with bated breath for the show to get started, but nothing happened.

Another Q announcement, that Hillary Clinton would be imprisoned in 2018 after her staff was systematically rounded up, also failed to deliver.

As with cults that make failed doomsday predictions, some abandoned QAnon, dismissing it as a fan fiction hoax that had duped them (some have compared it to Live Action Role Playing, or LARPing), but for others with a stronger level of cognitive dissonance, alternate explanations were put forth. One theorist suggested that prominent Democrats were secretly under arrest and wearing ankle monitors hidden under their clothes. Photos depicting weird pantleg bulges were offered as evidence.

QAnon ignored the misses and looked for hits. Trump himself, QAnon believes, has given what they call "proofs"—scraps of wink-wink nudge-nudge confirmations that he is listening to them.

"Following Q is like working a 50,000 piece puzzle. It's slow, intriguing and fun—as we wait for clues and put the pieces together," an author of *QAnon: An Invitation to the Great Awakening* wrote.

One of the oddest proofs started when a member of QAnon suggested on an 8chan message board, the day before President Trump's State of the Union address on January 30, 2018, that "maybe Q can work the phrase 'tip-top' into the State of the Union."

Months later, Q posted, "It was requested, did you listen today?" Q was referring to an Easter appearance that Trump made, flanked by Melania and an aide in a dopey-looking Easter Bunny costume on April 2, 2018.

Trump thanked Melania for her work getting the White House ready for the event. "We keep it in tip-top shape. We sometimes call it *tippy-top* shape," he told the crowd waiting to start the traditional Easter egg hunt.

Although the phrase hadn't happened in the State of the Union or the daily tweets, press interviews, rallies, and other appearances between January 29 and April 2, QAnon was blown away by the "tippy-top" comment paired by the presence of a white rabbit.

"How many times have you heard anyone use that phrase? Even for those who were on the fence about Q saw that one as a clear sign that President Trump was talking directly toward us," an author of *QAnon: An Invitation to the Great Awakening* wrote. Another of the book's authors recalled, "That did it for me. That's the day I knew Q wasn't a hoax."

ON JULY 31, 2018, Trump held a rally in Tampa, Florida, where he wanted to hammer home that he wasn't a Washington insider.

"I was probably in Washington in my entire life 17 times," Trump said. "True, 17 times. I don't think I ever stayed overnight. I've been there 17 times, never stayed there at night, I don't believe. You know what I'm getting at, right?" Trump shrugged, giving the "17 times" number a couple more mentions before moving on.

QAnon did know what he was getting at. Do I even have to tell you what the 17th letter of the alphabet is?

ON MAY 10, 2018, posts came in from Q numbered 72 through 76. Post 74 had a picture of an American flag in it. The same day, Trump made a deal with North Korea to release three American prisoners. Trump tweeted a video of the three Americans returning home, greeted by a giant flag being held up by two fire trucks. What was the vehicle number of one of the firetrucks?

That's right, Q74.

Q'S APPEAL IS PART of a more massive culture war. That's the direction sites like InfoWars have gravitated toward, too. The conspiracy is mixed with pieces aimed at making "triggered liberal snowflakes" look dumb or sinister. The fear of the liberal lifestyle agenda has led to the rise of conspiracy, as well as the alt-right and white identity movements.

Liberals view conservatives as Bible-thumping, racist, sexist, homophobic, uneducated gun nuts.

Conservatives, meanwhile, have hatred of a concept of a liberal New World Order full of words like white privilege, social justice, gun control, transgender, safe space, climate change, pro-choice, and multicultural. Anyone who doesn't agree with liberals gets labeled as a racist or sexist.

"Left Speak," as it is sneeringly called, is full of ideas about socialism, identity politics, abortion, and Sanctuary Cities. It's a snobby, elitist, and naïve worldview where reality is distorted to fit an agenda.

"Left speak is predicated on lying, on transforming rather than reporting. There are three forms of lying: omission, exaggeration, and misrepresentation," David Solway writes in an essay titled "The Lingo of the Left." "The left has mobilized all three commutations of the actual, leaving out what does not suit, inflating what does, and falsifying what may."

Many on the right view liberals as being damaging to "traditional family values."

"Globalist singer Celine Dion has introduced her new line of gender-neutral children's clothing designed to 'liberate' children from the traditional roles of boy and girl," writes Lori Colley, publisher of a newsletter called *Praying Citizen* and one of the authors of *QAnon: An Invitation to The Great Awakening*. "It's not just harmless fashion, folks, it's a satanic mindset—organized and strategic. Without a nuclear family, held together by a genetic male husband and a genetic female wife, we are doomed. The global elites' goal is an end to monogamy, God-given genders, and normal procreation."

THE CLINTON BODY COUNT

ONE OF THE THINGS that makes the Clintons so sinister, in the minds of far-right conspiracists, is a theory called the "Clinton Body Count" that suggests the political power couple has climbed the ladder by putting out a hit on a number of people who have stood in their way, from the start of their careers in Little Rock to the present day. This "body count" of lawyers, journalists, and politicians runs from a dozen to over a hundred, depending on the theorist and how far they are willing to stretch the degree of separation between the Clintons and the alleged victims. The theories also suggest that the Clintons ran a drug empire, a child trafficking ring, and other sinister enterprises.

The usual starting point for this theory is the suicide of Vince Foster. Foster was an Arkansas lawyer and a friend of the Clintons who became Bill Clinton's Deputy White House Counselor. Suffering from depression, Foster shot himself in Fort Marcy Park in Virginia in 1993. A line from his suicide note read "I was not meant for the job or the spotlight of public life in Washington. Here ruining people is considered sport." Theories quickly spread that Foster knew too many Clinton secrets and that Hillary and Bill had arranged a hit, making it look like a suicide. Despite there being no evidence Foster was murdered by anyone, the Clinton Body Count theory took off, spread on the airwaves by people like Rush Limbaugh. Soon anyone tangentially related to the Clintons who had died was added to the conspiracy.

A more recent alleged victim, and a point that QAnon rallies behind, is the death of Democratic National Committee employee Seth Rich, who conspiracists believe was murdered for being a potential whistleblower. On July 10, 2016, Rich, who worked as the DNC's Voter Expansion data director, was shot twice in the back. His murder is unsolved but suspected to be an attempted robbery. Doubt was cast on this conclusion when it was revealed that Rich still had his wallet, phone, and watch on him—it appeared nothing was stolen.

Conspiracy theories were soon put forth on Reddit threads and the conspiracy site Whatdoesitmean.com that Rich was murdered for his involvement in the DNC e-mail dump of 2016, sending the e-mails to WikiLeaks to help damage Hillary's campaign from the inside. In an interview, Julian Assange helped the theory grow when he hinted their source could have been Rich (without confirming or denying) and offering a $20,000 reward for information on who killed him. Rich being assassinated by the Deep State DNC was too juicy a conspiracy not to share and was soon disseminated into the Internet by InfoWars and other famous conspiracists.

Roger Stone, who has promoted the Clinton Body Count theory since the '90s, shared the Seth Rich theory as being just the latest Clinton-sanctioned murder. Stone claimed that there was an attempted assassination on his own life in 2016, as he first reported on InfoWars, and later told CNN's Anderson Cooper in 2018 that he had been poisoned by radioactive polonium, which had left him "extremely ill" and caused lesions on his face. Soon after that he was "T-boned in a hit and run" that had been unsolved. Though he didn't mention his longtime enemies the Clintons, he said that "the Deep State moves in strange ways" and that the attempt on his life was meant to "frame the Russians."

The Seth Rich theories made their way into the mainstream, where they were covered by FOX News, promoted by Sean Hannity, among others.

FOX later issued a retraction, and Rich's family sued FOX (it was dismissed) and *The Washington Times* (who issued an apology) for their part in spreading the conspiracy theory. But the retractions were too late. Rich has entered into the mythology of conspiracy, and signs asking "Who killed Seth Rich?" with his photo are still spotted at rallies.

"OBSESSIVELY DELUSIONAL"

IF YOU DON'T THINK conspiracy theory affects you, consider a *Vice* article titled "People Tell Us How QAnon Destroyed Their Relationships," where writer Mack Lamoureux compiled stories of people who had lost their loved ones down the QAnon rabbit hole. Among the stories was a woman who described how her mother, who has bipolar disorder and PTSD, began obsessively watching QAnon YouTube videos, with the theories eventually causing a rift between the two, daughter avoiding mother and her constant QAnon talk. Another woman told of how her husband, whom she had been with for eight years, had gone from "Prince Charming, a super cool guy," to someone unrecognizable and frightening after he dived into the world of QAnon. After constant demands to watch QAnon videos, they split up.

In September 2019, the *Phoenix New Times* reported how Mesa Community College in Arizona fired professor Douglas Belmore after discovering he had shown a 14-minute-long QAnon video to his class. Students interviewed by the *New Times* said Belmore "spent a significant portion of their classes talking about QAnon and its relation to the mainstream media, pornography, and human trafficking," with one student saying Belmore's teachings were "just babbling, basically."

As conspiracy continues to grow in prevalence, expect more believers to try to slip topics like QAnon, Pizzagate, and Flat Earth into school curriculum as legitimate theories.

ON JUNE 15, 2018, traffic backed up for miles around the Hoover Dam when 30-year-old Matthew Phillip Wright of Henderson, Nevada, armed with a rifle, handgun, and flash-bang explosives, parked an armored truck across U.S. Highway 93 on a bridge over the Colorado River connecting Nevada and Arizona. Like Richard, he was a former Marine who was unemployed but had worked as a metal fabricator.

Wright faced down the angry traffic stuck as far as the eye could see for a 90-minute standoff. He was holding a sign that read "RELEASE THE OIG REPORT" inside the armored vehicle until police chased him into the desert and arrested him in Arizona.

The inspiration for his protest came from QAnon, and perhaps a level of burnout from Q's failed predictions. The report Wright's sign referred to was the unredacted Justice Department Office of Inspector General report, which examined the department's handling of the Hillary e-mail probe.

"No more lies. No more bullshit. We the people demand full disclosure," Wright said in a video message recorded inside his truck, appearing to address Trump. "We elected you to do a duty. You said you were going to lock certain people up when you were elected. You have yet to do that. Uphold your oath."

The OIG report was released the day before Wright's bridge protest. But to the disappointment of Q followers, it was not packed with the bombshells implicating Hillary and the rest of the Deep State in crimes that would lead to their collective arrest. Cognitive dissonance took over again, with Q followers scrutinizing perceived font discrepancies that they said were clear signs the report had been tampered with, and the real story was still hidden. That disclosure of a secret report is perhaps what Wright was protesting.

There is no evidence you can present to a conspiracy theorist—studies, photographs, eyewitnesses, statements—that cannot be dismissed as a Deep State forgery.

Wright was charged with several felonies, including terrorist acts, unlawful flight from authorities, carrying a weapon in the commission of a crime, and misconduct involving weapons.

From prison, he attempted to write President Trump, the FBI, CIA, and members of Nevada's congressional delegation. After finding out about the letters, a concerned judge raised Wright's bail from $25,000 to a million dollars.

The signature line on Wright's letters bore the QAnon motto: "Where we go one, we go all."

MORE DETAILS OF ANTHONY COMELLO, who managed to assassinate the boss of the Gambino crime family, emerged in Comello's first court appearance.

"Mr. Comello's support for 'QAnon' went beyond mere participation in a radical political organization," Anthony Comello's lawyer wrote in a court document, explaining his client's motivation for murdering Frank Cali. "It evolved into a delusional obsession."

Comello, after absorbing QAnon ideas, "became certain that he was enjoying the protection of President Trump himself, and that he had the president's full support." Like other QAnon followers, he believed a full orchestra of sinister forces—Democrats, Satanists, the mafia, were all gathered like the Legion of Supervillains at the same table. In the month leading up to shooting Cali, Comello had twice tried to place New York Mayor Bill de Blasio under citizen's arrest at the mayoral home in Manhattan. When that failed, he decided to enlist United States Marshals at Federal District Court in Manhattan to help him arrest Democratic Representatives Maxine Waters and Adam Schiff (both of whom have clashed with Trump) but "he was rebuffed."

Comello's next step in hunting down the Deep State was to drive to Cali's house, crashing his truck into his car. When Cali emerged from his home, Comello, who had brought handcuffs with him, told the mafia leader that he was placing him under citizen's arrest.

Cali was not receptive to Comello's demand, but as he reached toward his waistband for his gun, Comello grabbed a 9mm from his truck and shot him repeatedly, then took off. He was arrested three days later, and when he appeared in court, "he displayed symbols and phrases associated with QAnon scrawled on his hand in pen."

"After everything is known about the case, it's going to show that the hate that's spewed on the Internet by QAnon and other right-wing conspiracy websites have an effect," Comello's defense attorney, Robert Gottlieb, told the press. While Comello awaits trial, the facility he is being detained in is being kept a secret from the public, as the possibility of a revenge killing by another inmate makes him a "dead man walking." His family has also reportedly received threats.

DESPITE THE DISAPPOINTING RELEASE of the Mueller Report, which QAnon hoped would be the catalyst for the Storm, Q maintains a following that still believes that their time will come.

> Q3349 Mar 20 2019 13:45:07 (EST)
> Ask yourself a very simple Q.
> Would the FAKE NEWS media (& other controlled assets) expend this amount of time and resource attacking [attempt to discredit-cast as conspiracy- LARP] this movement IF IT DID NOT POSE A SIGNIFICANT THREAT [Danger]?
> YOU ATTACK THOSE WHO THREATEN YOU THE MOST.
> Logical thinking.
> Q

CHAPTER EIGHTEEN

THE JONES CHARACTER

The joy of Trump's victory began to be overshadowed for Alex Jones starting in 2017, when he found himself becoming overwhelmed by lawsuits from all directions. The first was a public and ugly custody battle between Jones and his ex-wife (they divorced in 2015), Kelly Jones, for their three children, aged 14, 12, and 9 (at the time of the lawsuit). Kelly characterized Alex as "unhappy, unwell," "emotionally abusive," and "not a stable person," pointing to his show as evidence.

"He says he wants to break Alec Baldwin's neck. He wants J. Lo to get raped," the ex-Mrs. Jones said. After Jones made threats about House Intelligence Committee member Adam Schiff, a California Democrat, Kelly testified, "I'm concerned he's engaged in felonious behavior, threatening a member of Congress," pointing out that he broadcasted from home, where his children are. Jones called Schiff a "fairy" and said he would "beat his goddamn ass."

She also pointed out his badgering of Bernie Sanders at LAX, bringing his son along for the ambush. Jones and his family were transferring planes to head to Hawaii on vacation when they spotted Sanders. Jones and son began to pursue him through the airport. Jones called Sanders "the living embodiment of communist and socialist evil" and accused him of "running away" from him as an aide stepped in and asked Jones if he planned to apologize to the Sandy Hook families.

Jones countered Kelly's accusations by trying to have her custody taken away. After a long, bitter (and strange) battle the parents were issued joint custody, granting Kelly the decision to determine where the children live, but giving Alex visitation rights.

The former Kelly Jones continued a public campaign against her former husband for a while, setting up sites like "Kelly Jones Custody Wars," before she decided to move on to focus on "raising awareness about domestic violence," according to her Twitter page.

The most insightful thing to come from the custody lawsuit was when Jones' lawyer, Randall Wilhite, tried to dismiss the evidence from his InfoWars appearances by making the argument that Alex Jones was a "performance artist" and that the person you saw on InfoWars was him "playing a character," kind of like a WWE wrestler.

I asked Dr. Daniel White about this revelation. Did conspiracy theorists believe what they were saying, or was it an act? Richard McCaslin was no doubt a true believer, as were others I had talked to, like 9/11 Truther Matt Naus. But what about someone like Alex Jones, who has obtained a net worth of $10 million from his conspiracy peddling?

"In some cases, I think they do genuinely believe what they are saying—and this goes back to the concept that they are simply people trying to make sense of the world and getting it wrong. But in others, I am not so sure, particularly in those with a formalized structure like the Flat Earthers or UFOs. After all, it isn't like those at the top of the pyramid are going to admit that they made it all up," Dr. White says.

"I remember going to a UFO 'exposed' talk in Sydney a few years back with a speaker who had spent two hours talking, at times pretty incoherently, about crystal councils, lizard people inside the moon and celestial brotherhoods. I realized he was on to a really sweet deal—here was someone who got to travel all around the world, talk about his (I assumed) fantasy world, and not only have people listen but also pay him very well to do so. At the time, I also thought, 'damn, I am so in the wrong business,'" Dr. White joked. "I suspect that to a certain level it is similar to cults in that it may very well start as an 'easy money' scam or even as a way to get attention, but over time they start to believe what they are saying; after all, they are surrounded by people who are agreeing with them all the time. Psychologically, it is also really hard to come back from something like that."

THE ALEX JONES PLOT

TO SOME CONSPIRACY THEORISTS, the "performance artist" angle about Jones was nothing new. For many years, conspiracies about Jones himself have been circulated. He's rumored to be a government sellout, an agent of the Deep State.

This became Richard McCaslin's belief after Alex Jones declined to offer support and denounced his Bohemian Grove raid. Richard began to find Internet rumors and allegations about his old inspiration, now part of Richard's ever-growing conspiracy.

"I recently came across Internet reports that Alex Jones might be a COINTELPRO agent provocateur for the FBI," Richard wrote me.

Here is more conspiracy theory muddiness: the Counter Intelligence Program, or COINTELPRO, did exist. It is now known that this FBI surveillance program illegally tapped an "enemies list" of "subversive organizations"—a wide range of leaders and members of groups that they somehow determined were a threat. This list included the Socialist Workers Party, members of the civil rights movement (including Martin Luther King and Malcolm X), the labor movement, and other groups working for social change. Part of the program also chased after white supremacists. These organizations were targeted to be disrupted, discredited, infiltrated, spied on, harassed, and sabotaged. The program came to light after the FBI had a lawsuit filed against them by the Socialist Workers Party and the Young Socialist Alliance in 1973.

Richard is not the only one who suspects that Alex Jones is a double agent. Matthew Naus, the Truther I met in Milwaukee, showed me several pictures of himself and other Truthers with Jones in his photo album, but then a disappointed look crossed his face—he's parted ways with many of the people he was pictured with. The reason is that he now believes that the 9/11 cover-up is also a cover-up.

Naus believes the Truthers were either a party to the 9/11 plot or naïve stooges.

"Basically what this all is, is a second cover-up of 9/11. The first one was so obvious that they had to have..." Naus searched for the word. "...a *place* for all these people who figured it out, so they planned this way before 9/11. They planned this!" He flipped a page and pointed to a picture of him posing with Alex Jones in Manhattan at a 9/11 protest.

"You know about this guy... he's dirty. He's an agent of disinformation!"

Some of Alex Jones' most vocal critics have been rival talk show hosts, dating back to his elder, Milton William Cooper, the author of the classic, *Behold a Pale Horse*. Cooper bashed Jones on his show *The Hour of the Time*.

"Alex Jones, you are a bold-faced, miserable, stinking little coward liar," Cooper said on one episode of his show when he found that he had been dissed on *The Alex Jones Show*. Cooper's rant was inspired because Jones had stated that he had to cut Cooper off on his show because of "the foul language he had used." Cooper ripped Jones as a "sensationalist bullshit artist" who spreads "lies and deception."

"Don't ever lie about me, buddy, because I will chop you off at your ankles, I will chew you up, I will spit you out for the lying, stinking, rotten little coward that you are," Cooper broadcasted angrily.

Jones' rival Glenn Beck has also used his show on TheBlaze to rip Jones, calling him a "madman" and a "really spooky guy."

"He thought I was a CIA operative who helped orchestrate the cover-up of 9/11... anything that anyone would say about me on conspiracy theory, it's Alex Jones," Beck said on *The Glenn Beck Program*. "And when they try to make me look like a conspiracy theorist, they always use his arguments and assign them to me. I'm not the FEMA camp guy. I'm not the Birther guy. I'm not the World Trade Center guy. That's not me; it's him."

QANON VS. INFOWARS

INFOWARS ACTIVELY PROMOTED QANON before reversing course to dismiss it.

"You know, I've been told by five different Pentagon sources, high-level, that the whole 8chan thing is real, and that they're basically forecasting what they'd like to see happen, and giving you information," Jones initially told his audience, also saying that author and InfoWars correspondent Jerome Corsi was given the task of following the QAnon story.

But a few months later, Jones said it was time to "stick a fork" in QAnon, starting a rivalry between InfoWars and QAnon.

Jack Posobiec, an InfoWars guest, tweeted on August 4, 2018: "To be clear: Q is not real. It is either a big joke that got out of hand or a deliberate disinformation campaign by bad actors to steer people away from what's really going on- or worse leading to a mass hysteria event."

An entire chapter of *QAnon: An Invitation to the Great Awakening* is titled: "The Fake MAGA Problem & The Day I Helped Q Make Alex Jones Cry." In it, contributing author Dustin Nemos wrote:

"He screwed us over when it came to Sandy Hook. He let us down when it came to Pizzagate. He made us look like crazy gun nuts when it came to the Piers Morgan debate, and it's a pattern, a trend. Q has called him out multiple times."

Q did post a message, referring to Jones as AJ, and suggesting he was an agent of the Israeli Mossad, apparently a recruit to spread misinformation. Q's drop read:

> Why are the majority of 'Q' attacks by "PRO MAGA" supporters coming from AJ [MOS backed] and/or AJ known associates?
> Why are we a threat to them?

THE BILL HICKS THEORY

ONE OF THE MORE OUTLANDISH Alex Jones conspiracies, and one that proves Jones can dish it out but can't take it, suggests that Jones is deceased comedian Bill Hicks. Richard referenced the theory in his final Phantom Patriot video, where the side of his Jones jack-in-the-box read "Hicks-in-a-box" with the word "Hicks" crossed out and replaced with "Jones."

The comedian died from pancreatic cancer in 1994 at the age of 32, just a few years before Jones began his media career... *or did he?* The Hicks-Jones theory suggests that Hicks faked his death, then went to work for the CIA under the Jones character as a COINTELPRO-style agent of disinformation. Besides the fact that both Hicks and Jones were intense on the microphone, lots of random facts patched together built on the theory—a production company that Hicks was involved with, Sacred Cow Productions, also has ties to Jones, and an absurd amount of effort has been put forth analyzing how similar the two men's teeth are.

The conclusion by conspiracists, according to a report by *Vice*, is that all it took was a little "plastic surgery, testosterone, growth hormone, larynx surgery, and cosmetics" for Hicks to start a new life as a COINTELPRO-funded pseudo-conspiracy theorist. The theory has proliferated enough that Jones is sometimes confronted and called Bill Hicks while out in public, to his great annoyance.

"Bill Hicks is in the ground, folks," Jones said on his show. "This isn't funny; this is sick."

A group of people who were also not finding conspiracy to be funny were the Sandy Hook parents. After years of harassment from Jones and his followers, they were ready to fight back.

SANDY HOOK LAWSUITS

IN 2018, THE FLOODGATE OF lawsuits against Jones opened. Sandy Hook families sued Jones and InfoWars for defamation for his claims that they were crisis actors. Three Sandy Hook families filed in April 2018, followed by six more families in August 2018.

"He knew his claims were false, but he made them anyway to further a simple but pathetic goal: to make money by tearing away at the families' pain. This lawsuit seeks to hold Alex Jones and his financial network accountable for those disgraceful actions," Josh Koskoff, one of the lawyers for the families, told the media.

After the lawsuits were filed, Jones was accused in court of destroying evidence, including pages and videos related to InfoWars' coverage of Sandy Hook.

"Mr. Jones chose to destroy the evidence of his actual malice and defamatory conduct," the Sandy Hook families' lawyers stated in a court filing.

YOGURT COMPANY CHOBANI SUED JONES in 2017 for claims on InfoWars that the company's owner, Hamdi Ulukaya, was linked to a sexual assault case involving refugee children in Twin Falls, Idaho, where the company is based.

Jones issued a public retraction, stating, "I regret that we mischaracterized Chobani."

More lawsuits followed. In 2018 there were claims of discrimination and sexual harassment according to complaints to the Equal Employment Opportunity

Commission from two former InfoWars employees. Another legal action was from Marcel Fontaine, who InfoWars had claimed was the shooter in the Marjory Douglas High School shooting in Parkland, Florida. InfoWars broadcast a photo of Fontaine, wearing "communist garb," a.k.a. a Karl Marx T-shirt, but Fontaine was not the shooter and had never stepped foot in Florida. Brennan Gilmore, a witness who caught the car attack on protestors in Charlottesville, which led to the death of one person and injuries to several more on video, also filed against InfoWars. Jones had called Gilmore a "shill" for the "deep state," which led to a harassment campaign against Brennan and his family, according to Gilmore's defamation suit.

Matt Furie, creator of a cartoon character named Pepe the Frog, which had been co-opted as an alt-right symbol, won a suit against InfoWars for using the image on a poster sold on their website. A settlement required InfoWars to pay Furie $14,000 as well as donate $1,000 to an amphibian conservation charity called Save the Frogs.

The Sandy Hook lawsuits continued. In September 2019, Jones lost an appeal to one of the defamation lawsuits by Sandy Hook father Neil Heslin and was ordered to "pay all costs" related to the legal effort.

Heslin's attorney stated, "After InfoWars wasted everyone's time on a frivolous appeal, we can now return to the trial court where we intend to hold Mr. Jones fully accountable for his disgusting defamation of Mr. Heslin."

With eight more families and other lawsuits amassing, Jones can expect to spend a lot of time over the next years in court, and the forecast for him doesn't look good.

JONES WASN'T THE ONLY ONE being sued for spreading Sandy Hook conspiracies. Lenny Pozner and his HONR organization brought a suit against authors of the book *Nobody Died at Sandy Hook*, winning a defamation suit against them in June 2019. Author James Fetzer "acted with actual malice," according to court documents. Wolfgang Halbig, the Sandy Hooker who fed InfoWars with his obsession, was named in the lawsuits against Jones.

In another matter, InfoWars contributor and Trump advisor Roger Stone also found himself in court. In January 2019, Stone's home in Fort Lauderdale, Florida was raided in the early morning hours by FBI agents, armed and wearing night-vision goggles and paramilitary gear, who arrested Stone. The Mueller investigation charged him with obstruction of an official proceeding, five counts of false statements, and one count of witness tampering, all for his involvement of trying to obtain information from WikiLeaks for the Trump campaign[9].

When Stone stepped out onto the courthouse stairs to give a press conference, members of the crowd turned a chant he helped popularize against him: "Lock him up! Lock him up! Lock him up!"

DAY OF THE LONG KNIVES

THE SANDY HOOK LAWSUITS also led to a mass purge of InfoWars off of social media platforms—Twitter, YouTube, Apple, Spotify, Facebook, LinkedIn, Periscope, and more sites all removed *The Alex Jones Show* and other InfoWars pages. Jones got hit in the wallet when PayPal removed him. InfoWars announced that they had a new platform on Roku, but they were kicked off the next day after Roku received backlash.

"It's over a hundred platforms now," Jones said in an interview, lamenting his treatment by social media companies. "They literally are engaging in trying to put me in a digital gulag, and again it's because I'm exposing them." Jones would say in several interviews that banning him would be a slippery slope to shut down other commentators, Trump supporters, and free political thought in general.

In May 2019, Facebook (and Instagram, owned by Facebook) banned several conspiracy theorists and extremists from their platform. It was dramatically called the "Day of the Long Knives," by those given the boot (a reference to the Night of the Long Knives, where Hitler purged the Nazi Party of political enemies).

InfoWars was hit hardest, with the entire brand removed, including any pages or groups set up to share the platform's content. Alex Jones and Paul Joseph Watson's pages were also erased. Other figures swept out included controversial commentator Milo Yiannopoulos, white nationalist and political candidate Paul Nehlen, Nation of Islam leader Louis Farrakhan, and political stuntwoman Laura Loomer.

---

9   Trump in 2016: "WikiLeaks, I love WikiLeaks" and "this WikiLeaks is like a treasure trove" and "Boy, I love reading those WikiLeaks." Trump in April 2019, after Julian Assange is arrested at the Ecuadorian Embassy in London: "I know nothing about WikiLeaks."

Loomer is a conspiracist and InfoWars guest that spreads theories that shootings and attempted bombings are Democrat false flags. She was banned from Lyft and Uber when she sent a tweetstorm in 2017 complaining that she couldn't find a non-Muslim driver. Loomer fixated on theories about Minnesota Representative Ilhan Omar, including disrupting one of Omar's campaign events. When Loomer tweeted anti-Muslim comments about Omar, she was removed from the platform, which led her to handcuff herself to Twitter headquarters in protest.

Other Loomer stunts (in which she says her victims have been "Loomered") included crashing a Shakespeare in the Park production of *Julius Caesar*, where the title character looked similar to Trump. "Stop the normalization of political violence against the right!" she shouted after the Trump-like Caesar was assassinated in the play. Loomer also convinced some Hispanic men she met at a Home Depot to climb over Nancy Pelosi's fence and set up a tent on her lawn as a protest against immigration, as well as ambushing other events. Besides Twitter and Facebook, she's been banned from sites like PayPal and GoFundMe, a move to shut her down, Loomer says, by the "left-wing terrorists and tech tyrants."

Trump stepped in to tweet his support for those that had lost their social media.

"So surprised to see Conservative thinkers like James Woods banned from Twitter and Paul Watson banned from Facebook!" Trump wrote, mentioning the curmudgeonly conservative actor and InfoWars editor, respectively, and going on to say in other tweets that his administration would be "looking into" the ban. "Social Media & Fake News Media, together with their partner, the Democrat Party, have no idea the problems they are causing for themselves. VERY UNFAIR!" Trump tweeted.

As a reaction to this de-platforming, Trump hosted a "social media summit" on July 11, 2019. Tech giants like Twitter and Facebook weren't invited, with the guest list instead bringing around two hundred conspiracy theorists, alt-right trolls, meme generators, and far-right writers to the White House. Those present at the summit included many that had promoted Pizzagate, QAnon, the Clinton Body Count, and other conspiracies. InfoWars was not asked to participate directly, but the winner of an InfoWars meme contest and other guests of the platform were there. Alt-right cartoonist Ben Garrison had his invitation rescinded after misogynistic and anti-Semitic cartoons surfaced. The "summit" turned out to not have a point except to allow Trump to air a meandering list of media bias and wrongs perpetrated against him to a "parallel universe of Internet figures and journalists" (as a *New York Times* correspondent Katie

Rogers described) for an hour. He gave praise to the room full of supporters, telling them:

"And some of you are extraordinary. I can't say everyone, but..." Trump said as the room erupted into laughter. "No, but some of you are extraordinary. The crap you think of is unbelievable. True. Unbelievable."

THE JONES DEPOSITION

KASTAR, LYNCH, FARRAR & BALL LLP, lawyers for the Sandy Hook families, had a videotaped deposition of Alex Jones, over three hours long, which they posted on YouTube on March 29, 2019. A great deal of it is Jones evading answers by claiming he can't remember what he said due to the large amount of programming he produced every week and an inability to comment on the short clips he's shown of himself ranting about the Sandy Hook conspiracy. First, Jones tried to blame the media and lawyers for keeping his Sandy Hook conspiracies in the spotlight.

"I am not the only person to question Sandy Hook. And I legitimately asked those questions because I had concerns. I resent the fact that the media and the corporate lawyers and the establishment, the Democratic Party, try to make this my identity, brought it out, constantly brought it out, tricked me into debating it with them so they could say I was injuring people and I see the parties that continue to bring this up and drag these families through the mud are the real villains," Jones explained to the camera. "I do not consider myself to be that villain, and I could have done better in hindsight. I've apologized for that, but I've seen the very same corporate media and lawyers continue to say that I'm saying all these things and exaggerating and using it against the First Amendment and I think that's very dangerous and despicable."

For most of the deposition, Jones seems aloof and sometimes confused. But toward the end of the questioning, the "Jones character" is back. He blames his compounding lawsuits on his long-running super villain, Hillary.

"I know full well that when Hillary Clinton lost the election, that's when all this started... I remember when you first did this lawsuit you were like 'all Jones needs to do is say he's sorry,' some parents said that," Jones rambled. "And I'm like 'I am sorry this is all out of context, and your kids died, and that was all ignored,' so I've seen the disingenuousness and the fact this all just cold-blooded fit because Hillary lost the election."

"Do you think I work for Hillary Clinton or something? Or George Soros?" the prosecuting lawyer laughed.

"I know this—when Hillary lost, the light switch went on, and I never got sued, I got sued a bunch."

And then perhaps realizing blaming Clinton or trying a "just playing a character" defense would not be gaining traction, Jones decided to try a new approach: to claim a form of "psychosis" was behind his ranting about the Sandy Hook crisis actors theory.

"Why is the mainstream media lying so much, why is the government lying so much, the fact that the public doesn't believe what they're told anymore... we've allowed the government institutions to become so corrupt that people have lost any compass of what's real. And I myself have almost had a form of psychosis in the past where I basically thought everything was staged even though I'm now learning a lot of things aren't staged."

"You said false things about Sandy Hook because of *psychosis*?" the lawyer snapped back. "Correct?"

"I'm just saying the trauma of the media and the corporations lying so much... you don't trust anything anymore. Kind of like a child whose parents lie to them over and over again, so they don't know what reality is," Jones concluded.

CHAPTER NINETEEN

FREE AT LAST

W hen I imagine Richard and his conspiracy thoughts, I visualize him standing in the streets of a post-apocalyptic New World Order America in his Phantom Patriot costume. In the distance is a massive black storm cloud, lightning flashing within it, rolling across the horizon, consuming everything in its path. Flying out of this behemoth cloud are rows of black helicopters, swooping over the war-torn streets below. Security cameras are mounted everywhere, hundreds of miles of wire, agents of disinformation in trenchcoats and sunglasses peek around corners. Above, chemtrails crisscross the sky.

The storm is always on the horizon, and there is no escaping it, but it never arrives.

As Richard's conspiracies began to network, they formed a "super-conspiracy" which ran to all corners of his life. He began to see intricate weavings of theories and symbolism everywhere.

I sometimes found Richard's ideas interesting or amusing, in their theatrical creativity, but also sad. His messages to me were almost always tense, depressed, frustrated, angry. The conspiracy web had led to him concluding that Stan Lee was a "Reptilian hybrid" and that Chely Wright was part of a government brainwashing program. Conspiracy crept up on him everywhere, to the point that existence itself was a Matrix-like lie.

"There is no God/gods outside ourselves. We and everything else in the multiverse are part of an infinite, eternal consciousness. Everything is energy, and we are sentient energy. The 'physical' universe, our bodies, and even our deaths are mind-programmed illusions," Richard wrote to me, sharing things he had learned from David Icke.

I HAD ANOTHER ARGUMENT with Richard after I returned home from my visit to him in Pahrump in 2015. I e-mailed him to tell him I was working on this book and planned on wrapping it up. He responded with a list of demands. Some were reasonable—he wanted a dozen copies of the book and a percentage of sales, which I would have worked out with him. Some items on his list—complete editorial control of the manuscript, reprinting his "My Memories of Chely Wright" document in its entirety—weren't going to fly, I told him. He blew up at me in an angry tirade, and we exchanged heated messages back and forth. He accused me of being a deceptive journalist, and I responded that I thought I was being more than fair to him. He came up with a plot where I was going to ask him to bankroll publishing this book, but I told him I was never going to ask him for money. After a few messages, still angry, he finally relented. "I'm OK with you doing the book yourself, as long as you don't slander me... I probably brought this grief on myself, because I broke my own rule: NEVER TRUST THE PRESS!!!"

We didn't communicate for a month, but things got back on track, and we talked more about the book in a positive light. We began to exchange e-mails regularly again—Richard would message me to update me on the video projects he was working on, and when he saw something suspicious on the news. He rarely took time to say hello to me before diving right into some evil plot, and I imagined this impending cloud of doom was taking a toll on Richard.

This time, my idea about him was right.

ON MARCH 27, 2019, I saw that I had a message from Richard's friend Lon Gowan. I hadn't spoken to him since interviewing him about four years earlier. The message from him was asking me to call as soon as I could. As soon as I saw it, I knew that something terrible had happened to Richard and I guessed he was either dead or had gone off the deep end for some reason and ended up back in prison. But then I remembered the interview I had done where we talked about prison and he said "they'd have to shoot me before I go back there."

I called Lon as soon as I could, and my first instinct was right. Lon told me that sometime in October 2018, Richard had loaded up his truck in Pahrump. His neighbor had seen him leave and assumed he was taking a trip to Las Vegas. But instead, Richard had driven to Washington, D.C., where he had taken his own life. Months later, the neighbor called in a missing persons report.

Even though Richard had left a will addressed to Lon, police determined that one of Richard's cousins was his next of kin. This cousin wasn't close to Richard, hadn't spoken to him in years and didn't know much about him. That was the reason five months had passed without anyone knowing he was dead. That was all the info Lon had at the moment, but he told me he would update me as more came in.

Somewhat at a loss for words, I thanked him and hung up. I was caught off-guard but not entirely surprised. Alone in the desert, he had not been able to find any employment, money was dwindling, and his attempts at creating a viral hit Phantom Patriot show hadn't been a success. I looked at my e-mail and found my last correspondence with Richard was in July 2018. He had e-mailed me, asking what I knew about an upcoming HOPE Real-Life Superhero meet-up in San Diego and we exchanged a couple of messages.

I felt guilt. Could I have kept Richard more engaged in life? Even though I didn't agree with him, could I have tried to help more with his projects? Maybe talked to him more or helped him build a support group of RLSH?

I think those things could have been done, but Richard had been descending this path for a long time, over 20 years.

That night, I slept fitfully. I had a dream about Richard still being alive. He knocked on my door, and I went out on my front porch to talk to him. I was surprised to see him alive. He had faked his death, he told me, then opened up a jacket he was wearing to reveal his chest was strapped with plastic explosives. He smiled and then laughed heartily and told me he was going to sneak into the Bohemian Grove and finally blow up the Great Owl of Bohemia.

I WOKE UP EARLY the next morning, brewed coffee, and flipped open my computer. The first thing I saw on Facebook was an article titled "Ranting, Raving Alex Jones Laughed Out Of A Texas Chicken Restaurant."

Alex Jones and his new wife were getting food at Lucy's Fried Chicken when a group of people began heckling him. An angry Jones turned on his camera and huffed and puffed his most tiresome lines, calling the group "libtards," telling one heckler "you're not an American, you're a slob," and saying they had "extra chromosomes."

"America is awake to anti-free speech like you and bullies like you!" he screamed. But here was the beautiful part—the group just jeered and laughed at him, and Jones looked like a crazy, ranting, disheveled clown.

Eventually Jones, after persistent but polite prompting by an employee, walked off in a cloud of anger to find fried chicken somewhere else.

"Bye! Bye, Alex, have a good night!" someone laughed and called after him. I was never happier to see Alex Jones fail.

LATER THAT DAY, IMPATIENT to learn more, I tried to see if I could shake down any paperwork on Richard's death. I contacted the coroner's office, who couldn't give me much info as I wasn't a family member, but they gave me a police report number, and after contacting the D.C. Metro police department, I got a Public Incident Report. The report notes that Richard died on October 15, 2018. Richard was found in his truck, parked in an alleyway off of 15th Street. I did a virtual tour of the block where he was found on Google Street View. It seemed like an average neighborhood, with some brick apartment buildings covered in ivy.

But then I noticed it, looming across the street and taking up most of the block: the House of the Temple. Built in 1915, the House of the Temple is headquarters for the Scottish Rite of Freemasonry, and Richard had protested in front of it during his 2011 Thoughtcrime tour. Freemason Brigadier General Albert Pike, author of *Morals and Dogma of the Ancient and Accepted Scottish Rite of Freemasonry* (1871), is buried in the Temple. It stands just about a mile north of the White House.

ABOVE: The Scottish Rite of Freemasonry's House of the Temple in Washington, D.C.
CREDIT: WIKIMEDIA COMMONS/AGNOSTICPREACHERSKID.

Was Richard's final act of protest to kill himself next to a Freemason headquarters? I tried to imagine what Richard's death would look like through his own eyes. Richard's last days are a mystery, and he was found shot in a truck across the street from the Freemason headquarters. Did Richard want it to look like a conspiracy? Would conspiracists say he was a victim of the Clinton Body Count or a CIA assassination? What if it *was* a conspiracy?

LON, MUCH LIKE HE DID after Richard's arrest in 2002, slowly began to unravel what had happened to Richard and began processing what he had left behind. In between his time spent on movie and TV show sets, he filed paperwork to get Richard's cremated remains from the D.C. morgue, saving them from a fate of being dumped in a numbered mass grave of the unclaimed. He dealt with the IRS and made sure insurance and taxes were paid on his property in Pahrump, and reviewed Richard's living will.

It took Lon a while to talk about the details of Richard's death. They were, as he noted, "horrific and gruesome," and I think he needed some time to process it.

Richard, as a felon, was not allowed to purchase firearms. He always considered himself "principled," as Lon noted, so he was unlikely to pursue finding a gun on the black market. As such, he purchased a captive bolt pistol, commonly called a "cattle gun," as his suicide weapon. A captive bolt gun fires a metal cylinder using compressed air in a forceful but shallow shot before the cylinder retracts. It was made famous as the weapon of choice for hitman Anton Chigurh in *No Country for Old Men.*

It isn't an effective way to commit suicide. In an incident report, a witness says they saw Richard's truck "at 10:30 a.m., and again 11:15 a.m." the morning of October 14 and police were called, so Richard must have shot himself sometime that morning. Police found he was "suffering from head trauma," and he was transported to a hospital. He was pronounced dead at 4:35 p.m. the next day, October 15, 2018, at least 30 hours after he was called in.

As he struggled and gasped for air, about a mile away the nation's most powerful conspiracy theorist was sitting in the White House, perhaps sipping a Diet Coke and watching FOX News.

And right around the same time Richard's truck was surrounded by police cars, a fire truck, and an ambulance, down in Austin, Texas, *The Alex Jones Show* was preparing to go on air. The show opened with a baritone narrator saying, "crashing through the lies and disinformation... it's Alex Jones!" Jones launched into the airwaves with his story of the day—the October 2 murder of Saudi Arabian journalist Jamal Khashoggi in Turkey. Within the first three minutes of the show, Jones had pinned the death as a "false flag" with ties to the "Deep State," including Barack Obama and Hillary Clinton.

"A very very clear picture has emerged that this is a false flag to basically draw Saudi Arabia in and then to basically destabilize Saudi Arabia and have a coup in the Saudi kingdom and put something far worse in, so this has Iran and Obama and of course Hillary written all over it, trying to kill the peace plans that Trump has been trying to develop," Jones rasped breathlessly into the mic.

Later in the show, he ranted about his de-platforming, including recently being kicked off PayPal, and compared himself to a "Jew in Nazi Germany, in a ghetto that can't buy or sell anything." He talked about George Soros and revisited a favorite topic—how bad Hillary Clinton must smell, saying he'd been told she has an odor like "like a rotting pile of corpses." He plugged a 50% off holiday sale on InfoWars supplements and at the end of the show Roger Stone dropped by to talk about Congressman Ted Deutch, who Stone says "pressured" Facebook into de-platforming InfoWars and was plotting to overthrow Nancy Pelosi.

October 14, according to InfoWars, was just another day in Conspiracy World America.

LON TOLD ME THAT in addition to his remains, he had filed paperwork to get Richard's other possessions he had with him when he died. Among them was a black three-ring binder that had been found next to Richard on the passenger seat of his truck. After Lon acquired it, he mailed it to me.

Richard's death hit me for a second time when I opened the package Lon sent me. I remembered the first manila envelope filled with letters and comics I had received from Richard in 2010. Here was Richard's determined handwriting again, capturing his last words in a document titled "Final Thoughts of an Extreme Altruist." There had been an effort in the RLSH community by some to separate themselves from the "superhero" label by referring to themselves as "Extreme Altruists" or "X-Alts." Richard's three-ring binder contained the document, followed by a variety of printouts of articles related to conspiracies, and a collection of photos from protests he had staged over the years.

Richard's final writing features 21 thoughts over five pages talking about his decision to kill himself and his legacy. His first point describes deteriorating health: "tinnitus/early-onset Alzheimer's, arthritis/joint erosion, restless leg syndrome, sciatica." He notes, "I don't want to spend my remaining years degenerating into a broken-down, bitter old hermit, living on pills." He also notes "toxic 5G Wi-Fi radiation" and states, "I don't want to live to see World War III and the completion of UN agendas 21 and 2030." Agenda 21 is a conspiracy favorite. It calls for voluntary efforts for governments to work on ways to combat poverty and pollution and other actions to make the world sustainable. But theorists say the agenda is a Trojan horse for globalism and a New World Order. Agenda 2030 is a similar list of goals toward sustainability to reach by the year 2030.

Point five of Richard's document reads: "Everyone leaves this life, eventually. I am simply choosing the time, place, and circumstances. My passing, during this divisive time in history, will be meaningful."

He addresses the location of his suicide briefly: "I want the last thing I do, in this life, to be an act of defiance against the corrupt, Masonic Establishment." His truck was decked out with protest signs, designed to be an eye-catching last stand. A large sign in the bed of his vehicle read: "Warning! Albert Pike's 1871 Illuminati plan called for... Terrorism, 3 World Wars, Luciferian Religion, Global Dictatorship." A sign in the driver's window read: "When fascism comes to America it will be wrapped in the flag and carrying a cross — Sinclair Lewis. IT CAN HAPPEN HERE!"

Other points in his document ponder religion: "I realize that we are all unique aspects of the Infinite Consciousness... the true Supreme Being. We are all eternal spirits, having a temporary, human experience," Richard wrote.

Statements 10 through 14 "condemn" or "call out" several people, including the "equally corrupt Democrat and Republican parties," and states "America is now a failing democracy; well on its way to becoming a globalist/socialist police state."

"I condemn the ruling blue blood 'elite' of this world whether their names are Rothschild, Rockefeller, Soros, Netanyahu, Bush, Cheney, Gore, Obama, Biden, Trump, Pence, May, Blair, Cameron, Putin, or Pope Francis... among others." Richard also calls out mainstream media and then zeroes in on conspiracy theory:

(13) I call out Bill Hicks a.k.a. "Alex Jones" (who I met in 2001) as a false patriot and controlled opposition. Despite reporting a distorted version of the truth, his divisive act has led many, genuine truthseekers astray.

(14) Federal psy-op YouTube channels, like QAnon, Project Veritas, etc., function in a similar way to Bill Hicks/Alex Jones. They also trick people into trusting some mythical "white hat patriots" and Trump (a sociopathic Illuminati billionaire, who is bloodline cousins with Hillary and has committed incest with Ivanka) to "drain the swamp." Here's some advice, America... liberate yourselves!

Richard added points noting his appreciation for David Icke for "his efforts to reveal the true nature of reality" and "his few friends that remain," listing 11 people, including Lon, the guys from Las Vegas Motion Pictures who produced his videos, a couple of his neighbors, the guys who worked at the comic shop he got his weekly comic books from, and Denny Mozena (his former teenage sidekick, Iron Claw). I was on the list, too.

Points 17 to 19 express his regrets and disappointment. He mentions the Chely Wright country music Project Monarch theory and that despite his protest attempts, "the Las Vegas media and authorities continue to lie about the October 1, 2017, false flag attack," Richard wrote, referring to the deadliest mass shooting in our history. Stephen Paddock shot concertgoers from the 32nd floor of the Mandalay Bay Hotel, killing 58 and wounding over four hundred more. Richard had ridden his Phantom-Cycle around the hotel several times, protesting. Richard also reflects on his failed attempt at the Bohemian Grove:

"Perhaps things would have turned out differently if the idiots in my jury had taken me seriously and Judge Elliott Lee Daum and prosecutor Charles Arden hadn't been tools of the Bohemian Club."

His last point reads:

"(21) I truly hope that my struggle against the New World Order will inspire people to take back their freedom from the political, religious, and corporate 'snakes,' who stole it from them."

LON REPORTED THAT RICHARD, in death, did a last act of helping others. Being an organ donor was not the type of superheroics Richard had envisioned, but it helped save the lives of five people.

"Each of his lungs, his kidneys, and his liver were all viable and a match for five recipients. At last update, all recipients were doing great and had a wonderful

Christmas with their families," Lon informed an e-mail group of people Richard had listed as friends.

On November 12, 2019, I voyaged back to Pahrump to say goodbye to Richard. I flew into Las Vegas late the night before. As I walked sleepily through the terminal, the flashing slot machines reminded me of my 2015 trip to Nevada, where I was met by Richard leaning against the airport wall in his "Where the Heck is Pahrump?" shirt.

THE NEXT MORNING, Walter Marin and Mitch Teich of Las Vegas Motion Pictures, the company Richard hired to do his video production work, picked me up from my hotel. While I waited for them, I watched CNN, or as Trump might call the outlet, "fake news" and "the enemy of the people." Trump's impeachment inquiry hearings were about to get underway, and as I traveled, I spent my downtime watching it unfold.

After I got picked up by Walter and Mitch, we made the trip to Richard's house through the desolate terrain of Nevada. It was a strange feeling driving this route, a path I never thought I'd be revisiting. We passed the "Welcome to Pahrump" sign (now forever linked in my mind with the "Welcome to Dark Side Hee Haw" vandalism). We cruised by the fireworks stores, casinos, and fast food joints until we arrived at Richard's home. The yard was littered with dried-out tumbleweeds and other wilted plants, but his property looked to be in good shape despite being abandoned for a little over a year. Lon was already there, looking through a file of paperwork he had found in Richard's closet. Two of Richard's neighbors were there, too. They had been keeping an eye on his property as best they could. Someone had recently broken into the house through the back door, stealing Richard's TVs and a couple shelves of his prized comic book collection.

There was not much else of value to steal. Richard's bedroom had just his bed, neatly made, and an AM/FM alarm clock next to it. His closet had a pair of pants and two shirts hanging in it. There were no other clothes; he had perhaps donated those along with other household items before leaving for D.C.

His living room had his couch, a TV stand with a dust outline of where his stolen TV once stood. On his coffee table was a small photo album full of pictures of himself posing in his various superhero costumes, and next to it was a note he had handwritten:

"I could have committed suicide in the comfort and privacy of my own home. Instead, I chose to drive to Washington DC, warn the American people one last time, and die with honor."

Another small room had some costumes he had made for his videos, a box full of *The Stardust and Fantomah Show* DVDs, art supplies, and a couple of unfinished scripts. One appeared to be a script for a dramatization of part of his life titled "Bohemian Grove Reenactment." The other incomplete text was a start to a second episode of *The Stardust and Fantomah Show*. Next to the scripts was another short note, addressed to the people involved in his video productions: "If I were to choose a known actor to portray me in a movie, it would be Sam Worthington (*Avatar, Wrath of the Titans*)."

Another room contained his remaining comic book collection and a stack of books by David Icke and other conspiracy tomes, but other than that, the house was empty.

We headed into The Outpost next. Things were neat and orderly inside. G'nik sat silently on one side of The Outpost, staring silently at the row of mannequins lined up across from him. The exercise equipment and his crossbow target with the Reptilian mask on it were still there, along with his empty meeting table and his Patriot-Cycle, parked in a corner with a sign on top of it that read: "Politicians Are Really Parasites Who Live On Our Taxes!"

"I thought you might want to see this," Lon said, pointing out a black plastic case resting on a crate to me. I looked at it, puzzled, then flipped it open. There was a foam insert that had a bottle brush and a small bottle of oil. I squinted in the shadows (the electricity had been shut off, but the bright desert sun poured through the door) and unfolded a yellow copy of a receipt.

"Oh damn," I said, recoiling slightly. I looked back down at the case. There was a large chunk of space where a bolt pistol used to be.

RICHARD'S NEIGHBORS, LON, WALTER, MITCH, and I gathered in Richard's backyard. Lon, after a lot of time and paperwork, had acquired Richard's cremated remains. We took turns spreading them by the roots of a tree in his yard near his bedroom window. His neighbor, with a tear in her eye, told us it was a good place for Richard to rest because a flock of mourning doves liked to congregate in the tree. She had painted some rocks with the American flag on them and placed them on the ground next to it. She recalled what a friendly neighbor Richard was. She laughed and told us that when her female friends would visit, they would peek out the window at Richard doing yardwork shirtless, like schoolgirls, admiring what good shape he was in. She could count on him going for a run every morning, but when she stopped seeing him on his daily routine, she suspected something was wrong with him.

Lon said a few words, and his ashes were spread. We were silent for a moment, then headed back into his house. We talked for a bit, and then I headed back to Las Vegas with Walter and Mitch. As they spoke of video production, I stared out the window at the rocky desert and mesas passing by as we left Pahrump.

To many who encountered him, Richard was just a guy in a wacky costume on the Vegas strip, holding a sign that accused Obama of being a Reptilian. But I saw his life in whole—Richard as a boy trying to escape into a comic book he was reading while his dad screamed at his mom about bills, a puffy-haired evangelist on the TV in the background, proclaiming that Jesus could gift you money if you prayed hard enough. I see Richard, heartbroken and afraid of dying as he joins the Marines. I feel his excitement as he pursues his American dream of being a Hollywood action star and signs up for stunt school. My thoughts cloud as I think of those terrible years where his parents died and his life fell apart with nothing to lean on but the words of Alex Jones.

I thought of Richard's final costume, a shirt he had made that he wore when he committed suicide. He had placed a photo of it in the binder he left behind, the last photo in the book. It was a striped prison shirt, like his Thoughtcrime outfit, and in the style of the Phantom Patriot, it had a red Republican R on one shoulder, and a blue Democrat D on the other, both struck out.

On the chest of the shirt, in red, white, and blue letters are the words: FREE AT LAST.

The phrase was also found in one of the last points of Richard's "Final Thoughts" document:

"(20) The ancients Gnostics believed that the body was a prison for the spirit. With the death of my body, my pronoia (true self) is now FREE AT LAST!

I look forward to leaving this Archon-controlled virtual reality and finding a better existence beyond the Ouroboros, in the Upper Aeons."

Richard is referring to terms from Gnosticism here—the Archons are demons who rule the universe. The Ouroboros is the ancient symbol of a serpent or dragon eating its tail, which symbolizes eternity and the soul of the world. The Upper Aeons are described as a pure and luminous realm, a place full of divine potential and ideals.

I hope that Richard traveled there peacefully.

WHAT IF...?

I n 2019, I saw the phantom of Richard McCaslin frequently. A group of dozens of Anti-vaxxers showed up at the 2019 San Diego ComicCon, protesting in the style of Anonymous, wearing matching costumes of the character V from *V for Vendetta*. They held signs that read "Vaccines are Made from Aborted Fetal Cells" and "Vaccines Can Cause Injury and Death." I wondered what Richard would have thought of these comic-book-style conspiracists. He might have joined them, but then again might have dismissed them as a George Soros-backed group of infiltrators.

The viral "Storm Area 51, They Can't Stop All of Us" event may have started as a joke, but at its heart, it shared Richard's belief that the government is hiding something that needs to be exposed. About three thousand people showed up to the area for the September 20, 2019 "Alienstock" events, but only approximately one hundred made their way to protest outside the gates with goofy signs and alien costumes. A couple of people were detained for alcohol and public urination charges, and one for trying to sneak past the gates.

I think Richard probably would have driven out there to meet these people and try to rally them to his cause. Maybe he would have inspired a viral "Raid Bohemian Grove" page.

On August 10, 2019, wealthy financier and sex offender Jeffrey Epstein was found dead in his jail cell after committing suicide. Within minutes of his death being reported, I watched in disbelief as my social media feeds flooded with conspiracy theories (I was surprised to see quite a few of my friends sharing them). They ranged from the plausible—Epstein had paid off guards to look the other way while he killed himself—to the outlandish, like Epstein's body being replaced by a dead homeless man while he escaped on a private jet to the Middle East to get plastic reconstructive surgery on his face.

These ideas weren't being parroted from Alex Jones or Donald Trump (though both would join in before the day was over) but were being put forth from people's own natural conspiracy instincts.

Richard certainly would have had something to say about the death of Epstein, and I think he would have found a certain level of vindication. Here was the corrupt force Richard had waged war against: a rich and powerful pedophile with ties to the royal family, Bill Clinton, Donald Trump, and other influential people. He entertained at his tropical island—Little Saint James in the Virgin Islands, nicknamed by locals as "Pedophile Island."

The Alex Jones Show opened the day of Epstein's death with Jones saying that the news was "causing a Matrix-level awakening, the man-behind-the-curtain awakening, we're going to break down why it's captivating, why it's flipping the paradigm so massively."

Jones flatly dismissed theories Epstein had made a getaway.

"Dead men tell no tales, ladies and gentlemen," Jones croaked. "This is also a message to everyone else to keep their mouths shut and to absolutely understand that the Clintons and the evil spider globalist system that hides behind them is ready to kill anybody and everybody they need to."

A guest host on the show that day, Tom Pappert, talked about drone video footage that had been captured on Epstein's island in 2014.

"You've seen these disturbing images of the island itself. You got what appears to be Moloch the Owl, a popular scene from Bohemian Grove, and you can check out the old InfoWars documentary where Alex Jones got that on tape... we know it's got this bizarre temple," Pappert reported, referring to something strange found in the drone footage—a small temple-like building (though it could also be an observatory or a gaudy beach house) on top of the highest point of the island. It has a dome flanked by two large gold owl statues[10].

---

10 New July 2019 drone footage showed that the gold dome and owls on the "temple" were gone and that the building appeared to be filled with ladders and buckets of paint.

Here was the sinister place Richard had visualized in the Bohemian Grove, an island of pedophilia and owl worship.

All of these stories led me to think Richard was perhaps ahead of his time. When I first started corresponding with him it was easy to dismiss his ideas as coming from a lone eccentric. But when the President of the United States is retweeting a post that suggests Epstein was murdered as part of the Clinton Body Count, and hosting conspiracy theorists in a social media summit, I have to think that Richard is a zeitgeist. He is someone who attempted to soar into the American dream like Superman, but instead belly-flopped into the rabbit hole of an American nightmare.

THERE'S A CLASSIC MARVEL comic book series titled *What If...?* that first premiered in 1977. The series imagined an alternate-reality Marvel Universe. Richard had probably read them. Typical storylines imagined *What if* Spider-Man had joined the Fantastic Four? or *What if* Doctor Doom had become a hero?

Richard's brain was stuck in a pretty constant *What If...?* mode, and I can't help but think that way myself about him. *What if* the chain of events in Richard's life had been just slightly different? Would he still be alive?

When I interviewed the attorney from his case, Jeff Mitchell, he said he also thought it was a string of small moments that altered Richard's path that led him to the Bohemian Grove, Soledad, and, I would add, eventually led to his suicide.

"Had he not inherited the amount of money he did, he wouldn't have the money to do any of this," Mitchell said. "And then he said in his interviews that if he had a relationship, had kids, wasn't alone, he wouldn't have done this. And if he wouldn't have stumbled on that Alex Jones tape he never would have gone down this path, so along the road, there's these certain points, if any of those things had not happened, he wouldn't have done it."

Who is to blame for Richard's downward spiral into madness? Alex Jones? David Icke? His parents? Or is it a failure of the American dream in general?

Whatever the cause, conspiracy theory killed Richard. It entered his life at a point when he was weak with emotional devastation. His belief in material put forward by Alex Jones caused his raid of the Bohemian Grove. Six years of prison and three years of parole followed. When he was "free," he was viewed by society not as someone who was misguidedly trying to save the lives of children, but merely as a five-time felony arsonist who had engaged police officers in an armed standoff. He couldn't find employment. His conspiracy paranoia made it challenging to establish relationships, and so he isolated himself out in the desert.

I considered Richard to be a friend. My goal was to be objective, and I think I have been in examining his life. But he was someone I met and corresponded with for eight years and journeyed through part of my life with. Although I almost never agreed with his assessment, I miss hearing his interpretation of world events.

CONSPIRACY BELIEF IS NOT always wrong, and when I interviewed Dr. Daniel White, he said that there are times when these beliefs can even be healthy. It's an act of self-preservation.

"Healthy skepticism is important—questioning how and why things are the way they are is the only way that we progress, or any new discoveries are made. However, I would say that the skepticism needs to be partnered with the tools needed to discover the 'truth' and a strong dose of self-doubt and self-reflection—a willingness to step back and go 'hang on, have I got this completely wrong?'" Dr. White explained. "I would say that is also the line dividing truth seekers from conspiracy theorists—both are questioning and willing to challenge the status quo to find out what is going on, but one has both the tools needed to find the truth and the willingness to accept that they might be wrong."

It's impossible to stop people like Richard, Maddison Welch (the Pizzagate raider), the QAnon fanatics, and other people who have made dangerous plans to wrong conspiracy rights. Better education and not giving legitimacy to theories with no factual basis like Flat Earth and QAnon in classrooms might help prevent future cases, as well as better mental health care systems and support networks. But I'm confident in saying we will see the Richard McCaslin story repeat over and over with people pushed over the edge by conspiracy ideas.

I believe the First Amendment must be protected, but if you engage in libel or slander by telling people they are crisis actors and that their murdered children never existed, you should be sued, and that private companies have the right to decide to drop you from their platforms for violating their terms of agreement.

I BECAME OBSESSED WITH working on this book. It was a story about Richard McCaslin, a comic book artist, former Marine, stuntman, traveler, protestor, and conspiracy theorist, but there was also the story of the dark American underbelly that somehow affects us all.

There were periods where I hardly left the house for days on end, as I kept the coffee rolling, sitting at my desk in my pajamas, poring over old letters and e-mails from Richard, reading conspiracy manifestos and articles on case studies, and scouring the depths of the Internet for missing bits of info. It was draining and took a mental toll on me. I was becoming as bugged out as anyone you read about in these pages.

I guess if we're asking what ifs, by the way, and to give the benefit of the doubt to Richard one last time, we should also offer this possibility... *what if*... Richard was right about all of it? The Bohemian Grove, the Masons, the false flags, the Reptilians, the brainwashing programs? What if I'm wrong and it was all true?

You know what? I think it's finally time for me to climb out of the rabbit hole and get out of here.

ACKNOWLEDGEMENTS

So many people to thank in the web of my life.

First and foremost, this book is dedicated to Richard. All he wanted was for someone to tell his story. I think there are parts of this book he would take issue with, and I would probably have gotten a long, angry e-mail. But ultimately, I think he would be glad that someone finally told his story.

Lon Gowan was incredibly helpful in getting me material. He is extremely kind and really proves that we don't always choose our friends, but that we should try to be a good friend regardless. Other people who gave me insight and were helpful in piecing this story together include Jeff Mitchell, Matthew Naus, Mary Moore, Philip Weiss, Walter Marin, Dr. Daniel White, Denny Mozena, and my friends in the RLSH community, especially Rock n Roll and Night Bug of the California Initiative, Razorhawk, and Motor-Mouth.

Les Claypool, I love your music and I hope I didn't freak you out. To Chely Wright, I'm sorry this got dragged out, but I had to follow the story wherever it went.

My family and my friends who have been supportive of me and this project in particular, I appreciate it. Thanks to J. Jason Groschopf, David Beyer, Tim Demeter, Jan Christensen, Lee Gutowski, Paul Kjelland, Andrew Kjelland, Stephen Anderson, Allison Jornlin, Mike Huberty and Wendy Staats.

A huge thank you to Jessica Parfrey and Christina Ward of Feral House, who put in a lot of hard work to help this book reach its full potential.

And last, to Kate. This poor woman has listened to me ramble on about Reptilians and JFK and Flat Earth repeatedly and has taken it in stride. Thanks, Kate.

GENERAL

My sources of information about Richard McCaslin came from handwritten letters, e-mails, and in-person interviews between October 2, 2010 and the last e-mail I got from him July 18, 2018, as well as accounts he wrote. I also reviewed court transcripts of his trial and other legal documents, and received 172 pages of documents from a Freedom of Information Act request from the United States Secret Service.

THE RABBIT HOLE

Krulos, Tea. *Heroes in the Night: Inside the Real Life Superhero Movement*. Chicago Review Press, 2013.

The Matrix (film, 1999), directed by The Wachowskis.

INTO THE GROVE

Dark Secrets: Inside Bohemian Grove (film, 2000), directed by Alex Jones.

Finn, Maria. "Insider's Guide to San Francisco," *The Wall Street Journal*, October 9, 2010. Accessed here: www.wsj.com/articles/SB1000142 4052748704631504575532063842966330

Garnett, Porter. *The Bohemian Jinks: A Treatise*, published by the Bohemian Club, 1908. Accessed here: books.google.com/books/about/ The_Bohemian_Jinks.html?id=KTBIAAAAIAAJ

Van der Zee, John. *The Greatest Men's Party on Earth: Inside the Bohemian Grove*, Harcourt Brace Jovanovich, 1974.

Domhoff, G. William. *The Bohemian Grove and Other Retreats: A Study in Ruling-Class Cohesiveness*, Harper & Row, 1974.

Flock, Elizabeth. "Bohemian Grove: Where the rich and powerful go to misbehave," *The Washington Post*, June 15, 2011. Accessed here: www.washingtonpost.com/blogs/blogpost/ post/bohemian-grove-where-the-rich-and- powerful-go-to-misbehave/2011/06/15/ AGPV1sVH_blog.html?utm_term=.5560c8d081fb

Kramer, Larry. "Bohemian Grove—Where Big Shots Go to Camp," *The New York Times*, August 14, 1977. Accessed here: www.nytimes. com/1977/08/14/archives/bohemian-grove- where-big-shots-go-to-camp.html

Warren, James. "Nixon on Tape Expounds on Welfare and Homosexuality," *Chicago Tribune*, November 7, 1999. Accessed here: www.chicagotribune.com/news/ct-xpm-1999- 11-07-9911070165-story.html

Rothkopf, David. *Superclass: The Global Power Elite and the World They are Making*, Farrar, Straus and Giroux, 2009.

Wikipedia entry "List of Grove Plays," accessed here: en.wikipedia.org/wiki/List_of_Grove_Plays

Kovner, Guy. "Retired Gen. Stanley McChrystal, Conan O'Brien highlight secretive Bohemian Grove gathering," The *Press Democrat*, July 12, 2013. Accessed here: www.pressdemocrat.com/ news/2209308-181/retired-gen-stanley- mcchrystal-conan?sba=AAS

Rosellini, Lynn. "The Call of the Camp," *The New York Times*, July 19, 1982. Accessed here: www. nytimes.com/1982/07/19/us/the-call-of-the- camp.html

Mary Moore, interview with the author, December 21, 2012.

Weiss, Philip. "Masters of the Universe Go To Camp: Inside the Bohemian Grove," *Spy* Magazine, November 1989. Accessed here: www. scribd.com/ document/101806446/Weiss-Philip-Masters- of-the-Universe-Go-to-Camp-Inside-the- Bohemian-Grove-Spy-Magazine-Nov-1989- Pp-58-76

Philip Weiss, interview with the author, January 10, 2013.

Clogher, Rick. "Bohemian Grove: Inside the Secret Retreat of the Power Elite," *Mother Jones*, August 1981. Accessed here: www.scribd. com/doc/101807583/Clogher-Rick-Bohemian- Grove-Inside-the-Secret-Retreat-of-the-Power- Elite-Mother-Jones-Aug-1981

"Bohemian Grove: The Story *People* Magazine Censored," projectcensored.org, July 12, 2015. Accessed here: www.projectcensored.org/17- bohemian-grove-the-story-people-magazine- censored/

Shoumatoff, Alex. "Bohemian Tragedy," *Vanity Fair*, May 2009. Accessed here: www.vanityfair. com/culture/2009/05/bohemian-grove200905 *Brad Meltzer's Decoded*, season one, episode nine, "Secret Societies," aired January 27, 2011.

SUPERHERO-IN-TRAINING

"Retirement Living in Zanesville-Muskingum County-Ohio," best-place-to-retire.com, accessed June 6, 2019 here: www.best-place-to-retire.com/retire-in-zanesville-muskingum-county-oh

Richard sent me photocopied pages of his appearances in the letter pages of *X* #14 (Dark Horse Comics, May 1995), *Night Man* #17 (Malibu Comics, February 1995), and *Madman Comics* #7 (Dark Horse Comics, May 1995).

"All dressed up with no place to go: Casualties of the fifth annual Wizard Halloween Costume Contest," *Wizard* #63, November 1996.

Denny Mozena, interview with the author, January 5, 2013.

Martinez, Al. "NY Times on Kim Kahana," reprint of a February 4, 1982 article, accessed here: www.kahanastuntschool.com/nytimes.pdf

Martinez, Al. "He is a tiger dozing in the sun now, a predator at peace with the jungle: A Smile on the Face of a Tiger," *Los Angeles Times*, January 14, 1985.

Kim Kahana, interview with the author, February 22, 2013.

Lon Gowan, interview with the author, July 13, 2015.

Marines barrack roommate "John Smith," interview with the author, June 30, 2015.

WHO SHOT JFK?

I attended the 7th Annual JFK Assassination Conference and visited the Sixth Floor Museum November 20–23, 2019.

deHaven-Smith, Lance. *Conspiracy Theory in America*, University of Texas Press, 2014.

Marks, John D. *The Search for the "Manchurian Candidate": The CIA and Mind Control: The Secret History of the Behavioral Sciences*, W.W. Norton & Company, revised edition, 1991.

Gentry, Margaret. "'Umbrella Man' Theory Destroyed," *The Times-News*, September 26, 1978. Accessed here: news.google.com/newspapers?id=pmdPAAAAIBAJ&sjid=cyQEAAAAIBAJ&pg=6975%2C3133954

Marrs, Jim. *Crossfire: The Plot that Killed Kennedy*, Basic Books, revised edition, 2013.

Jacobson, Mark. *Pale Horse Rider: William Cooper, the Rise of Conspiracy, and the Fall of Trust in America*, Blue Rider Press, 2018.

Schutze, Jim. "Dallas Has Now Lost 82 Cases Against Robert Groden. Somebody Call Guinness," *Dallas Observer*, September 8, 2016.

Schutze, Jim. "For JFK Conspiracy Wedding, Reception at Campisi's, Where Else?", *Dallas Observer*, November 20, 2019.

Vary Baker, Judyth. *Me & Lee: How I Came to Know, Love and Lose Lee Harvey Oswald*, TrineDay, 2011.

638 Ways to Kill Castro (film, 2007), directed by Dollan Cannell.

McAdams, John. *JFK Assassination Logic: How to Think About Claims of Conspiracy*, University of Nebraska Press, 2014.

ALEX FUCKING JONES

Zaitchik, Alexander. "Meet Alex Jones," *Rolling Stone*, March 2, 2011.

Kyanka, Richard "Low Tax." "Silencing Alex Jones is a Threat to America's Freedom and Democracy!!!" SomethingAwful, August 7, 2018, accessed here: www.somethingawful.com/news/alex-jones/

Ronson, Jon. *Them: Adventures with Extremists*, Simon & Schuster, reprint, 2003.

Dark Secrets: Inside Bohemian Grove (film, 2000), directed by Alex Jones.

Mary Moore, interview with the author, December 21, 2012.

Philip Weiss, interview with the author, January 10, 2013.

McCaslin, Richard. *Phantom Patriot* booklet #1, self-published, August 2001.

TRUTHERS

Matthew Naus, author interview, December 7, 2012.

Walker, Hunter. "Conspiracy Theorist Jeff Boss Launches Mayoral Bid," observer.com, December 26, 2012.

Loose Change 9/11 (film, 2015), directed by Dylan Avery.

Wood, Judy. *Where Did the Towers Go? Evidence of Directed Free-Energy Technology on 9/11*, self-published, 2010.

BURN THE OWL

McCaslin, Richard. *Prison Penned Comics*, self-published, 2008.

The Order of Death (film, 2005), directed by Alex Jones.

MTV News Staff. "Country Beat: Chely Wright, Jim Reeves, Bellamy Brothers..." MTV.com, June 13, 2001. Accessed here: www.mtv.com/news/1444472/country-beat-chely-wright-jim-reeves-bellamy-brothers/

Wright, Chely. *Like Me: Confessions of a Heartland Country Singer*, Pantheon, 2010.

Jeff Mitchell, interview with the author, January 29, 2016.

THE PEOPLE VS RICHARD McCASLIN

Jeff Mitchell, interview with the author, January 29, 2016.

Les Claypool, interview with the author, January 14, 2016.

"Bohemian Grove Secrets and Stories Told by Bob Weir," YouTube video, September 12, 2012, accessed here: www.youtube.com/watch?v=J0UMENa_IAg

Shady, Bethany. "Harry Shearer," *Tastes Like Chicken*, accessed June 25, 2019 here: www.tlchicken.com/article.php?ARTid=53

The *Teddy Bears' Picnic* reviews were pulled from Rotten Tomatoes: www.rottentomatoes.com/m/1113733_teddy_bears_picnic

Vega, Cecilia M. "Bohemian Grove conducting own probe of break-in," The *Press Democrat*, February 1, 2002.

McCaslin, Richard. *Prison Penned Comics*, self-published, 2008.

Joseph Krukowski, interview with the author, via handwritten letters exchanged 2015–2016.

IT'S CALLED ART THERAPY!

McCaslin, Richard. *Prison Penned Comics*, self-published, 2019.

Dr. Daniel White, author interview, May 9, 2019.

Chapman University. "What do Americans fear? Chapman University's 3rd Annual Survey of American fears released," eurekaalert.org, October 12, 2016, accessed here: www.eurekalert.org/pub_releases/2016-10/cu-wda101216.php

Monmouth University. "Public Troubled by 'Deep State,'" monmouth.edu, March 19, 2018, accessed here: www.monmouth.edu/polling-institute/reports/monmouthpoll_us_031918/

Hamblin, James. "The Most Dangerous Way to Lose Yourself," *The Atlantic*, September 25, 2019.

REPTOID ROYALTY

Krulos, Tea. *Monster Hunters: On the Trail with Ghost Hunters, Bigfooters, Ufologists, and Other Paranormal Investigators*, Chicago Review Press, 2015.

Icke, David. *Children of the Matrix: How an Interdimensional Race Has Controlled the Planet for Thousands of Years—And Still Does*, Bridge of Love, 2001.

Conspiracy Theory with Jesse Ventura, "Reptilian," season 3, episode 1, originally aired November 7, 2012.

Flanigan, Jake. "How YouTube Became a Breeding Ground for a Diabolical Lizard Cult," *The New Republic*, June 3, 2019. Accessed here: newrepublic.com/article/154012/youtube-became-breeding-ground-diabolical-lizard-cult

THE THOUGHTCRIME TOUR

Richard's "My Open Letter to All RLSH" was hand-written and sent to me, then typed by me and posted on Therlsh.net forum, which no longer exists.

Razorhawk, interview with the author, July 19, 2015.

Quad City Times

I met Richard for stops on his Thoughtcrime Tour July 26 in Milwaukee and July 27 in Chicago, 2011.

Robbins, Alexandra. *Secrets of the Tomb: Skull and Bones, the Ivy League, and the Hidden Paths of Power*, Little, Brown and Company, 2002.

McChesney, Rashah. "Alcoa protester believes Obama is an alien," *Quad City Times*, June 29, 2011.

CRISIS ACTORS

The Guardian. "Alex Jones' pro-gun tirade at Piers Morgan on British presenter's own show," January 8, 2013.

Warzel, Charlie. "We Sent Alex Jones' Infowars Supplements To A Lab. Here's What's In Them," *BuzzFeed News*, August 9, 2017, accessed here: www.buzzfeednews.com/article/charliewarzel/we-sent-alex-jones-infowars-supplements-to-a-lab-heres

Bennett, Kaitlin. "Triggered Feminist Gets Destroyed by Kaitlin Bennett," InfoWars.com, February 12, 2019.

Martin, Adam. "Bombing Truther Crashes Boston Press Conference," *New York*, April 15, 2013.

Southern Poverty Law Center, "Mike Cernovich," accessed September 1, 2019, here: www.splcenter.org/fighting-hate/extremist-files/individual/mike-cernovich

Yardley, William. "White House Shooting Suspect's Path to Extremism," *The New York Times*, November 20, 2011.

Dicker, Ron. "Alex Jones Says Hillary Clinton And Obama Are Real Demons," huffpost.com, October 11, 2016.

YouTube video, "Alex Jones 'Turning the Freaking Frogs Gay,'" February 18, 2017, accessed here: www.youtube.com/watch?v=_ePLkAm8i2s

Pitosky, Marina. "Thousand Oaks shooting victim's mother pleads, 'I don't want thoughts. I want gun control,'" *USA Today*, November 9, 2018.

The Guardian. "Conspiracy theorist Alex Jones seeks to dismiss Sandy Hook defamation lawsuit," August 1, 2018.

Williamson, Elizabeth. "Sandy Hook Families Gain in Defamation Lawsuits Against Alex Jones," *The New York Times*, February 7, 2019.

Williamson, Elizabeth. "How Alex Jones and Infowars Helped a Florida Man Torment Sandy Hook Families," *The New York Times*, March 29, 2019.

Levitz, Eric. "Brooklyn Man Runs in Charity Race for Sandy Hook Victim So He Can Run Truther Theory by Her Family," *New York*, November 11, 2015.

Segarra, Lisa Marie. "Sandy Hook Conspiracy Theorist Gets Prison Time for Threatening 6-Year-Old Victim's Father," *Time*, June 8, 2017.

Wiedeman, Reeves. "The Sandy Hook Hoax," *New York*, September 5, 2016.

HONR, "Sandy Hook," accessed here September 1, 2019: www.honrnetwork.org/sandy-hook

Nashrulla, Tasneem. "Father Of A Sandy Hook Victim Apparently Killed Himself At A Newton Town Hall," Buzzfeed News, March 26, 2019.

RETURN OF THE PHANTOM PATRIOT

O'Brien, Cathy with Phillips, Mark. *Trance: Formation of America*, Reality Marketing, Inc., 1995.

I met with Richard January 20–21, 2012, in San Francisco for the Bohemian Club protest.

PIZZAGATE AND THE OTHER NEW RICHARDS

Yuhas, Alan. "'Pizzagate' gunman pleads guilty as conspiracy theorist apologizes over case," *The Guardian*, March 25, 2017.

American Intelligence Report. "What is Pizza Gate? Why People Think it is Real in Under 14 Mi...," December 5, 2016, accessed here: www.facebook.com/AmericanIntelligenceReport/videos/374973606180350/

Cauterucci, Christina, and Jonathan L. Fischer. "Comet is D.C.'s Weirdo Pizza Place. Maybe That's Why It's a Target," Slate.com, December 6, 2016.

Wenzel, John. "The definitive guide to Denver International Airport's biggest conspiracy theories," *The Denver Post*, October 31, 2016.

Goldman, Adam. "The Comet Ping Pong Gunman Answers Our Reporter's Questions," *The New York Times*, December 7, 2016.

Krulos, Tea. *Apocalypse Any Day Now: Deep Underground With America's Doomsday Preppers*, Chicago Review Press, 2019.

Hamilton, John. "Progressive Hunter," mediamatters.org, October 4, 2010.

Bross, Dan. "Plot to attack HAARP facility in Gakona stopped by Georgia police," alaskapublic.org, November 1, 2016.

THE INFOWARS PRESIDENT

C-SPAN. "President Obama and Seth Meyers Remarks at the 2011 White House Correspondents' Dinner," accessed here: www.c-span.org/video/?c4533998/president-obama-seth-meyers-remarks-2011-white-house-correspondents-dinner

Taddonio, Patrice. "WATCH: Inside the Night President Obama Took on Donald Trump," pbs.org, September 22, 2016.

Get Me Roger Stone (film, 2017), directed by Daniel DiMauro, Dylan Bank, Morgan Pehme.

Toobin, Jeffrey. "Roger Stone's And Jerome Corsi's Time In The Barrel," The New Yorker, February 11, 2019.

Matishak, Martin. "Intelligence head warns of more aggressive election meddling in 2020," politico.com, January 29, 2019.

Cole, Samantha. "This Deepfake of Mark Zuckerberg Tests Facebook's Fake Video Policies," Vice, June 11, 2019.

Karimi, Faith. "Pipe bomb suspect Cesar Sayoc describes Trump rallies as 'new found drug,'" cnn.com, April 24, 2019.

Hauser, Christine. "Coast Guard Officer Called a 'Domestic Terrorist' Pleads Guilty to Gun and Drug Charges," The New York Times, October 3, 2019.

WHERE THE HECK IS PAHRUMP?

I visited Richard in Pahrump May 19–23, 2015.

Phantom Patriot: An Inside Look (film, 2013), directed by Richard McCaslin.

Phantom Patriot Report 2013 (film, 2013), directed by Richard McCaslin.

Phantom Patriot Retro Cinema Episode 01 (film, 2015), directed by Richard McCaslin.

Phantom Patriot Retro Cinema Episode 02 (film, 2016), directed by Richard McCaslin.

Phantom Patriot Retro Cinema Episode 03 (film, 2016), directed by Richard McCaslin.

The Stardust and Fantomah Show (film, 2018), directed by Richard McCaslin.

THE WAR AGAINST SCIENCE

Garwood, Christine. Flat Earth: The History of an Infamous Idea, Thomas Dunne Books, 2007.

Behind the Curve (film, 2018), directed by Daniel J. Clark.

BBC News. "YouTube aids flat earth conspiracy theorists, research suggests," February 18, 2019, accessed here: www.bbc.com/news/technology-47279253

Weil, Kelly. "YouTube Tweaks Algorithm to Fight 9/11 Truthers, Flat Earthers, Miracle Cures," thedailybeast.com, January 25, 2019.

Ham, Ken. "Does the Bible Teach a Flat Earth?", answersingenesis.org, August 2, 2019.

Sargent, Mark. Flat Earth Clues: End of the World, self-published, 2019.

I attended the Wisconsin United for Freedom Rally on May 18, 2019.

Boseley, Sarah. "Andrew Wakefield found 'irresponsible' by GMC over MMR vaccine scare," The Guardian, January 28, 2010.

Brown, DeNeen L. "'You've got bad blood': The horror of the Tuskegee syphilis experiment," The Washington Post, May 16, 2017.

Modernhealthcare.com. "Anti-vaxxers take rowdy protests to CDC meetings," April 13, 2019, accessed here: www.modernhealthcare.com/government/anti-vaxxers-take-rowdy-protests-cdc-meetings

Q

Watkins, Ali. "Why a QAnon Believer Killed a Mob Boss," The New York Times, July 22, 2019.

WWG1WGA. QAnon: An Invitation to The Great Awakening, Relentlessly Creative Books, 2019.

Wootson, Jr., Cleve R. "Trump confidant Roger Stone can't stop claiming he was poisoned by polonium," The Washington Post, April 7, 2018.

Lamoureux, Mack. "People Tell Us How QAnon Destroyed Their Relationships," Vice, July 11, 2019.

Hsieh, Steven. "Mesa College Fires Professor Who Promoted QAnon Conspiracy Theory," Phoenix New Times, September 16, 2019.

Baer, Stephanie K. "An Armed Man Spouting A Bizarre Right-Wing Conspiracy Theory Was

Arrested After A Standoff At The Hoover Dam," BuzzfeedNews, June 17, 2018.

Hawkins, Dave. "Bail raised to $1M for Hoover Dam bridge barricade suspect," *Las Vegas Review-Journal*, July 17, 2018.

THE JONES CHARACTER

Siemaszko, Corky. "InfoWars' Alex Jones Is a 'Performance Artist,' His Lawyer Says in Divorce Hearing," nbcnews.com, April 17, 2017.

Dr. Daniel White, author interview, May 9, 2019.

TruNews, "A Blast From the Past for Alex Jones," August 7, 2018, accessed here: www.facebook.com/trunews/videos/2135592993141464/?v=2135592993141464

YouTube video, "Glenn Beck mocks Alex Jones," July 29, 2014, accessed here: www.youtube.com/watch?v=VfrGYb_uVjk

WWG1WGA. *QAnon: An Invitation to The Great Awakening*, Relentlessly Creative Books, 2019.

Lamoureux, Mack. "Digging Deep Into the Only Conspiracy Alex Jones Doesn't Like," *Vice*, March 4, 2017.

Silva, Daniella. "Alex Jones 'Resolves' Lawsuit With Chobani Yogurt, Issues Retraction," nbcnews.com, May 17, 2017.

Lartey, Jamiles. "InfoWars sued by man Alex Jones falsely identified as Parkland gunman," *The Guardian*, April 3, 2018.

Hughes, Roland. "Charlottesville: Why one man is suing Alex Jones for defamation," *BBC News*, August 11, 2018.

Neuman, Scott. "Alex Jones To Pay $15,000 In Pepe The Frog Copyright Infringement Case," npr.org, June 11, 2019.

Rosza, Matthew. "Alex Jones loses his appeal of Sandy Hook defamation lawsuit—and he has been ordered to pay up," salon.com, September 5, 2019.

Dukakis, Ali. "What you need to know about the indictment against Roger Stone," abcnews.go.com, November 15, 2019.

YouTube video, "Alex Jones 'I'm Ready to Die'-Exclusive Interview After Being Banned," September 13, 2018, accessed here: www.youtube.com/watch?v=xvqdhphHrh0

Marantz, Andrew. "Behind the Scenes with the Right-Wing Activist Who Crashed 'Julius Caesar,'" *The New Yorker*, June 20, 2017.

All Things Considered, "White House Social Media Summit Recap," July 13, 2019, accessed here: www.npr.org/2019/07/13/741485104/white-house-social-media-summit-recap

Feinberg, Ashley. "Things Donald Trump Said Today, Verbatim," slate.com, July 11, 2019.

Infowarslawsuit.com. "Breaking News: Watch Alex Jones Video Deposition," March 29, 2019.

FREE AT LAST!

Mazza, Ed. "Ranting, Raving Alex Jones Laughed Out Of A Texas Chicken Restaurant," huffpost.com, March 28, 2019.

The Alex Jones Show, October 15, 2018.

I visited Pahrump for the memorial November 12, 2019.

WHAT IF...?

Orac. "Antivaxxers invade San Diego Comic-Con," respectfulinsolence.com, July 22, 2019.

The Alex Jones Show, August 11, 2019.

TEA KRULOS IS THE AUTHOR of *Heroes in the Night* (2013), *Monster Hunters* (2015), *Apocalypse Any Day Now* (2019), and a contributor to *The Supernatural in Society, Culture, and History* (2018). He freelances for a wide range of publications and writes a column, "Tea's Weird Week," on his website, teakrulos.com. He lives in Milwaukee, WI.